# Learning

# C#.Net 4.0

# Learning

# C#.Net 4.0

**Ramesh Bangia**
*B.Sc., Comp. Sc. (IIT - Delhi)*
*Formerly* Managing Editor, Software Today
*Formerly* Incharge Computer Centre, Hindustan Copper Ltd., New Delhi

KHANNA BOOK PUBLISHING CO. (P) LTD.
DELHI

Learning C#.NET 4 — Ramesh Bangia



First Edition 2012

*Published by:*
**Khanna Book Publishing Co. (P) Ltd.**
4C/4344, Ansari Road, Darya Ganj, New Delhi-110 002
Phone: 011-23244447, 23244448
E-mail: contact@khannabooks.com
Website: www.khannabooks.com

*Regd. Off:* 1694-95, 1st Floor, Nai Sarak, Delhi-110006 (India)
Phone: 011-23283211, 23256658
Fax: 011-23256658

Printed in India by SPS Printers and Binders, Delhi

# PREFACE

Learning of a software is both easy and difficult. It depends upto what level you are planning to learn. If you are learning only for the working use, then it is very easy. But, when you try to go deep into it, then you realise how difficult it is to master it.

This book has been written in mind to make you aware of the options available in the software and how they can be used. It is like telling the child about the steps and stairs. You are the one who is to climb the stair. This book will just guide you how to use the stairs.

I am indeed debited to my publishers Khanna Book Publishing Co. Pvt. Ltd. for their suggestions and encouragement given in producing this book.

Suggestions for improvement of the book are indeed welcome.

**Author**

# CONTENTS

CHAPTER 1

# Introduction to C#.NET 4.0

***In this chapter you will read about:***

- Program.
- .NET Framework 4.0.
- Variables, Comment, Operators.
- Arrays, Procedure, Controls.
- Events, Forms, Message Boxes.

## What is a Program?

Program is made up of predefined commands. These commands are the keywords already have some meaning and action associated. Every language has its own keywords, rules and methods. Using them you create a program. There are varieties of languages available in the market for writing a program. Mainly used are C++, JAVA, C#, Visual Basic 2008 etc.

In general, a program is a set of instructions.

## Why Visual C# for programming?

In simple terms, it is now really very fast to write a program using Visual C#. You do not need to write complete code in Visual C#. Its IntelliSense feature is fantastic.

Suppose you want to display the message. Visual C# provides the Messagebox class for this purpose. Messagebox class is having Show method where you pass the string which you want to display. So to call Show method you need to type "." After Messagebox command but amazing thing is you do not need to type Show because IntelliSense will automatically bring all methods and properties associated with this class and you can select from its box.

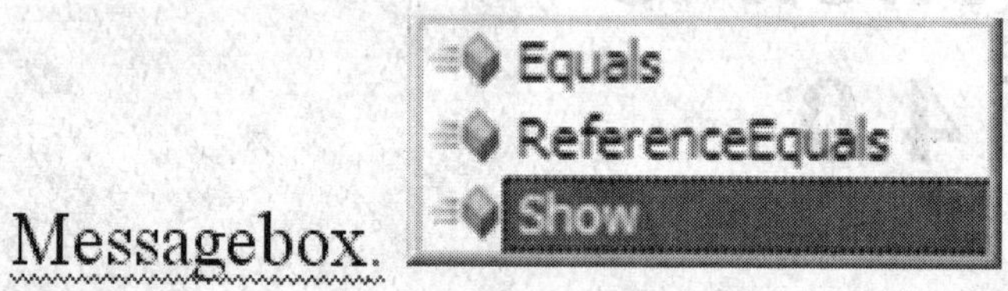


Like this you can save lot of time and you do not need to fill your brain with the complete list of methods and properties name. IntelliSense will show automatically.

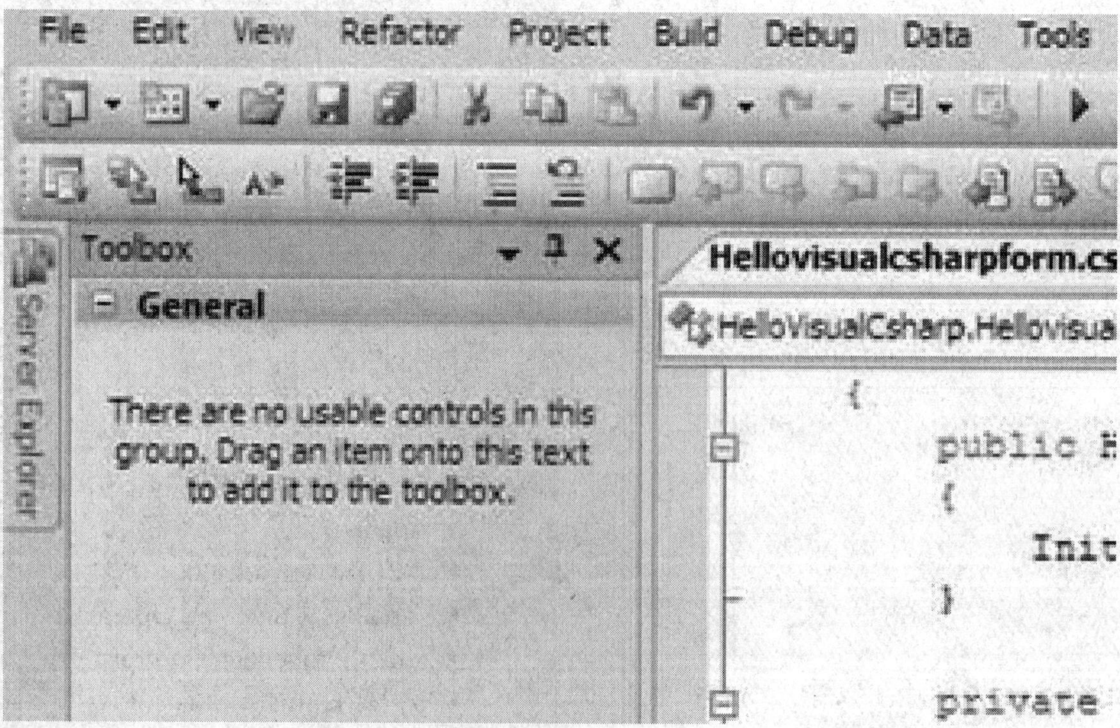

You can also press Ctrl + Spacebar on your keyboard to generate IntelliSense.

There are number of reasons for using Visual C#. One more is it provides many built-in controls for better appearance and easy coding.

For example:You do need to create code for text input. Visual C# provides textbox control for this purpose. All such common controls are located in Toolbox. You can view Toolbox by using Ctrl + Alt + X shortcut key.

One appreciable thing in Visual C# is You can easily deploy the program only through clicks.

## .Net Framework 4.0

In Visual Studio environment you generally use class for the development of program. For example if you want to display the message then you have Messagebox class available with you for this purpose. Instantly know this that all these classes are available in .Net Framework 4.0 library.

Visual Studio 2008 comes with many languages like Visual Basic, Visual C#, Visual J++, Visual C++. All these languages use common environment of .Net Framework 4.0. All languages use the Messagebox class from .Net Framework 4.0 library for displaying the message. The benefit here is you have variety of languages available for programming and if you are coming from C++ background then you can choose Visual C++. If you are upgrading from VB6 platform then you can choose Visual Basic 2008 because almost syntax is same.

Second benefit is if you are shifting from Visual C# to Visual Basic language because your company is focusing mainly in Client-Server application development then you do not need to learn all classes separately. Still all classes are same because they are located centrally in .Net Framework 4.0.

I'm sure that now you are familiar with .Net Framework environment.

## What is Visual Studio then?

Visual Studio provides you graphical interface for designing forms and it is very easy to write code because it provides design time environment for setting properties values and off course lot of code has been generated by it.

For example: If you want to perform certain action if user clicks on button control then you do not need to write event handler code for button control. Visual Studio environment will automatically generate it for you.

There are two ways for this:

1. If you will double-click on button control in design time then Visual Studio will open the code window with generated code as shown below:

```
private void button1_Click(object sender, EventArgs e)
        {

        }
```

The complete code would be like this:

```
using System;
using System.Collections.Generic;
using System.ComponentModel;
using System.Data;
using System.Drawing;
using System.Text;
using System.Windows.Forms;

namespace WindowsApplication2
{
```

```
    public partial class Form1 : Form
    {
        public Form1()
        {
            InitializeComponent();
        }

        private void button1_Click(object sender, EventArgs e)
        {

        }
    }
}
```

2. You can directly open the Code window. At top you can see two drop-down boxes. First is related to Types 

and second is related to Members 

.

## Variable

Variable stores the data. In Visual C# you can declare variable but for this you have to mention the data type also like Integer or String. One more thing to notice here is Visual C# is a case sensitive.

For example: Here both variables str or STR will be treated as different variables.

You can declare variable like this.

For example:

String x;

## Data Types

You can store string or integers or Boolean values in variable. There are many type of Data Types available in Visual C#. Let me explain few one of them to you.

## String Variable

It stores the characters like:

- Ram
- ABC123
- 12/23, Peterganj, Shahpur, New Delhi.
- .....

Remember this that string is always enclosed in double upper quotes.

Example: String namevarxyz;

Once the variable is declared then you can assign value in it like this:

X = "12/23, Peterganj, Shahpur, New Delhi";

## Integer variable

This kind of data type stores numbers.

For example:

- 7
- 123

- 677
- ....

You can declare integer variable like this:

int age;

Once the variable is declared then you can assign value in it like this:

age = 23;

You should not store the string value inside the Integer type variable otherwise you will encounter with error.

This is not allowed:

int age;

age = "ram";

## Boolean Variable

It is used for storing True / False values. These are helpful when you want to perform the code on yes/no logic basis.

You can declare Boolean variable like this:

Boolean xx;

To check this run the following code:

```
Boolean xx;
        xx = true;
        MessageBox.Show(xx.ToString());
```

Assigning value with variable declaration

You can also assign values while declaring the variable types.

For example:

```
String x = "ram";
  int age = 30;
```

The following code will demonstrate this properly.

Perform the following steps:

1. Click on File menu.
2. Click on New Project menu item.

   Or

   Use Shortcut key Ctrl + Shift + N
3. New Project dialog box will appear.
4. At the left side of dialog box, beneath Project Types, expand the Visual C# by clicking + sign if not expanded.
5. Select Windows.
6. At the right side of dialog box beneath Templates: you can see several Visual Studio installed Templates.
7. Select Windows Application.
8. In Name field type assigningvalues.

9. Click Ok.
10. In Solution Explorer click on the icon of Form1.cs for selection.
11. In the Properties window change the File Name property from Form1.cs to assigningvaluesform.cs.
12. Press Enter.
13. Click the form displayed in the Design window.
14. In the Properties window locate the Text property.
15. Type Assigning values form.
16. Press Enter.
17. Notice the Title bar of the Form which is changed with the text you have recently typed in the Text property of the Form.
18. In the Properties window locate the Size field and type 400, 300 to specify the width and height of the form.
19. Press Enter.
20. Add button control to the form.
21. Be sure that button control is selected; if not then click it once for the selection.
22. In Properties window locate the Text property.
23. Type, Click here.
24. In the Properties window locate the Location field and type 170, 113.

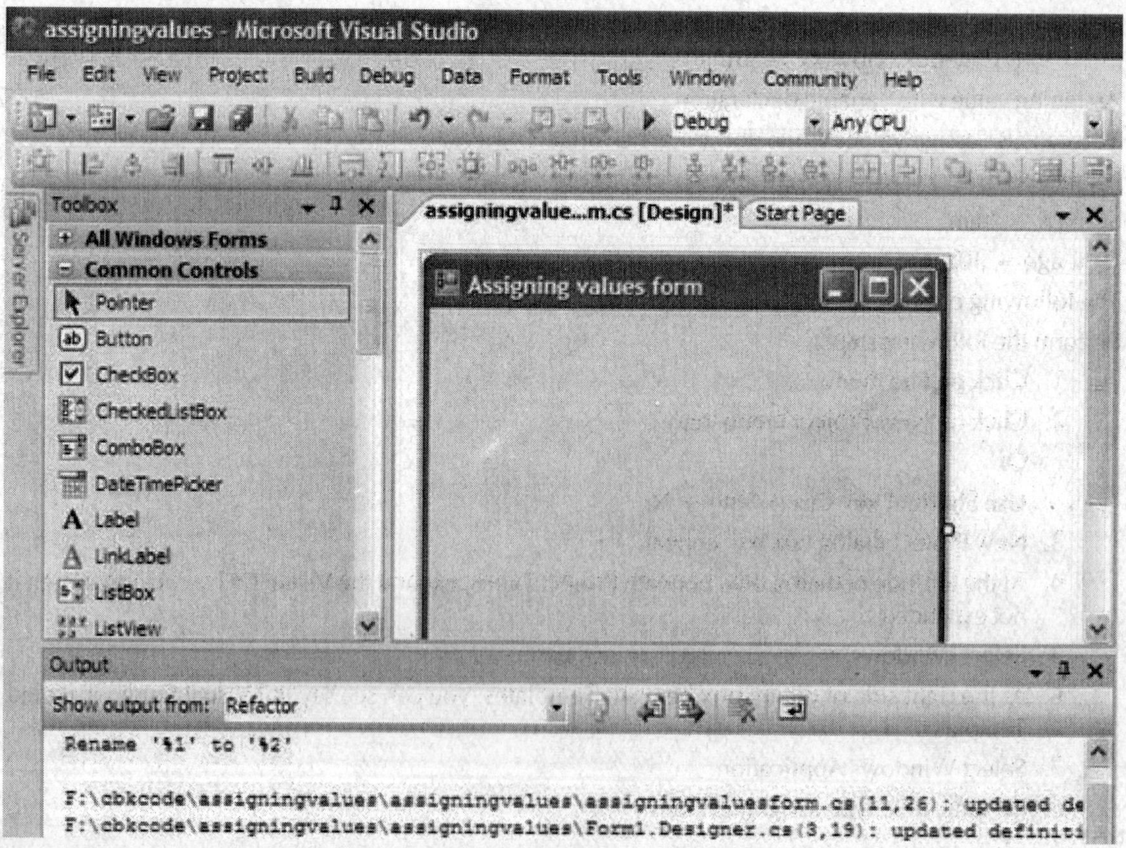

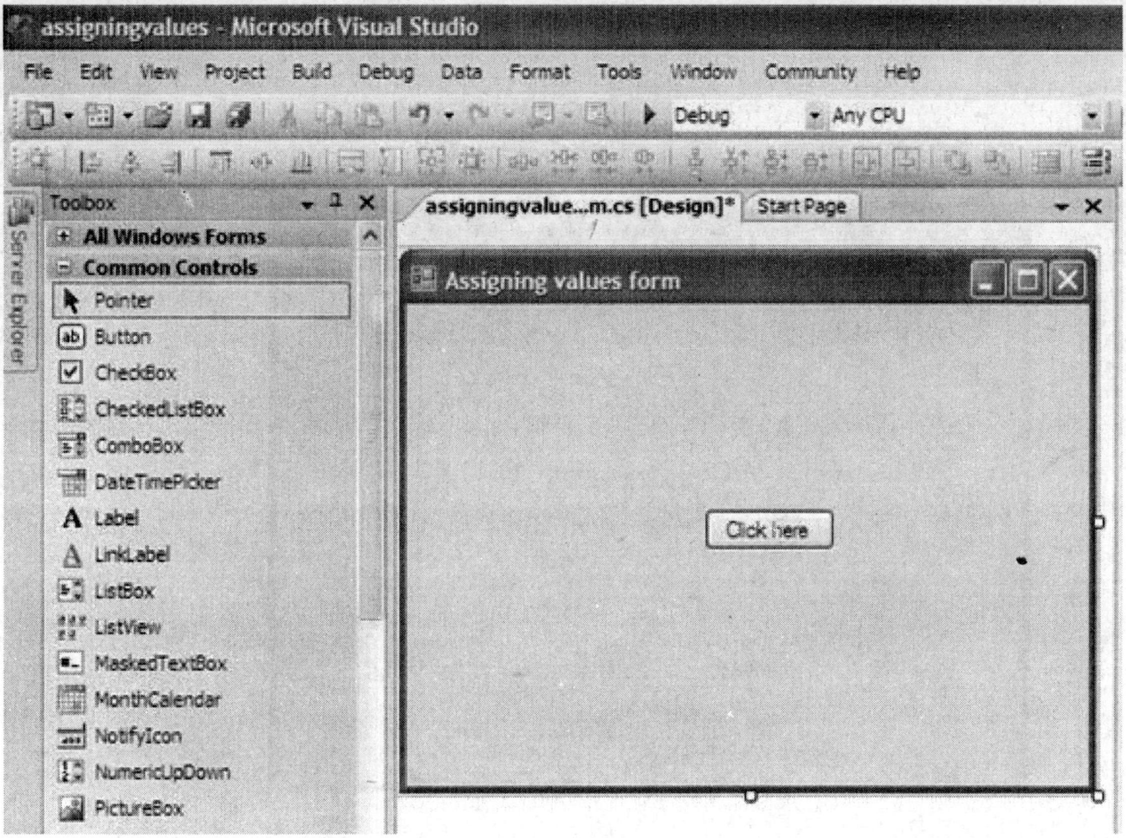


25. This time your form will appear like this:
26. Open the code window.
27. Type following code:

```
using System;
using System.Collections.Generic;
using System.ComponentModel;
using System.Data;
using System.Drawing;
using System.Text;
using System.Windows.Forms;

namespace assigningvalues
{
    public partial class assigningvaluesform : Form
     {
        public assigningvaluesform()
         {
            InitializeComponent();
         }

        private void button1_Click(object sender, EventArgs e)
         {
         String str = "Visual C#";
         int i = 2005;
         Boolean bol = true;
```

```
            MessageBox.Show(str + " " + i + " " + bol);
        }
    }
}
```

28. Now this is the time to run program by pressing F7 key on your keyboard.

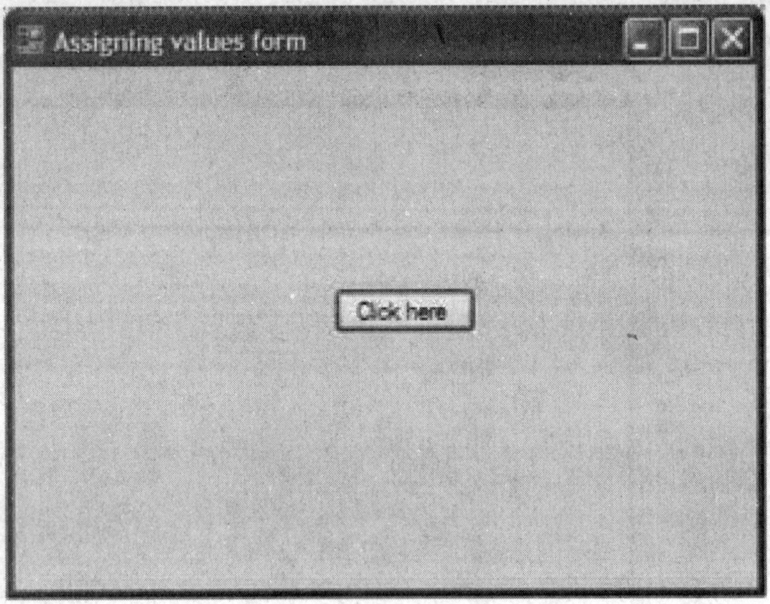


29. Click on the button control to get output.

Inside the button control event handler we had assigned the values while declaring variables.

Messagebox.show class here is used for displaying message. You may notice this that I have used + to join data. This is known as concatenation.

You can join strings or variables collectively using +.

For example:

```
String x;
x = "Ram";
string y;
y = "Sharma";
int z;
z = 76;
string str;
Str = " The age of := " + x  + " " + y + " " + " is  " + z
```

Amazing! Visual C# is very flexible.

## Semicolon

You have noticed this in above examples I have used semicolon after the end of every statement or command line. It is compulsory then and only Visual C# understands that your one command is complete and you are writing next command so after every semicolon each command is treated separate. If you will not write semicolon then you will encounter with error(s).

Never forget to write semicolon after the end of every statement.

For example:

```
int x;
String y;
```

## Comment

It is very easy to declare a line comment in Visual C#. For this you have to use two front slashes // before the code which you want Visual C# to treat as comment. The line which is declared as comment is not executed whiles the execution of other code inside the procedure or function.

For example:

```
private void button1_Click(object sender, EventArgs e)
        {
            // This is a assignment example
        String str = "Visual C#";
        int i = 2008;
        Boolean bol = true;
    MessageBox.Show(str + " " + i + " " + bol);
        }
```

## Arithmetic Operators

Visual C# provides operators for performing addition, subtraction, multiplication etc.

| *Operator* | *Description* | *Example* |
|---|---|---|
| + (Addition) | It will return the sum of two operands | 8 + 3 |
| - (Subtraction) | It will return the difference of two operands | 8 – 3 |
| * (Multiplication) | It will return the product of two operands | 8 * 3 |
| / (Division) | It will return the quotient of two operands | 8 / 3 |

You may also perform the operation while declaring variable.

For example:

```
private void button1_Click(object sender, EventArgs e)
        {
            int x = 14 + 5;
        MessageBox.Show(x.ToString());

        }
```

## Comparison Operators

Comparison operators are used when you want to compare two or more values or variables.

| Operator | Description | Examples |
|---|---|---|
| = = (Equals) | It will return True if the number on the left-hand side is equal to the number on the right-hand side. | 8 = 5 (false)5 = 8 (false)5 = 5 (true) |
| != (Not Equal to) | It will return True if the number on the left is not equal to the number on the right. | 8 <> 5 (true)5 <> 8 (true)8 <> 5 (false) |
| > (Greater than) | It will return True if the number on the left is greater than the number on the right. | 7 > 3 (true)3 > 7 (false)3 > 3 (false) |

CHAPTER 1

< (Less than) — It will return True if the number on the left is less than the number on the right.
7 < 3 (false)3 < 7 (true)3 < 3 (false)

> = (Greater than or Equal to) — It will return True if the number on the left is greater than or equal to the number on the right.
7 > = 3 (true)3 > = 7 (false)3 > = 3 (true)

< = (Less than or Equal to) — It will return True if the number on the left is less than or equal to the number on the right.
7 < = 3 (false)3 < = 7 (true)3 < = 3 (true)

## Condition

There might be a situation when you have to perform the code on condition basis. You can implement conditions using If keyword.

Like,

```
If  (name="Raj")
{
' Perform the following code...
'........
'.....
}
else
{

' Perform the following code...
'........
'.....

}
```

If condition, plays the vital role in programming. You can easily perform the code on the basis of condition. If condition returns True then all code will be executed defined before else keyword and if condition returns False then all code will be executed which are mentioned after else keyword.

Note: To check the conditions you can use comparison operators.

For example:

```
private void button1_Click(object sender, EventArgs e)
        {
        int x;
        x = 5;
       if(x > 3)
            {
            MessageBox.Show(" X > 3 ");
            }
            else
            {
            MessageBox.Show(" X < 5 ");
            }
        }
```

Above code will return the following output:

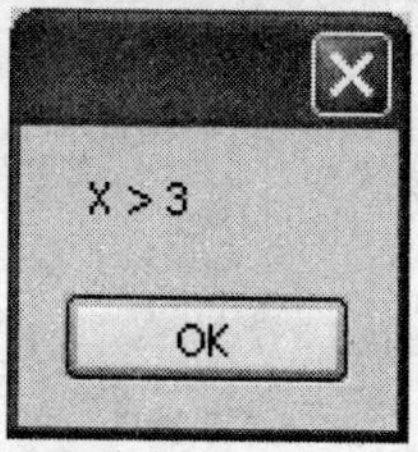


## ElseIf

If you want to check more conditions before else keyword then for this purpose you can use else if as many times as many times you want.

Pseudo code:

```
If condition then
' perform following steps...
...
ElseIf condition then
' perform following steps...

ElseIf condition then
            ' perform following steps...

Else

' perform following steps...
            End If
        End If
End If
```

This code will better explain the use of elseif.

```
private void button1_Click(object sender, EventArgs e)
        {
        int x;
        x = 5;
       if(x > 3)
            {
           MessageBox.Show(" X > 3 ");
            }
            else if (x == 3)
            {
                MessageBox.Show(" X == 3");
            }
            else
            {
                MessageBox.Show(" X < 5 ");
            }
        }
```

This program will return the following output:

## For Loop

Sometimes you need to repeat actions. For example, suppose if you want to displays a series of numbers on screen. This loop allows you to specify a number, and then it repeats the code contained within that loop for the specified number of times.

The following code will explain this:

```
private void button1_Click(object sender, EventArgs e)
        {

            for(int i=1;i<=5;i++)
            {
                MessageBox.Show("hello");
            }
        }
```

Above code will display hello five times.

## Error handling in Visual C#

Visual C# is really smart in error handling. There is a chance that you will encounter with an error when you run the code in run time.

For example: You have written code for database connectivity and due to some reason database has been moved for maintenance purpose. So in such case you can write such code inside Try block. Even if error encounters your program will not be crashed or hanged out and keeps continue running.

```
Try
    {
    //Code you want to perform
    }
Catch
    {
    // Error catching
    }
```

## Arrays

Arrays make you possible to store multiple values in variable.

For example:

String[] x;

X = new string[5];

Here the first statement declares x as an array and second defines that this string array is having 10 string elements.

## Procedure

What ever code you write in Visual C# actually you are placing them in a procedure. Technically, procedure is a group of code statements which performs a specific task or function. You can also call a procedure from code in another procedure. Procedure can also return value.

General procedure declaration is like this:

```
Public void xpro()
{
//statements…
}
```

Procedure which is returning value..

```
Public string xpro()
{
Return "cool";
}
```

## Properties

In Visual C# every control has set **of properties** like Size, Text, Location, Visible, Font, ForeColor, BackColor etc.

You can set these properties in design time or run time. In design time you can set these properties using properties window and in run time you can set these properties like this:

label1.Text = = "Hello";

**Size:** This property is used to set the size of control

**Text:** This property is used to display the text.

**Location**: This property is used to set the location of control.

**Visible**: This property is used to make control visible or invisible in run time. To make control invisible in run-time just set this property to False.

**Font**: This property is used to set the Font for control.

**ForeColor**: This property is used to set the ForeColor of control.

**BackColor**: This property is used to set the BackColor of control.

**Enable**: If you set this property to False then user is unable to use that particular control in run-time whose Enable property is set as False.

## Events

When you click on button control then click event occurs. Once the event is occured then Visual C# executes the code inside the event handler of that particular event which has been occured.

For example:

```
private void button1_Click(object sender, EventArgs e)
        {
                // Your code here…
```

```
        }
```

Many types of events are associated with the control.

For example: when you move your mouse over the button control then Mousemove event will occur:

```
private void button1_MouseMove(object sender, MouseEventArgs e)
        {
            MessageBox.Show("Mouse move event");
        }
```

Now position your mouse over the button control you will receive the following message:

## Controls

Visual C# provides lot of ready made control in Toolbox. You do not need to write code for input or displaying the message.

**Button**: This control is used to perform action if user clicks on it.

**Checkbox**: This control is used to select multiple values.

**CheckedListbox**: This control is used to select values from list and you can check or uncheck the list too.

**ComboBox**: This control is used to select value and you have also option available to type item list in text box.

**DateTimePicker**: This control is used to select or set Date and Time.

**Label**: This control is used to display text in Form.

**ListBox**: This control is used to select value from List.

**MonthCalendar**: This control is used to display Calendar.

**PictureBox**: This control is used to display pictures.

**RadioButton**: This control is used to select one item from group of items.

**TextBox**: This control is used to input text.

**ToolTip**: This control is used to display ToolTips.

In Control chapter I have explained few controls in depth with step by step exercises which have much more use in creating professional application.

## Messagebox

You can display messages in a box using Messagebox class

For example:

```
Messagebox.Show("Hello");
```

## Form

You can say that Form is the main heart of any Visual C# program. You add all controls to the Form. In a project you can add more than one form too.

For this perform the following steps:

1. Click on Project menu.
2. Click Add New Item.
3. Select Windows Form.
4. Click Add.

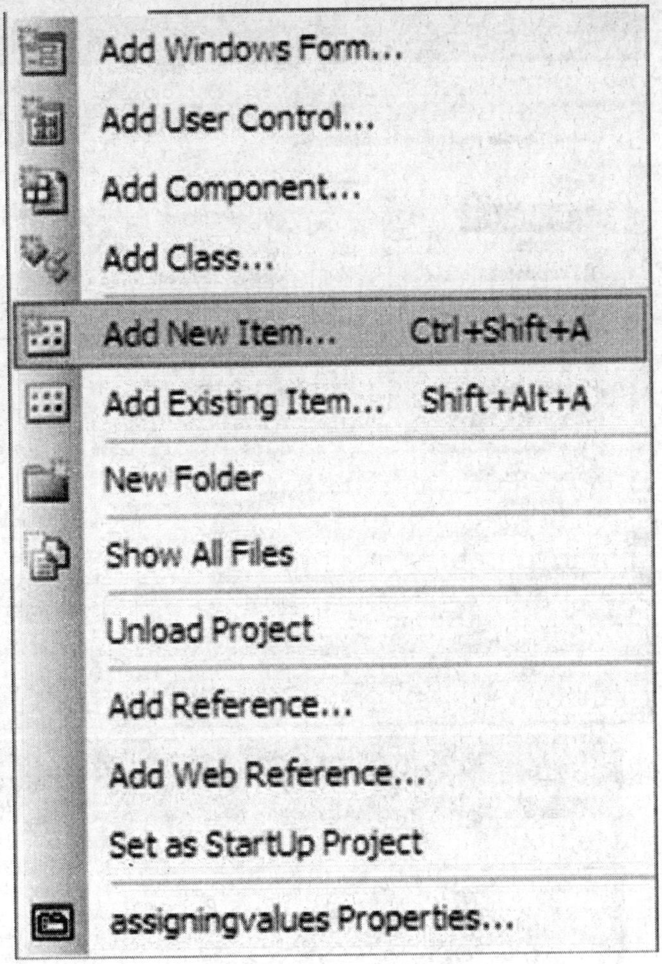


5. The new form has been added.

If you want to set the title of the Form then for this purpose you can use its Text property. If you set its MaximizeBox and MinimizeBox property to False then you are not able to Maximize or Minimize the form Like this you can restrict the user.

If you want to display the form in center then set its StartPosition property to CenterScreen.

To fill the form to entire screen set its WindowState property to Maximized.

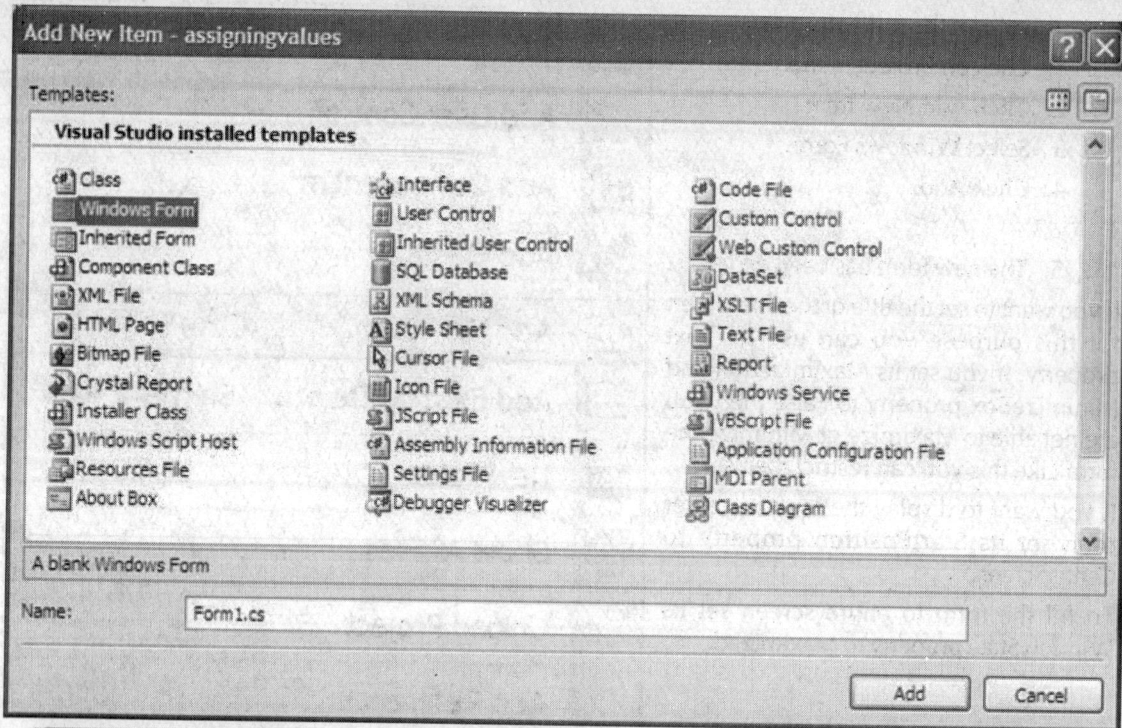
Add New Item - assigningvalues
Templates:
Visual Studio installed templates
Class
Windows Form
Inherited Form
Component Class
XML File
HTML Page
Bitmap File
Crystal Report
Installer Class
Windows Script Host
Resources File
About Box
Interface
User Control
Inherited User Control
SQL Database
XML Schema
Style Sheet
Cursor File
Icon File
JScript File
Assembly Information File
Settings File
Debugger Visualizer
Code File
Custom Control
Web Custom Control
DataSet
XSLT File
Text File
Report
Windows Service
VBScript File
Application Configuration File
MDI Parent
Class Diagram
A blank Windows Form
Name:
Form1.cs
Add
Cancel

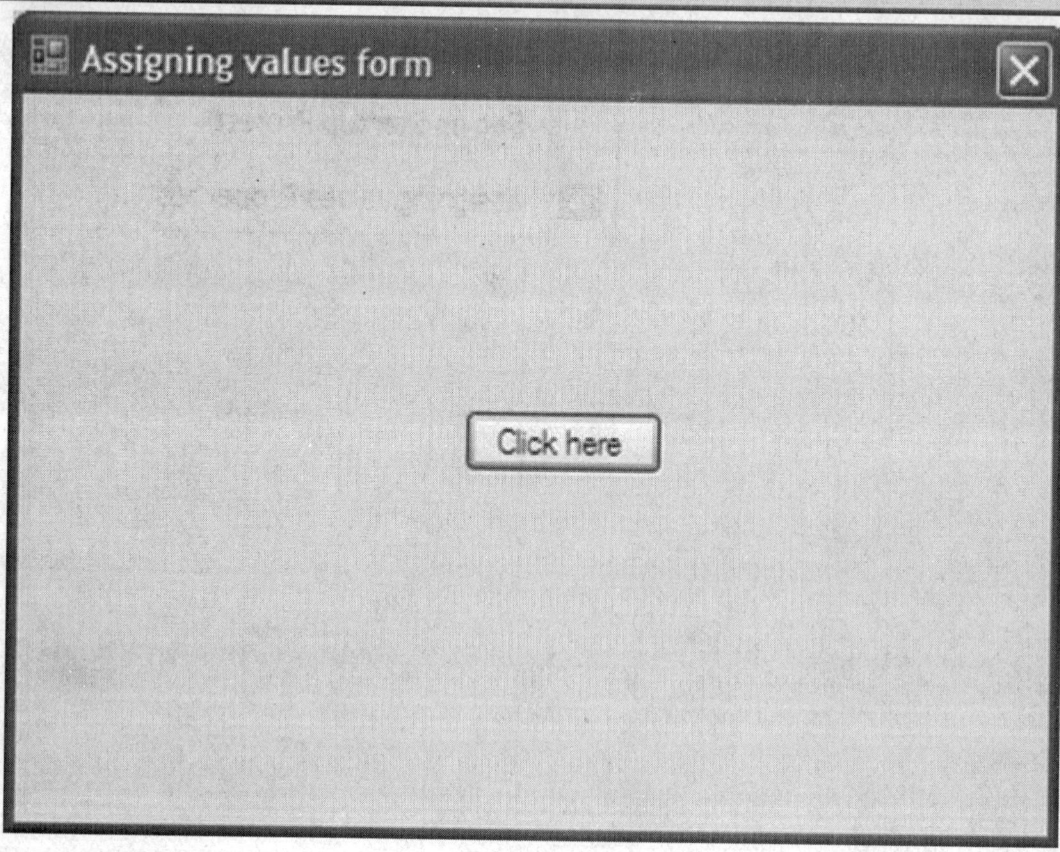
Assigning values form
Click here

CHAPTER 2

# Introducing Classes and Objects

***In this chapter you will read about:***

- Class Fundamentals.
- Constructors.
- Garbage Collection and Destructors.
- Using Parameters.
- Object Creations.

## Class Fundamentals

We have been using classes since the start of this book. Of course, only extremely simple classes have been used, and we have not taken advantage of the majority of their features. Classes are substantially more powerful than the limited ones presented so far.

Let's begin by reviewing the basics. A *class* is a template that defines the form of an object. It specifies both the data and the code that will operate on that data. C#ii$e8mdftss specification to construct *objects*. Objects are *instances* of a class. Thus, a class is essentially a set of plans that specify how to build an object. It is important to be clear on one issue: A class is a logical abstraction. It is not until an object of that class has been created that a physical representation of that class exists in memoiy.

## The General Form of a Class

When you define a class, you declare the data that it contains and the code that operates on it. While very simple classes might contain only code or only data, most real-world ckss es contain both.

In general terms, data is contained in *data members* defined by the class, and code is contained *in function members*. It is important to state at the outset that C# defines several specific flavors of data and function members. For example, data members (also called *fields)* include instance variables and static variables. Function members include Methods, constructors, destructors, indexers, events, operators, and properties. For now, we wBJlUinit our discussion of the class to its essential elements: instance variables and methods. Later in this chapter constructors and destructors are discussed.

A class is created by use of the keyword **class.** Here is the general form of a simple **class** definition that contains only instance variables and methods:

```
class chassname {
    // declare instance variables
    access typevarl;
    access type var2;
    // ...
    access type varN;

    // declare methods
    access ret-type methodl(parameters) {
    // body of method
    }
    access ret-type method2(parameters) {
    // body of method
    }
    // ...
    access ret-type methodN(parameters) {
        // body of method
    }
}
```

Notice that each variable and method declaration is preceded with access. Here, access is an access specifier, such as public, which specifies how the member can be accessed. As mentioned earlier, class members can be private to a class or more accessible. The access specifier determines what type of access is allowed. The access specifier is optional, and if absent, then the member is private to the class. Members with private access can be used only by other members of their class. For the examples in this chapter, all members (except for the **Main**() method) will be specified as public, which means that they can be used by all other code—even code defined outside the class.

Although there is no syntactic rule that enforces it, a well-designed class should define one and only one logical entity. For example, a class that stores names and telephone numbers will not normally also store information about the stock market, average rainfall, sunspot cycles, or other unrelated information. The point here is that a well-designed class groups logically connected information. Putting unrelated information into the same class will quickly destructure your code.

Up to this point, the classes that we have been using have had only one method: **Main()**. However, notice that the general form of a class does not specify a **Main()** method. A **Main()** method is required only if that class is the starting point for your program.



## Define a Class

To illustrate classes, we will be evolving a class that encapsulates information about buildings, such as houses, stores, offices, and so on. This class is called **Building,** and it will store three items of information about a building: the number of floors, the total area, and the number of occupants.

The first version of **Building** is shown here. It defines three instance variables: **Floors, Area,** and **Occupants.** Notice that **Building** does not contain any methods. Thus, it is currently a data-only class. (Subsequent sections will add methods to it.)

```
class Building {
public int Floors; // number of floors
public int Area; // total square footage of building
public int Occupants; // number of occupants
}
```

The instance variables defined by **Building** illustrate the way that instance variables are declared in general. The general form for declaring an instance variable is shown here:

```
access type var-name;
```

Here, *access* specifies the access; *type* specifies the type of variable; and *var-name* is the variable's name. Thus, aside from the access specifier, you declare an instance variable in the same way that you declare local variables. For **Building,** the variables are preceded by the public access modifier. As explained, this allows them to be accessed by code outside of **Building.**

**A class** definition creates a new data type. In this case, the new data type is called **Building.** You will use this name to declare objects of type **Building.** Remember that a class declaration is only a type description; it does not create an actual object. Thus, the preceding code does not cause any objects of type **Building** to come into existence.

To actually create a **Building** object, you will use a statement like the following:

```
Building house = new Building!); // create an object of type building
```

After this statement executes, **house** will be an instance of **Building.** Thus, it will have "physical" reality. For the moment, don't worry about the details of this statement

Each time you create an instance of a class, you are creating an object that contains its own copy of each instance variable defined by the class. Thus, every **Building** object will contain its own copies of the instance variables **Floors, Area, and Occupants.** To access these variables, you will use the member access operator, which is a period. It is commonly referred to as the *dot operator.* The dot operator links the name of an object with the name of a member. The general form of the dot operator is shown here:

```
object.member
```

Thus, the *object* is specified on the left, and the *member* is put on the right. For example, to assign the **Floors** variable of **house** the value 2, use the following statement:

In general, you can use the dot operator to access both instance variables and methods. Here is a complete program that uses the **Building** class:

```
// A program that uses Ihe Building class,
using System;
class Building {
```

```
    public int Floors;   // number of floors
    public int Area;     // total square footage of building
    public int Occupants;     // number of occupants
  }
// This class declares an object of type Building, class BuildingDemo {
    static void Main() {
    Building house = new Building(); // create a Building object
    int areaPP;                     // area per person

    // Assign values to fields in house,
    house.Occupants = 4;
    house.Area = 2500;
    house.Floors = 2;

    // Compute the area per person.
    areaPP = house.Area / house.Occupants;

    Console.WriteLine("house has:\n " +
                 house.Floors + " floors\n " +
          house.Occupants + "        occupants\n " +
          house.Area + " total area\n " +
       areaPP + " area per person");
    }
  }
```

This program consists of two classes: **Building and BuildingDemo.** Inside **BuildingDemo, the Main()** method creates an instance of **Building** called **house.** Then the code within **Main()** accesses the instance variables associated with **house,** assigning them values and using those values. It is important to understand that **Building and BuildingDemo** are two separate classes. The only relationship they have to each other is that one class creates an instance of the other. Although they are separate classes, code inside **BuildingDemo** can access the members of **Building** because they are declared **public.** If they had not been given the **public** access specifier, their access would have been limited to the **Building** class, and **BuildingDemo** would not have been able to use them.

Assume that you call the preceding file **UseBuilding.es.** Compiling this program creates a file called **UseBuilding.exe.** Both the **Building and BuildingDemo** classes are automatically part of the executable file. The program displays the following output:

```
house has:
    2 floors
    4 occupants
    2500 total area
    625 area per person
```

It is not necessary for the **Building** and the **BuildingDemo** classes to actually be in the same source file. You could put each class in its own file, called **Building.cs and BuildingDemo.es,** for example. Just tell the C# compiler to compile both files and link them together. For example, you could use this command line to compile the program if you split it into two pieces as just described:

```
esc Building.es BuildingDemo.es
```

If you are using the Visual Studio IDE, you will need to add both files to your project and then build.

Before moving on, let's review a fundamental principle: Each object has its own copies of the instance variables defined by its class. Thus, the contents of the variables in one object can differ from the contents of the variables in another. There is no connection between the two objects except for the fact that they are both objects of the same type. For example, if you have two **Building** objects, each has its own copy of **Floors, Area, and Occupants,** and the contents of these can (and often will) differ between the two objects. The following program demonstrates this fact:

```
// This program creates two Building objects.
using System;

class Building {
    public int Floors;   // number of floors
    public int Area;     // total square footage of building
    public int Occupants; // number of occupants
}

// This class declares two objects of type Building.
class BuildingDemo {
    static void Main() {
        Building house = new Buildingf);
        Building office = new Building ();

        int areaPP; // area per person

        // Assign values to fields in house.
        house .Occupants = 4;
        house. Area = 2500;
        house . Floors = 2;

        // Assign values to fields in office.
        office .Occupants = 25;
        office. Area = 4200;
        office. Floors - 3;

        // Compute the area per person in house.
        areaPP = house .Area / house .Occupants;

        Console .WriteLine (     "house has : \n " +
                                 house. Floors + " floorsXn " +
                        house. Occupants + " occupants\n
                        house. Area + " total area\n " +
                    areaPP + " area per person");
        Console.WriteLine ();

        // Compute the area per person in house.
        areaPP = house .Area / house .Occupants;

        Console.WriteLine(       "ofties has:\n " +
                                 office.Floors + " floors\n " +
                                 office.Occupants + " occupants\n
                                 office.Area + " total area\n " +
                                 areaPP + " area per person");
```

The output produced by this program is shown here:

```
house has:
   2 floors
   4 occupants
   2500 total area
   625 area per person

office has:
   3 floors
```

```
5 occupants
4200 total area
168 area per person
```

As you can see, **house's** data is completely separate from the data contained in **office.** Figure 6-1 depicts this situation.

## How Objects Are Created

In the preceding programs, the following line was used to declare an object of type **Building:**

```
Building house = new Building();
```

This declaration performs three functions. First, it declares a variable called **house** of the class type **Building.** This variable is not, itself, an object. Instead, it is simply a variable that can *refer to* an object. Second, the declaration creates an actual, physical copy of the object.

| | | |
|---|---|---|
| house | Floors | 2 |
| | Area | 2500 |
| | Occupants | 4 |
| office | Floors | 3 |
| | Area | 4200 |
| | Occupants | 25 |

This is done by using the **new** operator. Finally, it assigns to **house** a reference to that object. Thus, after the line executes, **house** refers to an object of type **Building.**

The new operator dynamically allocates (that is, allocates at runtime) memory for an object and returns a reference to it. This reference is then stored in a variable. Thus, in C#, all class objects must be dynamically allocated.

As you might expect, it is possible to separate the declaration of **house** from the creation of the object to which it will refer, as shown here:

```
Building house:                  // declare refernce to object
house = new Building();          // allocate a Building object
```

The first line declares house as a reference to an object of type **Building.** Thus, **house** is a variable that can refer to an object, but it is not an object, itself. The next line creates a new **Building** object and assigns a reference to it to **house. Now, house** is linked with an object.

The fact that class objects are accessed through a reference explains why classes are called *reference types.* The key difference between value types and reference types is what a variable of each type means. For a value type variable, the variable, itself, contains the value. For example, given

```
int x;
x = 10;
```

x contains the value 10 because x is a variable of type **hit,** which is a value type. However, in the case of

```
Building house = new Building();
```

**house** does not, itself, contain the object. Instead, it contains a reference to the object.

## Reference Variables and Assignment

In an assignment operation, reference variables act differently than do variables of a value type, such as int. When you assign one value type variable to another, the situation is straightforward. The variable on the left receives a *copy* of the *value* of the variable on the right. When you assign one object reference variable to another, the situation is a bit more complicated because the assignment causes the reference variable on the left to refer to the same object to which the reference variable on the right refers. The object, itself, is not copied. The effect of this difference can cause some counterintuitive results. For example, consider the following fragment:

```
Building housel = new Building();
Building house2 =- housel;
```

At first glance, it is easy to think that **housel and house2** refer to separate and distinct objects, but this is not the case. Instead, **housel and house2** will both refer to the *same* object. The assignment of **housel** to **house2** simply makes **house2** refer to the same object that **housel** does. Thus, the object can be acted upon by either **housel** or **houseZ.** For example, after the assignment

```
housel.Area = 2600
```

executes, both of these **WriteLine<)** statements

```
Console.WriteLine(housel.Area);
Console.WriLeLine(house2.Area);
```

display the same value: 2600.

Although **housel and house2** both refer to the same object, they are not linked in any other way. For example, a subsequent assignment to **house2** simply changes what object **house2** refers to. For example:

```
Building housel = new Building ();
Building house2 = housel;
Building house3 = new Building));

house2 = house3; // now house2 and house3 refer to the same object.
```

After this sequence executes, **house2** refers to the same object as **house3.** The object referred to by **housel** is unchanged.

## Methods

As explained, instance variables and methods are two of the primary constituents of classes. So far, the **Building** class contains data, but no methods. Although data-only classes are perfectly valid, most classes will have methods. *Methods* are subroutines that manipulate the data defined by the class and, in many cases, provide access to that data. Typically, other parts of your program will interact with a class through its methods.

A method contains one or more statements, hi well-written C# code, each method performs only one task. Each method has a name, and it is this name that is used to call the method. In general, you can name a method using any valid identifier that you please. However, remember that **Main()** is reserved for the method that begins execution of your program. Also, don't use C#'s keywords for method names.

When denoting methods in text, this book has used and will continue to use a convention that has become common when writing about C#. A method will have parentheses after its name. For example, if a method's name is **GetVal,** then it will be written GetVaK ) when its name is used in a sentence. This notation will help you distinguish variable names from method names in this book.

The general form of a method is shown here:

```
access ret-type name(pammeter-list) {
// body of method
}
```

Here, *access* is an access modifier that governs what other parts of your program can call the method. As explained earlier, the access modifier is optional. If not present, then the method is private to the class in which it is declared. For now, we will declare methods as **public** so that they can be called by any other code in the program. The *ret-type* specifies the type of data returned by the method. This can be any valid type, including class types that you create. If the method does not return a value, its return type must be **void.** The name of the method is specified by *name.* This can be any legal identifier other than those that would cause conflicts within the current declaration space. The *parameter-list* is a sequence of type and identifier pairs separated by commas. Parameters are variables that receive the value of the *arguments* passed to the method when it is called. If the method has no parameters, then the parameter list will be empty.

## Add a Method to the Building Class

As just explained, the methods of a class typically manipulate and provide access to the data of the class. With this in mind, recall that Main() in the preceding examples computed the area-per-person by dividing the total area by the number of occupants. Although technically correct, this is not the best way to handle this computation. The calculation of area-per-person is something that is best handled by the **Building** class, itself. The reason for this conclusion is easy to understand: The area-per-person of a building is dependent upon the values in the **Area** and **Occupants** fields, which are encapsulated by **Building.** Thus, it is possible for the **Building** class to perform this calculation on its own. Furthermore, by adding this calculation to **Building,** you prevent each program that uses **Building** from having to perform this calculation manually. This prevents the unnecessary duplication of code. Finally, by adding a method to **Building** that computes the area-per-person, you are enhancing its object-oriented structure by encapsulating the quantities that relate directly to a building inside **Building.**

To add a method to **Building,** specify it within **Building's** declaration. For example, the following version of **Building** contains a method called **AreaPerPersont)** that displays the area-per-person for a building:

```
// Add a method to Building.

using System;

class Building {
    public int E'loors;           // number of floors
    public int Area;              // total square footage of building
    public int Occupants;         // number of occupants

// Display the area per person,
public void AreaPerPerson () {
    Console.WriteLine(" " + Area / Occupants + " area per person");
    }
}

// Use the AreaPerPerson() method.
class BuildingDemo {
    static void Main(I (
        Building house = new Building{);
        Building office - new Building();

    // Assign values to fields in house,
        house .Occupants = 4 ;
        house.Area = 2500;
        house.Floors = 2;

    // Assign values to fields in office
    office.Occupants = 25;

    Console.WriteLine("house has:\n " +
                     house.Floors + " floors\n " +
             house.Occupants + " occupants\n
                 house.Area + " total area");
    house.AreaPerPerson();
```

```
    Console.WriteLine();

    Console.WriteLine( "offies has:\n " +
                       office.Floors + " floors\n " +
                       office.Occupants + " occupants\n
                       office.Area + " total area\n " +
                       areaPP + " area per person");
    office.AreaPerPerson();
   }
 }
```

This program generates the following output, which is the same as before:

```
house has:
    2 floors
    4 occupants
    2500 total area
    625 area per person
 office has:
    3 floors
    5 occupants
    4200 total area
    168 area per person
```

Let's look at the key elements of this program, beginning with the **AreaPerPerson()** method, itself. The first line of **AreaPerPersonC) is**

```
public void AreaPerPerson () {
```

This line declares a method called **AreaPerPerson()** that has no parameters. It is specified as public, so it can be used by all other parts of the program. Its return type is **void.** Thus, **AreaPerPerson()** does not return a value to the caller. The line ends with the opening curly brace of the method body.

The body of **AreaPerPerson()** consists solely of this statement:

```
Console.WrileLine{" " + Area / Occupants + " area per person");
```

This statement displays the area-per-person of a building by dividing **Area by Occupants.** Since each object of type **Building** has its own copy of **Area** and **Occupants,** when **AreaPerPerson()** is called, the computation uses the calling object's copies of those variables.

**The AreaPerPerson()** method ends when its closing curly brace is encountered. This causes program control to transfer back to the caller.

Next, look closely at this line of code from inside Main():

```
house.AreaPerPerson();
```

This statement invokes the **AreaPerPerson()** method on **house.** That is, it calls **AreaPerPerson()** relative to the object referred to by **house,** by use of the dot operator. When a method is called, program control is transferred to the method. When the method terminates, control is transferred back to the caller, and execution resumes with the line of code following the call.

In this case, the call to **house,AreaPerPerson()** displays the area-per-person of the building defined by **house.** In similar fashion, the call to **office.AreaPerPerson()** displays the area-per-person of the building defined by **office.** Each time **AreaPerPerson()** is invoked, it displays the area-per-person for the specified object.

There is something very important to notice inside the **AreaPerPerson()** method: The instance variables **Area and Occupants** are referred to directly, without use of the dot operator. When a method uses an instance variable that is defined by its class, it does so directly, without explicit reference to an object and without use of the dot operator. This is easy to understand if you think about it. A method is always invoked relative to some object of its class. Once this invocation has occurred, the object is known. Thus, within a method, there is no need to specify the object a second time. This means that **Area** and **Occupants** inside **AreaPerPerson()** implicitly refer to the copies of those variables found in the object that invokes **AreaPerPerson()**.

## Return from a Method

In general, there are two conditions that cause a method to return. The first, as the **AreaPerPerson()** method in the preceding example shows, is when the method's closing curly brace is encountered. The second is when a **return** statement is executed. There are two forms of **return:** one for use in **void** methods (those that do not return a value) and one for returning values. The first form is examined here. The next section explains how to return values.

In **a void** method, you can cause the immediate termination of a method by using this focm of **return:**

```
return;
```

When this statement executes, program control returns to the caller, skipping any remaining code in the method. For example, consider this method:

```
public void MyMeth()
    int 1;

    for(i=0; i<10; i++) {
        if(i == 5) return          // stop at 5
        Console.WriteLine();
    }
}
```

Here, the **for** loop will only run from 0 to 5, because once i equals 5, the method returns.

It is permissible to have multiple **return** statements in a method, especially when there are two or more routes out of it. For example,

```
public void MyMeth {} {
    // ...
    if (done) return;
    // . . .
    if (error) return;
}
```

Here, the method returns if it is done or if an error occurs. Be careful, however. Having too many exit points in a method can destructure your code, so avoid using them casually.

## Return a Value

Although methods with a return type of **void** are not rare, most methods will return a value. In fact, the ability to return a value is one of a method's most useful features. You have already seen an example of a return value when we used the **Math.Sqrt()** function earlier to obtain a square root.

Return values are used for a variety of purposes in programming. In some cases, such as with **Math.Sqrt()**, the return value contains the outcome of some calculation. In other cases, the return value may simply indicate success or failure. In still others, it may contain a status code. Whatever the purpose, using method return values is an integral part of C# programming.

Methods return a value to the calling routine using this form of **return:**

```
return value;
```

Here, *value* is the value returned.

You can use a return value to improve the implementation of **AreaPerPerson()**. Instead of displaying the area-per-person, a better approach is to have **AreaPerPerson()** return this value. Among the advantages to this approach is that you can use the value for other calculations. The following example modifies **AreaPerPerson()** to return the area-per-person rather than displaying it:

```
// Return a value from AreaPerPerson ().

using System;

class Building {
    public int Floors; // number of floors
    public int Area; // total square footage of building
    public int Occupants; // number of occupants

// Return the area per person,
public int AreaPerPerson () {
    return Area / Occupants;
    }
}

// Use the return value from AreaPerPerson{).
class BuildingDemo {
    static void Main() {
        Building house = new Building ();
        Building office = new Building!);
        int areaPP; // area per person

    // Assign values to fields in house,
    house.Occupants = 4;
    house.Area - 2500;
    house.Floors = 2;

    // Assign values to fields in office.
    office.Occupants = 25;
    office.Area = 4200;
    office.Floors = 3;

    // Obtain area per person for house.
    areaPP = house.AreaPerPerson ();

    Console.WriteLine("house has:\n " +
                      house.Floors + " floors\n " +
                      house.Occupants + " occupants\n
                      house.Area + " total area\n " +
                      areaPP + " area per person");

    Console .WriteLine () ;

    // Obtain area per person for office.
    areaPP = office. AreaPerPerson (} ;

    Console .WriteLine ("office has : \n " +
                      office.Floors + " floors\n " +
                office.Occupants + " occupants\n
                office.Area + " total area\n " +
```

```
            areaPP + " area per person");
    }
}
```



The output is the same as shown earlier.

In the program, notice that when **AreaPerPerson ()** is called, it is put on the right side of an assignment statement. On the left is a variable that will receive the value returned by **AreaPerPerson( ).** Thus, after

```
areaPP = house .AreaPerPerson ();
```

executes, the area-per-person of the **house** object is stored in **areaPP.**

Notice that **AreaPerPerson( )** now has a return type of int. This means that it will return an integer value to the caller. The return type of a method is important because the type of data returned by a method must be compatible with the return type specified by the method. Thus, if you want a method to return data of type **double,** then its return type must be type **double.**

Although the preceding program is correct, it is not written as efficiently as it could be. Specifically, there is no need for the **areaPP** variable. A call to **AreaPerPerson()** can be used in the **WriteLine()** statement directly, as shown here:

```
Console.WriteLine("house has:\n " +
                  house.Floors + " floors\n " +
                  house.Occupants + " occupants\n
                  house.Area + " total area\n " +
                  areaPP + " area per person");
```

In this case, when **WriteLine()** is executed, **house.AreaPerPerson()** is called automatically, and its value will be passed to **WriteLine()**. Furthermore, you can use a call to **AreaPerPerson()** whenever the area-per-person of a **Building** object is needed. For example, this statement compares the per-person areas of two buildings:

```
if(bl.AreaPerPerson() > b2.AreaPerPerson ())
    Console.WriteLine("bl has more space for each person");
```

## Use Parameters

It is possible to pass one or more values to a method when the method is called. A value passed to a method is called an *argument.* Inside the method, the variable that receives the argument is called a *format parameter,* or just *parameter,* for short. Parameters are declared inside the parentheses that follow the method's name. The parameter declaration syntax is the same as that used for variables. The scope of a parameter is the body of its method. Aside from its special task of receiving an argument, it acts like any other local variable. Here is a simple example that uses a parameter. Inside the **ChkNum** class, the method **IsPrime()** returns **true** if the value that it is passed is prime. It returns **false** otherwise. Therefore, **IsPrime()** has a return type of **bool.**

```
// A simple example that uses a parameter.

using System.

class ChkNum {
    // Return true if x is prime
    public tool IsPrime(int x) {
        if(x =<= 1) return false

for(int i=2; i <= x/i; i++)
    if ( (x %i) == 0) return false'

    return true;
```

```
    }
}

class ParmDemo {
    static void MainO {
    ChkNum ob = new ChkNum ();

    for(int i=2; i < 10; 1++)
        if(ob.IsPrimt(i) Console.WriteLine(1 + " is prime.");
        else Console.WriteLine(i + " is not prime: ");
    }
}
```

Here is the output produced by the program:

```
2 is prime.
3 i s prime.
4 i s not prime.
5 is prime.
6 is riot prime.
8
9
```

In the program, **IsPrime{** ) is called eight times, and each time a different value is passed. Let's look at this process closely. First, notice how **IsPrime(**) is called. The argument is specified between the parentheses. When **IsPrime(**) is called the first time, it is passed the value 2. Thus, when **IsPrime(**) begins executing, the parameter x receives the value 2. In the second call, 3 is the argument, and x then has the value 3. In the third call, the argument is 4, which is the value that x receives, and so on. The point is that the value passed as an argument when **IsPrime(**) is called is the value received by its parameter, x.

A method can have more than one parameter. Simply declare each parameter, separating one from the next with a comma. For example, here the **ChkNum** class is expanded by adding a method called **LeastComFactor(** ), which returns the smallest factor that its two arguments have in common. In other words, it returns the smallest whole number value that can evenly divide both arguments.

```
// Add a method that takes two arguments.

using System;

class ChkNum {
    // Return true if x is prime.
    public bool IsPrime (int. x) {
        if(x <- 1) return false;

        for(int i=2; i <= x/i; i++)
            if((x %1) == 0) return false;

        return true;
}

// Return the least common factor.
public int LeastComF'actor (int. a, int b) {
    int max;

    if(IsPrime(a) || IsPrime(b)) return 1;

    max = a < b ? a : b;
```

```
    for(int i=2; i <= max/2; i++)
        if(((a%1) == 0) && ((b%1) == 0)) return i;

    return 1;
    }
}

class ParmDemo {
    static void Main{) {
    chkNum ob = new ChkNum ();
    int a, b;

    for (int i=2; i < 10;
        if(ob. Is Prime (i) > Console.WriteLine (i + " is prime ." )
        else Console. WriteLine (i + " is not prime. ") ;

a = 7;
b = 8;
Console .WriteLine ("Least common factor for " +
                        a + " and " + b + " i s " +
                        ob.LeastComFactor (a, b) ) ;

a = 100;
b = 8;
Console .HriteLine ("Least common factor for " +
                        a + " and " + b + " is " +
                        ob.LeastComFactor (a, b) ) ;

a = 100;
b = 75;
Console.WriteLine ("Least common factor for " +
                        a + " and " + b + " is " +
                        ob. LeastComFactor (a, b) ) ;
    }
}
```

Notice that when **LeastComFactor()** is called, the arguments are also separated by commas. The output from the program is shown here:

```
2 is prime.
3 is prime.
4 is not prime.
5 is prime.
6 is *iot prime .
7 is prime.
8 is not prime.
9 is not prime.
Least common factor for 7 and 8 is 1
Least common factor for 100 and 8 is 2
Least common factor for 100 and 75 is 5
```

When using multiple parameters, each parameter specifies its own type, which can differ from the others. For example, this is perfectly valid:

```
int MyMeth(int a, double b, float c) {
    // . . .
```

## Add a Parameterized Method to Building

You can use a parameterized method to add a new feature to the **Building** class: the ability to compute the maximum number of occupants for a building assuming that each occupant must have a certain minimal space. This new method is called **MaxOccupant()**. It is shown here:

```
// Return the maximum number of occupants if each
// is to have at least the specified minimum area.
public int MaxOccupant (int minArea) {
    return Area / minArea;
}
```

When **MaxOccupanH )** is called, the parameter **minArea** receives the minimum space needed for each occupant. The method divides the total area of the building by this value and returns the result. The entire **Building** class that includes **MaxOccupanK )** is shown here:

```
/*
   Add a parameterized method that computes the
   maximum number of people that can occupy a
   building assuming each needs a specified
   minimum space
*/

using System;

class Building {
   public int Floor     // number of floors
   public int Area;     // total square footage of building
   public int Occupant  // number of occupants

 // Return the area per person.
 public int AreaPerPerson() {
    return Area / Occupants;
 }

 // Return the maximum number of occupants if each
 //  is to have at least the specified minimum area.
 public.int MaxOccupant (int minArea) {
    retunr Area / minArea;
    }
 }

 // Use MaxOccupant().
 class BuildingDemo {
    static void Main() {
        Building house = new Building();
        Building office – new Building ();

    // Assign values to fields in house.
    house.Occupants = 4;
    house.Area = 2500;
    house.Floors = 2;

    // Assign values to fields in office.
    office.Occupants = 25;
    office.Area = 4200;
```

```
        office.Floors = 3;

        Console.WriteLine <"Maximum occupants for house if each has '
                           300 + " square feet: " +
                           house.MaxOccupanl(300));

        Console.WriteLine("Maximum occupants for office if each has " +
                           300 + " square feet: " +
                           office.MaxOccupant(300));
        }
    }
```

The output from the program is shown here:

```
Maximum occupants for house if each has 300 square feet; 8
Maximum occupants for office if each has 300 square feet; 14
```

## Avoiding Unreachable Code

When creating methods, you should avoid causing a situation in which a portion of code cannot, under any circumstances, be executed. This is called *unreachable code,* and it is considered incorrect in C#. The compiler will issue a warning message if you create a method that contains unreachable code. For example:

```
public void MyMeth{) {
   char a, b;

   // ...

   if(a==b> {
      Console- WriteLine ("equal");
      return;
   } else {
      Console .WriteLine ("not. equal" ) ;
      return;
   }
   Console.WriteLine("this is unreachable");
}
```

Here, the method **MyMeth()** will always return before the final **WriteLine()** statement is executed. If you try to compile this method, you will receive a warning. In general, unreachable code constitutes a mistake on your part, so it is a good idea to take unreachable code warnings seriously.

## Constructors

In the preceding examples, the instance variables of each **Building** object had to be set manually using a sequence of statements, such as

```
house.Occupants = 4;
house.Area = 2500;
hose.floors = 2;
```

An approach like this would never be used in professionally written C# code. Aside from this approach being error prone (you might forget to set one of the fields), there is simply a better way to accomplish this task: the constructor.

A *constructor* initializes an object when it is created. It has the same name as its class and is syntactically similar to a method. However, constructors have no explicit return type. The general form of a constructor is shown here:

```
access class-name(pamm-list) {
// constructor code
}
```

Typically, you will use a constructor to give initial values to the instance variables defined by the class or to perform any other startup procedures required to create a fully formed object. Also, usually, *access* is **public** because constructors are normally called from outside their class. The *param-list* can be empty, or it can specify one or more parameters.

All classes have constructors, whether you define one or not, because C# automatically provides a default constructor that causes all member variables to be initialized to their default values. For most value types, the default value is zero. For **bool,** the default is false. For reference types, the default is null. However, once you define your own constructor, the default constructor is no longer used.

Here is a simple example that uses a constructor:

```
//A simple constructor.

using System;

class MyClass {
    public int x;

    public MyClass()
        x = 10;
    }
}

class ConsDemo {
    static void Main () {
        MyClass ti = new MyClass ();
        MyClass t2 = new MyClass ();

        Console . WriteLine (tl . x + " " + t2 . x) ;
    }
}
```

In this example, the constructor for MyClass is

```
public MyClass () {
    x - 10;
    }
```

Notice that the constructor is specified as public. This is because the constructor will be called from code defined outside of its class. This constructor assigns the instance variable x of MyClass the value 10. This constructor is called by new when an object is created. For example, in the line

```
MyClass ti = new MyClass();
```

the constructor MyClass() is called on the tl object, giving tl.x the value 10. The same is true for t2. After construction, t2.x has the value 10. Thus, the output from the program is

```
10 10
```

## Parameterized Constructors

In the preceding example, a parameterless constructor was used. While this is fine for some situations, most often you will need a constructor that has one or more parameters. Parameters are added to a constructor in the same way they are added to a method: just declare them inside the parentheses after the constructor's name. For example, here MyClass is given a parameterized constructor:

CHAPTER 2

```
/* A parametrized constructor.

using System;

class MyClass {
   public MyClass(int i) {
      x = 1;
   }
}

class ParmConsDemo {
   static void Mainf) {
      MyClass tl = new MyClass(10);
      MyClass t2 = new MyClass(88);

      Console.WriteLine(tl-x + " " + t2.x);
   }
}
```

The output from this program is shown here:

```
10 88
```

In this version of the program, the MyClass() constructor defines one parameter called i, which is used to initialize the instance variable, x. Thus, when the line

```
MyClass tl - new MyClass(10);
```

executes, the value 10 is passed to i, which is then assigned to x.

## Add a Constructor to the Building Class

We can improve the Building class by adding a constructor that automatically initializes the Floors, Area, and Occupants fields when an object is constructed. Pay special attention to how Building objects are created.

```
// Add a constructor is Building.

using System/

class Building {
   public int Flours; // number of floors
   public int Area; // total square footage of building
   public int Occupants; // number of occupants

   // A parameterized constructor for Building,
   public Buildingfint f, int a, int o) {
      Floors = f;
      Area = a;
      Occupants = o;
   }

   //Display the area per person.
   public int AreaPerPerson() {
      return Area / Occupants;
   }

   // Return the maximum number of occupants if each
   // is to have at least the specified minimum area.
```

```
    public int MaxOccupant{int minArea) {
        return Area / minArea;
    }
}

// Use the parameterized Building constructor,
class BuildingDemo [
    static void Mainf) (
        Building house - new Building(2, 2500,- 4);
        Building office = new Building(3, 4200, 25);

        Console.WriteLine("Maximum occupants for house if each has " +
                          300 + " square feel: " +
                          house .MaxOccupant (300) ) -,

        Console.WriteLine("Maximum occupants for office if each has" +
                          300 + " square feet: " +
                          office.MaxOccupant (300)) ;
    }
}
```

The output from this program is the same as for the previous version.

Both house and **office** were initialized by the **Building()** constructor when they were created. Each object is initialized as specified in the parameters to its constructor. For example, in the following line,

```
Building house = new Builciing(2, 2500, 4);
```

the values 2, 2500, and 4 are passed to the **Building()** constructor when **new** creates the object. Thus, **house's** copy of **Floors, Area,** and **Occupants** will contain the values 2, 2500, and 4, respectively.

## The new Operator Revisited

Now that you know more about classes and their constructors, let's take a closer look at the new operator. As it relates to classes, the **new** operator has this general form:

```
new class-name(arg-list)
```

Here, *class-name* is the name of the class that is being instantiated. The class name followed by parentheses specifies the constructor for the class. If a class does not define its own constructor, new will use the default constructor supplied by C#. Thus, new can be used to create an object of any class type.

Since memory is finite, it is possible that new will not be able to allocate memory for an object because insufficient memory exists. If this happens, a runtime exception will occur.

### Using new with Value Types

At this point, you might be asking why you don't need to use new for variables of the value types, such as int or float? In C#, a variable of a value type contains its own value. Memory to hold this value is automatically provided when the program is run. Thus, there is no need to explicitly allocate this memory using new. Conversely, a reference variable stores a reference to an object. The memory to hold this object must be allocated dynamically, during execution.

Not making the fundamental types, such **int** or **char,** into reference types greatly improves your program's performance. When using a reference type, there is a layer of indirection that adds overhead to each object access. This layer of indirection is avoided by a value type.

As a point of interest, it is permitted to use new with the value types, as shown here:

```
int i = new int ();
```

Doing so invokes the default constructor for type int, which initializes i to zero. For example:

```
// Use new with d vaiue type,

using System;

class newValue {
    static void Main() {
        int i = new int(); // initialize i to zero
        Console.WriteLine("The value of i is: " + i) ;
    }
}
```

The output from this program is

```
The value of i is: 0
```

As the output verifies, i is initialized to zero. Remember, without the use of new, i would be uninitialized, and it would cause an error to attempt to use it in the WriteLine() statement without explicitly giving it a value first.

In general, invoking new for a value type invokes the default constructor for that type. It does not, however, dynamically allocate memory. Frankly, most programmers do not use new with the value types.

## Garbage Collection and Destructors

As you have seen, objects are dynamically allocated from a pool of free memory by using the new operator. Of course, memory is not infinite, and the free memory can be exhausted. Thus, it is possible for new to fail because there is insufficient free memory to create the desired object. For this reason, one of the key components of any dynamic allocation scheme is the recovery of free memory from unused objects, making that memory available for subsequent reallocation. In many programming languages, the release of previously allocated memory is handled manually. For example, in C++, the delete operator is used to free memory that was allocated. However, C# uses a different, more trouble-free approach: *garbage collection.*

C#'s garbage collection system reclaims objects automatically—occurring transparently, behind the scenes, without any programmer intervention. It works like this: When no references to an object exist, that object is assumed to be no longer needed, and the memory occupied by the object is eventually released and collected. This recycled memory can then be used for a subsequent allocation.

Garbage collection occurs only sporadically during the execution of your program. It will not occur simply because one or more objects exist that are no longer used. Thus, you can't know, or make assumptions about, precisely when garbage collection will take place.

### Destructors

It is possible to define a method that will be called just prior to an object's final destruction by the garbage collector. This method is called a *destructor,* and it can be used in some highly specialized situations to ensure that an object terminates cleanly. For example, you might use a destructor to ensure that a system resource owned by an object is released. It must be stated at the outset that destructors are a very advanced feature that are applicable only to certain rare cases. They are not normally needed. They are briefly described here for completeness.

Destructors have this general form:

```
~class-name() {
    // destruction code
}
```

Here, *class-name* is the name of the class. Thus, a destructor is declared like a constructor except that it is preceded with a ~ (tilde). Notice it has no return type and takes no arguments.

To add a destructor to a class, you simply include it as a member. It is called whenever an object of its class is about to be recycled. Inside the destructor, you will specify those actions that must be performed before an object is destroyed.

It is important to understand that the destructor is called just prior to garbage collection. It is not called when a variable containing a reference to an object goes out of scope, for example. (This differs from destructors in C++, which *are* called when an object goes out of scope.) This means that you cannot know precisely when a destructor will be executed. Furthermore, it is possible for your program to end before garbage collection occurs, so a destructor might not get called at all.

The following program demonstrates a destructor. It works by creating and destroying a large number of objects. During this process, at some point the garbage collector will be activated, and the destructors for the objects will be called.

```
//Demonstrate a destructor.

using System;

class Destruct {
     public int x;

     public Destruct (ibt i) {
     }

     // Called when object is recycled.
     ~Destruct () {
     Console.WriteLine("Destructing " + x) ;
     }

     // Generates an object that is immedlately destroyed,
     public void Generator(int i) {
         Destruct o = new Destruct (i);
     }
}

class- DestructDemo {
     static void Main() {
         int count;

         Destruct ob = new Destruct (0);

     /* Now, generate a large number of objects. At some         point,
garbage collection will occur. Note: You might need         to increase
the number of objects generated in order to         force garbage collection.
*/

     for(count-1; count < 100000; count++)

         ob.Generator(count);

     Console.WriteLine("Done");
     }
}
```

Here is how the program works. The constructor sets the instance variable x to a known value. In this example, x is used as an object ID. The destructor displays the value of x when an object is recycled. Of special interest is Generator(). This method creates and then promptly destroys a Destruct object. The DestructDemo class creates an initial Destruct object called ob. Then using ob, it creates 100,000 objects by calling Generator! ) on ob. This has the net effect of creating and destroying 100,000 objects. At various points in the middle of this process, garbage collection will take place. Precisely how often or when is dependent upon several factors, such as the initial amount of free memory, the operating system, and so on. However, at some point, you will start to see the messages generated by the destructor. If you don't see the messages prior to program termination (that is, before you see the "Done" message), try increasing the number of objects being generated by upping the count in the for loop.

One important point; The call to WriteLineO inside ~Destruct() is purely for the sake of illustration in this rather contrived example. Normally, a destructor should act only on the instance variables defined by its class.

Because of the nondeterministic way in which destructors are called, they should not be used to perform actions that must occur at a specific point in your program. One other point: It is possible to request garbage collection. This is described in Part II, when C#'s class library is discussed. However, manually initiating garbage collection is not recommended for most circumstances, because it can lead to inefficiencies. Also, because of the way the garbage collector works, even if you explicitly request garbage collection, there is no way to know precisely when a specific object will be recycled.

## The this Keyword

Before concluding this chapter, it is necessary to introduce this. When a method is called, it is automatically passed a reference to the invoking object (that is, the object on which the method is called). This reference is called this. Therefore, this refers to the object on which the method is acting. To understand this, first consider a program that creates a class called Reel that encapsulates the width and height of a rectangle and that includes a method called Area() that returns its area.

```
using System;

class Rect {
   public int Width;
   public int Height;

   public Rect (int w, int h) {
      Width = w;
      Height = h;
   }

   public int Area () {

   return Width * Height;
   }
}

class UseRect {
   static void Main () {
      Rect rl = new Rect<4, 5);
      Rect r2 = new Rect (7, 9);

      Console.WriteLine ("Area of rl: " + rl.Area ()
      Console.WriteLine ("Area of r2: " + r2.Area ()
```

```
    }
}
```

As you know, within a method, the other members of a class can be accessed directly, without any object or class qualification. Thus, inside **Area()**, the statement

```
return Width * Height;
```

means that the copies of **Width and Height** associated with the invoking object will be multiplied together and the result returned. However, the same statement can also be written like this:

```
return this.Width * this.Height;
```

Here, **this** refers to the object on which **Area()** was called. Thus, **this.Width** refers to that object's copy of **Width, and this.Height** refers to that object's copy of **Height.** For example, if **Area<)** had been invoked on an object called x, then **this** in the preceding statement would have been referring to x. Writing the statement without using **this** is really just shorthand.

It is also possible to use **this** inside a constructor. In this case, **this** refers to the object that is being constructed. For example, inside **Rect()**, the statements

```
Width = w;
Height = h;
```

can be written like this:

```
this.Width = w;
this.-Height = h;
```

Of course, there is no benefit in doing so in this case.

For the sake of illustration, here is the entire **Rect** class written using the **this** reference:

```
using System;

class Rect {
    public int.Width;
    public int. Height;

    public Rect(int w, int h) {
    this. Width = w;
    this. Height = h;
}

public int Area ( ) {
    return this. Width * this. Height;
    }
}

class UseRect (
    static void Mainf) I
        Rect rl - new Rect(4, 5);
        Rect r2 = new Rect(7, 9);

    Console,WriteLine("Area of rl: " + rl.Area());
    Console.WriteLine("Area of r2: " + r2.Area());

    }
}
```

Actually, no C# programmer would use this as just shown because nothing is gained and the standard form is easier. However, this has some important uses. For example, the C# syntax permits the name of

CHAPTER 2

a parameter or a local variable to be the same as the name of an instance variable. When this happens, the local name *hides* the instance variable. You can gain access to the hidden instance variable by referring to it through this. For example, the following is a syntactically valid way to write the Rect() constructor:

```
public Rect(int Width, int Height) {
    this.Width = Width;
    this.Height = Height;
}
```

hi this version, the names of the parameters are the same as the names of the instance variables, thus hiding them. However, this is used to "uncover" the instance variables.

# CHAPTER 3

# Arrays and Strings

***In this chapter you will read about:***

- Arrays.
- One-dimensional array.
- Multidimensional array.
- Implicitly Typed Arrays.
- Assigning Array References.

## Introduction to Arrays

An *array* is a collection of variables of the same type that are referred to by a common name. In C#, arrays can have one or more dimensions, although the one-dimensional array is the most common. Arrays are used for a variety of purposes because they offer a convenient means of grouping together related variables. For example, you might use an array to hold a record of the daily high temperature for a month, a list of stock prices, or your collection of programming books.

The principal advantage of an array is that it organizes data in such a way that it can be easily manipulated. For example, if you have an array containing the dividends for a selected group of stocks, it is easy to compute the average income by cycling through the array. Also, arrays organize data in such a way that it can be easily sorted.

Although arrays in C# can be used just like arrays in many other programming languages, they have one special attribute: They are implemented as objects. This fact is one reason that a discussion of arrays was deferred until objects had been introduced. By implementing arrays as objects, several important advantages are gained, not the least of which is that unused arrays can be garbage-collected.

## One-Dimensional Arrays

A *one-dimensional array* is a list of related variables. Such lists are common in programming. For example, you might use a one-dimensional array to store the account numbers of the active users on a network. Another array might store the current batting averages for a baseball team.

Because arrays in C# are implemented as objects, two steps are needed to obtain an array for use in your program. First, you must declare a variable that can refer to an array. Second, you must create an instance of the array by use of new. Therefore, to declare a one-dimensional array, you will typically use this general form:

```
type{ \ array-name - new type[size\;
```

Here, *type* declares the *element type* of the array. The element type determines the data type of each element that comprises the array. Notice the square brackets that follow *type*. They indicate that a one-dimensional array is being declared. The number of elements that the array will hold is determined by *size*.

Here is an example. The following creates an int array of ten elements and links it to an array reference variable named sample.

```
int[] sample = new int [ 10];
```

The sample variable holds a reference to the memory allocated by new. This memory is large enough to hold ten elements of type int.

As is the case when creating an instance of a class, it is possible to break the preceding declaration in two. For example:

```
int[] sample;
sample = new int[101;
```

In this case, when sample is first created, it refers to no physical object. It is only after the second statement executes that sample refers to an array.

An individual element within an array is accessed by use of an index. An *index* describes the position of an element within an array. In C#, all arrays have 0 as the index of their first element. Because sample has 10 elements, it has index values of 0 through 9. To index an array, specify the number of the element you want, surrounded by square brackets. Thus, the first element in sample is sample[0], and the last element is sample[9]. For example, the following program loads sample with the numbers 0 through 9:

```
// Demonstrate a one-dimensional array.
```

```
using System;

class ArrayDemo {
    static void Main{) {
    int [ ] sample = new int [10];
    int i ;

    for(i = 0; i < 10; i = i+1)
        sample [i] = i;

    for (i = 0; i = 10; i = i+1)
        Console.WriteLine ("sample [" + i + "]:" + sample [i] ) ;
    }
}
```

The output from the program is shown here:

```
sample[0]:0
sample[1]:1
sample[2]:2
sample[3]:3
sample[4]:4
sample[5]:5
samp]e[6]:6
sample[7]:7
sample[8]:8
sample[9]:9
```

Arrays are common in programming because they let you deal easily with large numbers of related variables. For example, the following program finds the average of the set of values stored in the **nums** array by cycling through the array using a for loop:

```
// Compute the average of a set of values,

using System;

class Average (
    static void Main() {
        int [] nums = new int [10];
        int avg = 0;
    nums[0]:  99;
    nums[1]:  10;
    nums[2]:  100;
    nums[3]:  18;
    nums[4]:  78;
    nums[5]:  23;
    nums[6]:  63;
    nums[7]:  9;
    nums[8]:  87;
    nums[9]:  49;

    for (int i = 0; i < 10; i++)
        avg = avg + nums [i]'

    Console . WriteLine ("Average : " + avg);
    }
}
```

The output from the program is shown here:

```
Average: 53
```

## Initializing an Array

In the preceding program, the **nums** array was given values by hand, using ten separate assignment statements. While that is perfectly correct, there is an easier way to accomplish this. Arrays can be initialized when they are created. The general form for initializing a one-dimensional array is shown here:

```
type[ \ array-name = { vail, vail, vaB,.... valN };
```

Here, the initial values are specified by *vail* through *valN*. They are assigned in sequence, left to right, in index order. C# automatically allocates an array large enough to hold the initializers that you specify. There is no need to use the **new** operator explicitly. For example, here is a better way to write the **Average** program:

```
//Compute the average of a set of values.

using System;

class Average {
   static void Mainf) {
      int[] nums = ( 99, 10, 100, 18, 78, 23,
                     63, 9, 87, 49 };
   int avg - 0;

   for (int i=0; i < 10, i++)

      avg = avg / 10;

   Console.WriteLine("Average: " + avg);
   }
}
```

As a point of interest, although not needed, you can use new when initializing an array. For example, this is a proper, but redundant, way to initialize **nums** in the foregoing program:

```
int [] nums = new int = ( 99, 10, 100, 18, 78, 23,
                          63, 9, 87, 49 };
```

Although redundant here, the new form of array initialization is useful when you are assigning a new array to an already-existent array reference variable. For example:

```
int[] nums
nums = new int[] ( 99, 10, 100, 18, 78, 23,
                   63, 9, 87, 49 };
```

In this case, nums is declared in the first statement and initialized by the second.

One last point: It is permissible to specify the array size explicitly when initializing an array, but the size must agree with the number of initializers. For example, here is another way to initialize nums:

```
int[] nums = new int [10]( 99, 10, 100, 18, 78, 23,
                           63, 9, 87, 49 };
```

In this declaration, the size of **nums** is explicitly stated as 10.

## Boundaries Are Enforced

Array boundaries are strictly enforced in C#; it is a runtime error to overrun or underrun the ends of an array. If you want to confirm this for yourself, try the following program that purposely overruns an array:

```
// Demonstrate an array overrun.

using System;

class ArrayErr {
```

```
    static void Main() {
        int[] sample = new int [10];
        int 1;

        // GeneraLe an array overrun.
        for (i =— 0; i < 100; i = i+1)
    }
}
```

## Multidimensional Arrays

Although the one-dimensional array is the most commonly used array in programming, multidimensional arrays are certainly not rare. A *multidimensional array* is an array that has two or more dimensions, and an individual element is accessed through the combination of two or more indices.

### Two-Dimensional Arrays

The simplest form of the multidimensional array is the two-dimensional array. In a two-dimensional array, the location of any specific element is specified by two indices. If you think of a two-dimensional array as a table of information, one index indicates the row, the other indicates the column.

To declare a two-dimensional integer array table of size 10, 20, you would write

```
int[,] table = new int[10, 20];
```

Pay careful attention to the declaration. Notice that the two dimensions are separated from each other by a comma. In the first part of the declaration, the syntax

```
[,]
```

indicates that a two-dimensional array reference variable is being created. When memory is actually allocated for the array using new, this syntax is used:

```
int[10, 20]
```

This creates a 10x20 array, and again, the comma separates the dimensions.

To access an element in a two-dimensional array, you must specify both indices, separating the two with a comma. For example, to assign the value 10 to location 3,5 of array table, you would use

```
table[3, 5] - 10;
```

Here is a complete example. It loads a two-dimensional array with the numbers 1 through 12 and then displays the contents of the array.

```
// Demonstrate a two-dimensional array,

using System;

class TwoD {
    static void Main() {
        int t, i;
        int[,] table = new int[3, 4];

        for(t=0; t < 3; t- + t) {
            for(1=0; i < 4; ++i) {
                table[t,i] - (t*4)+i+1;
                Console.Write(table [t,i] + " ");
            }
            Console.WriteLine ();
        }
    }
}
```

In this example, table[0, 0] will have the value 1, table[0,1] the value 2, table[0, 2] the value 3, and so on. The value of table[2, 3] will be 12.

## Arrays of Three or More Dimensions

C# allows arrays with more than two dimensions. Here is the general form of a multidimensional array declaration:

```
type[,...,] name - new type[sizel, size!,..., sizeN];
```

For example, the following declaration creates a 4x10x3 three-dimensional integer array:

```
int[,,] multidim = new int[4, 10, 3];
```

To assign element 2, 4,1 of **multidim** the value 100, use this statement:

```
multidim[2, 4, 1] = 100;
```

Here is a program that uses a three-dimensional array that holds a 3x3x3 matrix of values. It then sums the value on one of the diagonals through the cube.

```
// Sum the values on a diagonal of a 3x3x3 matrix,

using System;

class ThreeDMatrix {
    static voi d Main() {
        int[,,] m - new int[3, 3, 3];
        int sum = 0;
        int n = 1;

        for (int x=0; x < 3; x + +)
            for(int y=0; y < 3; y+ + }
                for{int z=Q; z < 3; 7+1-)
                    mix, y, zI = n++;

        sum = m[0, 0, 0] +m[l, 1, 1] + m[2, 2, 2];

        Console.WriteLine("Sum of first diagonal: "+ sum);
    }
}
```

The output is shown here:

```
Sum of first diagonal: 42
```

## Initializing Multidimensional Arrays

A multidimensional array can be initialized by enclosing each dimension's initializer list within its own set of curly braces. For example, the general form of array initialization for a two-dimensional array is shown here:

```
type[,] array_name = {
    (val,val,val, ...,val),
    (val, val, val,..., val),
    .
    .
    .
    (val, val, val,..., val)
);
```

Here, *val* indicates an initialization value. Each inner block designates a row. Within each row, the first value will be stored in the first position, the second value in the second position, and so on. Notice that commas separate the initializer blocks and that a semicolon follows the closing}.

For example, the following program initializes an array called sqrs with the numbers 1 through 10 and their squares.

```
// initialise a two-dimensional array.
```

```
using Systems

class Squares {
  static void Main!) {
  int [,] sqrs = 1
      ( 1, 1 ),
      ( 2, 4 ),
      ( 3, 9 ),
      ( 4, 16 ),
      ( 5, 25 ),
      ( 6, 36 ),
      ( 7, 49 ),
      ( 8, 64 ),
      ( 9, 81 ),
      ( 10, 100 ),
   );
   int i, j;

   for (i = 0; i < 10; i++) {
     for (j = 0; j = 2; j++)
        Console.Write(sqrs[i,j] + " ");
     Console.WriteLine() ;
     }
   }
}
```

Here is the output from the program:

```
1  1
2  4
3  9
4  16
5  25
6  36
7  49
8  64
9  81
10 100
```

## Jagged Arrays

In the preceding examples, when you created a two-dimensional array, you were creating what is called a *rectangular array*. Thinking of two-dimensional arrays as tables, a rectangular array is a two-dimensional array in which the length of each row is the same for the entire array. However, C# also allows you to create a special type of two-dimensional array called a *jagged array*. A jagged array is an *array of arrays* in which the length of each array can differ. Thus, a jagged array can be used to create a table in which the lengths of the rows are not the same.

Jagged arrays are declared by using sets of square brackets to indicate each dimension. For example, to declare a two-dimensional jagged array, you will use this general form:

```
type[ ] [ \ array-name = new type[size][ ];
```

Here, *size* indicates the number of rows in the array. The rows, themselves, have not been . allocated. Instead, the rows are allocated individually. This allows for the length of each row to vary. For example, the following code allocates memory for the first dimension of jagged when it is declared. It then allocates the second dimensions manually.

```
int [] [] jaqqed = new int [3] [];
jagged[0] = new int[4];
jaqqed[1] = new int[3] ,
jaqqed[2] = new int[5];
```

It is easy to see how jagged arrays got their name!

Once a jagged array has been created, an element is accessed by specifying each index within its own set of brackets. For example, to assign the value 10 to element 2,1 of **jagged,** you would use this statement:

```
jagged [2][1] = 10;
```

Note that this differs from the syntax that is used to access an element of a rectangular array. The following program demonstrates the creation of a jagged two-dimensional array:

```
// Demonstrate jagged arrays.

using System;

class Jagged {
    static void Main() {
        int[] [J jaqqed = new int[3] [];
        jaqqed[0] = new int[4};
        jaqqed[11 = new int[ 3] ;
        jagged[2] =- new int. [5] ;

        int i;

        // Store values in third array.
        for(i=0; i < 5; i++)
            jagged[2][i] - i;

        // Display values in first array.
        for(i=0; i < 4; i++)
            jagged[1][i] = i;

        // Store value in third array
        for(i=0; i < 5; i++)
            jagged[2][i] = i;

        // Store valuse in third array
        for(i=0; i < 4; i++)
            Console.Write(jagged[0][i] + " ");

        Console.WriteLine(};

        // Display values in second array.
        for(i=0; i < 3; i++)
            Console.Write(jagged[1] [i] + " ");

        Console.WriteLine();

        // Display values in third array.
        for(i-^0; i < 5; i++)
            Console.Write(jagged[2][il + " ");
        Console.WriteLine();
    }
}
```

The output is shown here:

```
0123
```

```
012
01234
```

Jagged arrays are not used by all applications, but they can be effective in some situations. For example, if you need a very large two-dimensional array that is sparsely populated (that is, one in which not all of the elements will be used), then a jagged array might be a perfect solution.



One last point: Because jagged arrays are arrays of arrays, there is no restriction that requires that the arrays be one-dimensional. For example, the following creates an array of two-dimensional arrays:

```
int[][,] jagged = new int[3][,];
```

The next statement assigns jagged[0] a reference to a 4x2 array:

```
jagged[0] = new int [4, 2];
```

The following statement assigns a value to jagged[0111,0]:

```
jagged[01[1,0] - i;
```

## Assigning Array References

As with other objects, when you assign one array reference variable to another, you are simply making both variables refer to the same array. You are neither causing a copy of the array to be created, nor are you causing the contents of one array to be copied to the other. For example, consider this program:

```
// Assigning array reference variables.

using System;

class AssignARef {
    static void Main() {
        int i;

        int[] numsl = new int [10];
        int[] nums2 = new int [10];

        for(1=0; i < 10; i++) numsl[i] = i;
        for(i=0; i < 10; 14+) nuras2[i] = -i;

        Console.Write ("Here is numsl: ");
        for (1 = 0; i < 10; i++)
            Console.Write(numsl[i] + " ");
        Console.WriteLine ();

        Console.Write("Here is nums2: ");
        for{i=0; i < 10; i++)
            Console.Write(nums2[i] + " ");
        Console.WriteLine ();

        nums2 = numsl;   // now nums2 refers to numsl

        Console.Write("Here is nums2 after assignment: ");
        for (1=0; i < 10; 1 + + )
            Console.Write{nums2[i] + " ");
        Console.WriteLine {};

        // Next, operate on numsl array through nums2.
        nums2[3] - 99;

        Console.Write("Here is numsl after change through nums2: ");
        for(i=0; i < 10; i++) .
            Console.Write(numsl[i] + " ") ;
```

```
            Console.WriteLine ();
        }
    }
```

The output from the program is shown here:

```
Here is numsl: 0 1 2 3 4 5 6 7 8 9
Here is nums2: 0 -1 -2 -3 -4 -5 -6 -7 -8 -9
Here is nums2 after assignment: 0 1 2 3 4 5 6 7 8 9
Here is numsl after change through nums2: 0 1 2 99 4 5 6 7 8 9
```

As the output shows, after the assignment of **numsl to nums2,** both array reference variables refer to the same object.

## Using the Length Property

A number of benefits result because C# implements arrays as objects. One comes from the fact that each array has associated with it a Length property that contains the number of elements that an array can hold. Thus, each array provides a means by which its length can be determined. Here is a program that demonstrates this property:

```
// Use the length array property.
using System;

class LengthDemo {
    static void Main() {
        int[] nums = new int[10];

        Console.WriteLine("Length of nums is " + nums.Length);

        // Use Length to initialize nums.
        for(int i=0; i < nums.Length; i++)
            nums[i] = i * i;

        // Now use Length to display nums.
        Console.Write(Here as nums: ");
        for(int i=0; i < nums-Length; 1++}
            Console.Write(nums [i] + " " );

        Console.WriteLine();
    }
}
```

This program displays the following output:

```
Length of nums is 10
Here is nums: 0  1 4 9 16 25 36 49 64 81
```

In LengthDemo notice the way that nums.Length is used by the for loops to govern the number of iterations that take place. Since each array carries with it its own length, you can use this information rather than manually keeping track of an array's size. Keep in mind that the value of Length has nothing to do with the number of elements that are actually in use. Length contains the number of elements that the array is capable of holding.

When the length of a multidimensional array is obtained, the total number of elements that can be held by the array is returned. For example:

```
// Use the Length array property on a 3D array.

using System;
```

```
class LengthDemo3D {
    static void Main() {
        int[,,] nums = new int[10, 5, 6];

        Console.WriteLine("Length of nums is " + nums.Length);
    }
}
```

**The output** is shown **here:**

```
Length of nums is 300
```

As the output verifies. **Length** obtains the number of elements that **nums** can hold, which, is 300 (10x5x6) in this case. It is not possible to use **Length** to obtain the length of a specific dimension.

The inclusion of the **Length** property simplifies many algorithms by making certain types of array operations easier—and safer—to perform. For example, the following program uses **Length** to reverse the contents of an array by copying it back-to-front into another array:

```
// Reverse an array.

using System;

class RevCopy I
    static void Main() {
        int i, j ;
        int[] numsl = new int[10];
        int[] nums2 = new int[10];

        for(i = 0; i < numsl, Length; i++) numsl[i] = i;

        Console.Write("Original contents; ");
        for (i=0; < nums2.Length; i++)
            Console.Write(numsl[i] + " ");

        Console.WriteLine();

        // Reverse copy numsl Lc nums2.
        if(nums2.Length >= numsl.Length) // make sure nums2 is long enough
            for(i=0, j=numsl.Length-1; i < numsl.Length; i++, j==)
                nums2 [j] = numsl[i];

        Console.WriLc("Reversed contents:);
        for(i=0; i < nums.Length; i++)
            Console.Write(nums2[i] " ");

        Console.WriteLine();
    }
}
```

Mere is the output:

```
Original contents: 0 1 2 3 4 5 6 7 8 9
Reversed contents: 9 8 7 6 5 4 3 2 1 0
```

Here,. **Length** helps perform two important functions. First, it is used to confirm that the target array is large enough to hold the contents of the source array. Second, it provides the termination condition of the for loop that performs the reverse copy. Of course, in this simple example, the size of the arrays is easily known, but this same approach can be applied to a wide range of more challenging situations.

## Using Length with Jagged Arrays

A special case occurs when **Length** is used with jagged arrays. In this situation, it is possible to obtain the length of each individual array. For example, consider the following program, which simulates the CPU activity on a network with four nodes:

```
// Demonstrate Length with jagged arrays,

using System;

class Jagged {
    static void MainO {
        int[] [] network__nodes = new int[4] [];
        network_nodes[0] = new int [3!;
        network_nodes [1] = new int [71 ;
        network_nodes [2] = new int [2];
        network nodes[3] — new int[5];

        int i, j;

        // Fabricate some fake CPU usage data.
        for (i = 0; i < network__nodes. Length; i++)
            for(j=0; j < network_nodes[i].Length
                network nodesji] [j] = i * j + 70;

        Console.WriteLine("Total number of network nodes; " +
                    network_nodes.Length + "\n");

        for (i = 0; i < network_nodes,Length; i + +) )
            for(j=0; j < network__nodes [i] .Length; j+ + } {
                Console.Write("CPU usage at node " + i +
                        " CPU "+ j +":");
                Console.Write(network_nodes[i][j] + "% ");
                Console.WriteLine();
            }
            Console.WriteLine();
        }
    }
}
```

The'output is shown here:

```
Total number of network nodes: 4
CPU usage at node 0 CPU 0 : 70%
CPU usage at node 0 CPU 1 : 70%
CPU usage at node 0 CPU 2 : 70%

CPU usage at node 1 CPU 0 : 70%
CPU usage at node 1 CPU 1 : 71%
CPU usage at node 1 CPU 2 : 72%
CPU usage at node 1 CPU 3 : 73%
CPU usage at node 1 CPU 4 : 74%
CPU usage at node 1 CPU 5 : 75%
CPU usage at node 1 CPU 6 : 76%

CPU usage at node 3 CPU 0 : 70%
CPU usage at node 3 CPU 1 : 72%

CPU usage at node 3 CPU 0 : 70%
CPU usage at node 3 CPU 1 : 73%
CPU usage at node 3 CPU 2 : 76%
CPU usage at node 3 CPU 3 : 79%
CPU usage at node 3 CPU 4 : 82%
```

Pay special attention to the way Length is used on the jagged array network_nodes. Recall, a two-dimensional jagged array is an array of arrays. Thus, when the expression

```
network_ nodes.Length
```

is used, it obtains the number of *arrays* stored in network_nodes, which is four in this case. To obtain the length of any individual array in the jagged array, you will use an expression such as this:

```
network_nodes[0].Length
```

which, in this case, obtains the length of the first array.

## Implicitly Typed Arrays

C# 3.0 added the ability to declare implicitly typed variables by using the var keyword. These are variables whose type is determined by the compiler, based on the type of the initializing expression. Thus, all implicitly typed variables must be initialized. Using the same mechanism, it is also possible to create an implicitly typed array. As a general rule, implicitly typed arrays are for use in certain types of queries involving LINQ. In most other cases, you will use the "normal" array declaration approach. Implicitly typed arrays are introduced here for completeness. An implicitly typed array is declared using the keyword var, but you *do not* follow var with [ ]. Furthermore, the array must be initialized because it is the type of the initializers that determine the element type of the array. All of the initializers must be of the same or compatible type. Here is an example of an implicitly typed array:

```
var vals = new [ ] { 1, 2, 3, 4, 5 };
```

This creates an array of int that is five elements long. A reference to that array is assigned to vals. Thus, the type of vals is "array of int" and it has five elements. Again, notice that var is not followed by [ ]. Also, even though the array is being initialized, you must include new[]. It's not optional in this context.

Here is another example. It creates a two-dimensional array of double:

```
var vals = new[,] { {1.1, 2.2}, [3.3, 4.4),( 5.5, 6.6} };
```

In this case, vals has the dimensions 2x3.

You can also declare implicitly typed jagged arrays. For example, consider the following program:

```
// Demonstiale an Implicitly typed jagged array.

using System;

class Jagged {
    static void Main() {

        var jaqqed = new[] {
            new[] {1, 2, 3, 4 },
            new[] {9, 8, 7 },
            new[] {11, 12, 13, 14, 15}
        };

        for (int j = 0; -i < jagged.Length; j ++) {
            for (int i = 0; i < jagged [j].Length; i++)
                Console.Write(jaqqed[j][i] + " ");

            Console.WriteLine{};
        }
    }
}
```

The program produces the following output:

```
1 2 3 4
9 8 7
11 12 13 14 15
```

Pay special attention to the declaration of **jagged:**

```
val jagged - new[] {
    new [] {1, 2, 3, 4}.
    new [] {9, 8, 7},
    new [] {11, 12, 13, 14}
};
```

Notice how **new[]** is used in two ways. First, it creates the array of arrays. Second, it creates each individual array, based on the number and type of initializers. As you would expect, all of the initializers in the individual arrays must be of the same type. The same general approach used to declare **jagged** can be used to declare any implicitly typed jagged array.

As mentioned, implicitly typed arrays are most applicable to LINQ-based queries. They are not meant for general use. In most cases, you should use explicitly typed arrays.

**The foreach Loop**

C# defines a loop called **foreach,** but a discussion of that statement was deferred until later. The time for that discussion has now come. **The foreach** loop is used to cycle through the elements of a *collection.* A collection is a group of objects. C# defines several types of collections, of which one is an array. The general form of **foreach** is shown here:

```
foreach(h/pc loopvar in collection) statement;
```

Here, *type loopvar* specifies the type and name of an *iteration variable.* The iteration variable receives the value of the next element in the collection each time the **foreach** loop iterates. The collection being cycled through is specified by *collection,* which, for the rest of this discussion, is an array. Thus, *type* must be the same as (or compatible with) the element type of the array. The *type* can also be var, in which case the compiler determines the type based on the element type of the array. This can be useful when working with certain queries, as described later in this book. Normally, you will explicitly specify the type.

Here is how **foreach** works. When the loop begins, the first element in the array is obtained and assigned to *loopvar.* Each subsequent iteration obtains the next element from the array and stores it in *loopvar.* The loop ends when there are no more elements to obtain. Thus, the **foreach** cycles through the array one element at a time, from start to finish.

One important point to remember about **foreach** is that the iteration variable *loopvar* is read-only. This means you can't change the contents of an array by assigning the iteration variable a new value.

Here is a simple example that uses **foreach.** It creates an array of integers and gives it some initial values. It then displays those values, computing the summation in the process.

```
// Use the foreach loop.

using System;

class ForeachDemc {
    static void Main() {
        int sum = 0;
        int [] nums = new int [101 ;

    // Give nums some values.
    for (int i = 0; i < 10; i++)
        nums [i1 = 1;

    // Use foreach to display and sum the value.
    foreach(int x in nums) {
        Console.WriteLine("Value is: " + x);
    }
```

```
        Console.WriteLine("Summation; " + sum);
    }
}
```

The output from the program is shown here:

```
Value is: 1
Value is: 2
Value is: 3
Value is: 4
Value is: 5
Value is: 6
Value is: 7
Value is: 8
Value is: 9
Summation : 45
```

As this output shows, **foreach** cycles through an array in sequence from the lowest index to the highest.

Although the **foreach** loop iterates until all elements in an array have been examined, it is possible to terminate a **foreach** loop early by using a **break** statement. For example, this program sums only the first five elements of **nums:**

```
// Use break with a foreach.

using System;

class ForeachDemo {
    static void Main() {
        int sum = 0;
        int i ] nums = new int [10] ;

        // Give nums some values .
        for (int i = 0; i < 10; i++)
            nums [i] = i;

        // Use foreach to display and sum the values .
        foreach ( i nt x in nums) {
            Console .Write Line ("Value is : " + x) ;
            sum += x;
            if(x == 4} break; // stop the loop when A is obtained
        }
        Console . WriteLine ("Summation of first 5 elements : " + sum) ;
    }
}
```

This is the output produced:

```
Value is: 0
Value is: 1
Value is: 2
Value is: 3
Value is: 4
Summation of first 5 elements : 10
```

As is evident, the **foreach** loop stops after the fifth element has been obtained.

**The foreach** loop also works on multidimensional arrays. It returns those elements in row order, from first to last.

```
// Use lo reach on a two-dimensional array.

using System;
```

```
class ForeachDemo2 {
    static void Main() (
        int sum = 0;
        int[,] nums = new int[3,5];

        // Give nums some values.
        for{int i = 0; i < 3;
            for(int j=0; j < 5;
                nums[i,j] - (i + 1) Mj+D ;

        // Use foreach to display and sum the values
        foreach(int x in nums) {
            Console.WriteLine("Value is: " + x);
            sum += x;
        )
        Console.WriteLine("Summation: " + sum);
    }
}
```

The output from this program is shown here:

```
Value is: 1
Value is: 2
Value is: 3
Value is: 4
Value is: 5
Value is: 2
Value is: 4
Value is: 6
Value is: 8
Value is: 10
Value is: 3
Value is: 6
Value is: 9
Value is: 12
Value is: 15
Summation: 90
```

Since the **foreach** loop can only cycle through an array sequentially, from start to finish, you might think that its use is limited. However, this is not true. A large number of algorithms require exactly this mechanism, of which one of the most common is searching. For example, the following program uses a **foreach** loop to search an array for a value. It stops if the value is found.

```
// Search an array using foreach.

using System;

class Search {
    static void Main() {
        int[] nums = new int[10];
        int val;
        bool found = false;

        // Give nums some values.
        for(int i = 0; i < 10; i++)
            nums[i] = i;
        val = 5;

        // Use foreaeh to search nums for key;
        foreach(int x in nums) {
```

```
            if(x == val) {
                found = true;
                break;
            }
        }

        if (found)
            Console.WriteLine("Value found!");
    }
}
```

The output is shown here:

```
Value found!
```

The **foreach** loop is an excellent choice in this application because searching an array involves examining each element. Other types of foreach applications include such things as computing an average, finding the minimum or maximum of a set, looking for duplicates, and so on. As you will see later in this book, **foreach** is especially useful when operating on other types of collections.

## Strings

From a day-to-day programming standpoint, **string** is one of C#'s most important data types because it defines and supports character strings. In many other programming languages, a string is an array of characters. This is not the case with C#. In C#, strings are objects. Thus, string is a reference type. Although **string** is a built-in data type in C#, a discussion of **string** needed to wait until classes and objects had been introduced.

Actually, you have been using the **string** class, but you did not know it. When you create a string literal, you are actually creating a **string** object. For example, in the statement

```
Console.WriteLine("In C#, strings are objects.");
```

the string "In C#, strings are objects." is automatically made into a string object by C#. Thus, the use of the string class has been "below the surface" in the preceding programs. In this section, you will learn to handle them explicitly.

## Constructing Strings

The easiest way to construct a string is to use a string literal. For example, here **str** is a **string** reference variable that is assigned a reference to a string literal:

```
string str - "C# strings are powerful .";
```

In this case, str is initialized to the character sequence "C# strings are powerful." You can also create a **string** from a **char** array. For example:

```
char[] charray = {'t', 'e', 's', 't'};
string str = new string(charray);
```

Once you have created a string object, you can use it nearly anywhere that a quoted string is allowed. For example, you can use a string object as an argument to **WriteLine**(), as shown in this example:

```
// Introduce string.

using System;

class StringDemo {
    static void Main(){

        char() charray = {'A', ' ', 's', 't', 'r', 'i', 'n', 'g', '.', };
        string str1 = new string(charray);
        string str2 = "Another string.";
```

```
        Console.WriteLine(strl};
        Console.WriteLine(str?);
    }
}
```

The output from the program is shown here:

```
A string.
Another string.
```

## Operating on Strings

The string class contains several methods that operate on strings. Table 4-1 shows a few. Notice that several of the methods take a parameter of type **StringComparison.** This is an enumeration type that defines various values that determine how a comparison involving strings will be conducted. As you might guess, there are various ways in which two strings can be compared. For example, they can be compared based on the binary values of the characters that comprise them. This is called an *ordinal* comparison. Strings can also be compared in a way that takes into account various cultural metrics, such as dictionary order. This type of comparison is called *culture-sensitive.* (Culture sensitivity is especially important in applications that are being internationalized.) Furthermore, comparisons can either be case-sensitive or ignore case differences. Although overloads of methods such as **Compare(), Equals(), IndexOff(),** and **LastIndexOf()** do exist that provide a default string comparison approach, it is now considered best to explicitly specify what type of comparison you want. Doing so helps avoid ambiguity in this regard. (It also helps with internationalizing an application.) This is why these forms are shown here.

Tn general, and with some exceptions, if you want to compare two strings for sorting relative to the cultural norms, you will use **StringComparison.CurrentCulture** as the comparison approach. If you want to compare two strings based solely on the value of their characters, it is usually best to use **StringComparison.Ordinal.** To ignore case differences, specify either **StringComparison. CurrentCultureIgnoreCase or StringComparison. OrdinalIgnoreCase.** You can also specify an invariant culture.

Notice that in Table 4-1, **Compare()** is declared as static. The static modifier means that **Compare()** is called on its class name, not an instance of its class. Thus, to call **Compare(),** you will use this general form:

```
result = string.Compare(sfr7, str2, how);
```

where how specifies the string comparison approach.

The two methods **ToUpper()** and **ToLower(),** which uppercase or lowercase a string, respectively. The forms shown here both have a **CultureInfo** parameter. This is a class that describes the cultural attributes to use for the conversion. The examples in this book use the current culture settings. These settings are specified by passing **CultureInfo.CurrentCulture. The CultureInfo** class is in **System.Globalization.** As a point of interest, there are versions of these methods that use the current culture by default, but to avoid ambiguity on this point, this book will explicitly specify this argument.

The string type also includes the **Length** property, which contains the length of the string.

| **Method** | **Description** |
|---|---|
| static intComparejstringstrA, string strB, StringComparison comparison Type) | Returns less than zero if strA is less than strS, greater than zero if strA is greater than srrB, and zero if the strings are equal. How the comparison is conducted is specified by comparison Type. |
| bool Equals(string value, StringComparison comparison Type) | Returns true if the invoking string is the same as value. How the comparison is conducted is specified by comparison Type. |

| | |
|---|---|
| int IndexOf(char value) | Searches the invoking string for the first occurrence of the character specified by value. An ordinal search is used. Returns the index of the first match, or -1 on failure. |
| int IndexOffstringvafue, StringComparison comparison Type) | Searchesthe invokingstringforthefirstoccurrenceofthe substring specified by value. How the search is conducted is specified by comparison Type. Returns the index of the first j match, or -lonfailure. |
| int LastIndexOf(char value) | Searches the invoking string for the last occurrence of the character specified by value. An ordinal search is used. Returns the index of the first match, or -1 on failure. |
| int LastIndexOf(string value, StringComparison comparison Type} | Searches the invoking string for the last occurrence of the substring specified by value. How the search is conducted is specified by comparison Type. Returns the index of the last match, or-1on failure. |
| string ToLower( Culture Info.CurrentCultu re culture) | Returns a lowercase version of the invoking string. How the conversion is performed is specified by culture. |
| string ToUpper( Culture Info.CurrentCultu re culture} | Returns an uppercase version of the invoking string. How the conversion is performed is specified by culture. |

**Table 4-1** A Sampling of Common String Handling Methods

To obtain the value of an individual character of a string, you simply use an index. For example:

This displays "t", the first character of "test". Like arrays, string indexes begin at zero. One important point, however, is that you cannot assign a new value to a character within a string using an index. An index can only be used to obtain a character.

You can use the = = operator to test two strings for equality. Normally, when the = = operator is applied to object references, it determines if both references refer to the same object. This differs for objects of type string. When the = = is applied to two string references, the contents of the strings themselves are compared for equality. The same is true for the != operator: when comparing string objects, the contents of the strings are compared. In both cases, an ordinal comparison is performed. To test two strings for equality using cultural information, use Equals() and specify the comparison approach, such as StringComparison.CurrentCulture. One other point: the CompareO method is intended to compare strings to determine an ordering relationship, such as for sorting. To test for equality, use EqualsO or the string operators.

Here is a program that demonstrates several string operations:

```
// Some string operations.

using Systems
using System.Globalization;

class Strops {
    static void Main() {
    string strl = "When it comes to .NET programming, C# is #1
    string str2 = "When it comes to .NET programming, C# it; #1
```

```
string str3 = "C# strings are powerful.";
string strUp, strLow;
int result, idx;

Console .WriteLinef'strl: " + strl];

Console.WriteLine("Length of strl: " + strl.Length);

// Create upper- and lowercase versions of strl.
strLow = strl.ToLower(CultureInfo.CurrentCulture);
strUp = strl.ToUpper(Culturelnfo.CurrentCul ture);
Console.WriteLine("Lowercase version of strl:\n " + strLow);
Console.WriteLine("Uppercase version of strl:\n " + strUp);

Console.WriteLine();

// Display strl, one char at a time.
Console.WriteLine("Display strl, one char at a time."]
for(int i-0; i < strl.Length; i++)
   Console.Write(strl [i]);
Console.WriteLine("\n");

// Compare strings using == and !=. These comparisons are ordinal.
if (strl == str2)
   Console.WriteLine("strl == str2");
else
   Console.WriteLine("strl != str2");

if (strl == str3)
   Console.WriteLine("strl == str3");
else
   Console.Wri teLine("strl != str3");

// This compari son is culture-sensitive.
result = string. Compare (strl, str3, StringCompari son. Current.Culture)
if(result == 0)
   Console.WriteLine("strl and str3 are equal");
else if(result < 0)
   Console.WriteLine ("strl is less than str3");
else
   Console.WriteLine("strl is greater than str3");

Console.WriteLine (1 ;

// Assign a new string to str2.
str2 = "One Two Three One";

// Search a string.
idx = str2 . IndexOf ("One", StringCoinparison . Ordinal) ;
Console.WriteLine("Index of first occurrence of One: " + idx);
idx = str2.Lastlndexof("One" , StringComparison.Ordinal) ;
Console.WriteLine("Index of last occurrence oi One: " + idx) ;
```

This program generates the following output:

```
strl: When it comes to .NET programming, C# is #1. Length of strl: 44
Lowercase version of strl:
   when it comes to .net programming, r# is #1.
```

```
Uppercase version of strl;
   WHEN IT COMES TO .NET PROGRAMMING, C# IS #1.

Display strl, one char at a time.
When it comes to .NET programming, C# is #1.

strl == str2
strl != str3
strl is greater than str3

index of first occurrence of One: 0
index of last occurrence of One: 14
```

Before moving on, in the program notice that **Compare()** is called as shown here:

```
result = string.Compare(strl, str3, StiingComparison.CurrentCulture);
```

As explained, because **Compare()** is declared as **static,** it is called on its class name, not an instance of its class.

You can *concatenate* (join together) two strings using the + operator. For example, this statement:

```
string strl = "One" ;
string str2 = "Two" ;
string str3 = "Three" ;
string str4 = strl + str2 + str3;
```

initializes **str4** with the string "OneTwoThree".

One other point: The **string** keyword is an *alias* for (that is, maps directly to) the **System. String** class defined by the .NET Framework class library. Thus, the fields and methods defined by **string** are those of the **System. String** class, which includes more than the sampling described here. **System.String** is examined in detail in Part II.

## Arrays of Strings

Like any other data type, strings can be assembled into arrays. For example:

```
// Demonstrate string arrays.

using System;

class StringArrays {
   static void Main{) {
      string [ ] str = { "This" , "is", "a" , "test . " } ;

      Console. WriteLine ("Original array: "} ;
      for(int i^O; i. < str. Length; i + +)
         Console.Write (str [i] + " ");
      Console .WriteLine ( "\n" ) ;

      // Change a string .
      str[l] = "was";
      str[3] = "test, too!";

      Console. WriteLine ("Modified array: ");
      for (int i=0; i < str.Length; i++)
         Console .Write (str [i] + " " ) ;
   }
}
```

**Here is the output from this program:**

```
Original array :
```

```
This is a test.

Modified array:
This was a test, too!
```

Here is a more interesting example. The following program displays an integer value using words. For example, the value 19 will display as "one nine".

```
// Display the digits of an integer using words.

using System;

class ConvertDigitsToWords {
    static void Main() {
        int num;
        int next.digit;
        int numdiqits;
        int [] n = new int[20];

        string[] digits = { "zero", "one", "two",
                            "three", "four", "five",
                            "six", "seven", "eight",
                            "nine" };

    num = 1908;

    Console.WriteLine("Number: " + num);

    Console .Write ("Number in words: ");

    nextdigit = 0;
    numdigits = 0;

    // Get individual digits and store in n.
    // These digits are stored in reverse order .
    do {
        nextdigit = num % 10 ;
        n [numdlgi ts] - nextdi git;
        numdigits++;
        num = num / 10;
    } while {num > 01 ;
    numdigits==;

    // Display the words .
    for (; numdigits >= 0; numdigits==)
        Console.Write (digits [n [numdigits] ] + " "),

    Console. WriteLine();
    }
}
```

The output is shown here:

```
Number: 1908
Number in words: one nine zero eight
```

In the program, the string array digits holds in order the word equivalents of the digits from zero to nine. The program converts an integer into words by first obtaining each digit of the value and storing those digits, in reverse order, in the int array called n. Then, this array is cycled through from back to front. In the process, each integer value in n is used as an index into digits, with the corresponding string being displayed.

## Strings Are Immutable

Here is something that might surprise you: The contents of a **string** object are immutable. That is, once created, the character sequence comprising that string cannot be altered. This restriction allows strings to be implemented more efficiently. Even though this probably . sounds like a serious drawback, it isn't. When you need a string that is a variation on one that already exists, simply create a new string that contains the desired changes. Because unused string objects are automatically garbage-collected, you don't even need to worry about what happens to the discarded strings.

It must be made clear, however, that string reference variables may, of course, change which object they refer to. It is just that the contents of a specific **string** object cannot be changed after it is created.

To fully understand why immutable strings are not a hindrance, we will use another of **string's** methods: Substring(). The **Substring*)** method returns a new string that contains a specified portion of the invoking string. Because a new **string** object is manufactured that contains the substring, the original string is unaltered, and the rule of immutability is still intact. The form of **SubstringC)** that we will be using is shown here:

```
string Substring(int startlndex, int length)
```

Here, *starilndex* specifies the beginning index, and *length* specifies the length of the substring.

Here is a program that demonstrates **Substringt)** and the principle of immutable strings:

```
// Use Substring();

using System;

class SubStr {
    static voi d Main() {
        string orgstr = "C# makes strings easy.";

        // Construct a substring.
        string subtr = orgstr.Substring(5, 12);

        Console.WriteLine("orgstr; " + orgstr);
        Console.WriteLine("substr; " + substr);
    }
}
```

Here is the output from the program:

```
orgestr: C# makes strings easy.
substr: kes strings
```

As you can see, the original string **orgstr** is unchanged, and substr contains the substring.

One more point: Although the immutability of **string** objects is not usually a restriction or hindrance, there may be times when it would be beneficial to be able to modify a string. To allow this, C# offers a class called **StringBuilder,** which is in the **System.Text** namespace. It creates string objects that can be changed. For most purposes, however, you will want to use **string, not StringBuilder.**

### Strings Can Be Used in switch Statements

A string can be used to control a switch statement. It is the only non-integer type that can be used in the switch. The fact that strings can be used in switch statements makes it possible to handle some otherwise difficult situations quite easily. For example, the following program displays the digit equivalent of the words "one," "two," and "three":

```
// A string can control a switch statement.

using System;
```

```
class Stringwitch {
    static void Main() {
        string[] str = {"one", "two", 'three", "two", "one" }

        foreach(strings in strs)
            switch(s) (
                case "one":
                    Console.Write(1);
                    break;
                case "two":
                    Console.Write(2);
                    break;
                case "three":
                    Console.Write(3);
                    break;
```

The output is shown here:

```
12321
```

CHAPTER 4

# Operator Overloading

***In this chapter you will read about:***

- Operator Overloading.
- Overloading True and False.
- Overloading the Logical Operators.
- Conversion Operators.
- Handling Operators.

## Introduction

C# allows you to define the meaning of an operator relative to a class that you create. This process is called operator overloading. By overloading an operator, you expand its usage to your class. The effects of the operator are completely under your control and may differ from class to class. For example, a class that defines a linked list might use the + operator to add an object to the list. A class that implements a stack might use the + to push an object onto the stack. Another class might use the + operator in an entirely different way.

When an operator is overloaded, none of its original meaning is lost. It is simply that a new operation, relative to a specific class, is added. Therefore, overloading the + to handle a linked list, for example, does not cause its meaning relative to integers (that is, addition) to be changed.

A principal advantage of operator overloading is that it allows you to seamlessly integrate a new class type into your programming environment. This type extensibility is an important part of the power of an object-oriented language such as C#. Once operators are defined for a class, you can operate on objects of that class using the normal C# expression syntax. You can even use an object in expressions involving other types of data. Operator overloading is one of C#'s most powerful features.

## Operator Overloading Fundamentals

Operator overloading is closely related to method overloading. To overload an operator, use the operator keyword to define an operator method, which defines the action of the operator relative to its class.

There are two forms of operator methods: one for unary operators and one for binary operators. The general form for each is shown here:

```
// General form for overloading a unary operator
public static ret-type operator op(param-type operand)
{
    // operations
}
// General form for overloading a binary operator
public static ret-type operator op(param-typel operandl, pamm-typel operand2)
{
    // operations
}
```

Here, the operator that you are overloading, such as + or /, is substituted for op. The ret-type specifies the type of value returned by the specified operation. Although it can be any type you choose, the return value is often of the same type as the class for which the operator is being overloaded. This correlation facilitates the use of the overloaded operator in expressions. For unary operators, the operand is passed in operand. For binary operators, the operands are passed in operandl and operand!. Notice that operator methods must be both public and static.

For unary operators, the operand must be of the same type as the class for which the operator is being defined. For binary operators, at least one of the operands must be of the same type as its class. Thus, you cannot overload any C# operators for objects that you have not created. For example, you can't redefine + for int or string.

One other point: Operator parameters must not use the ref or out modifier.

## Overloading Binary Operators

To see how operator overloading works, let's start with an example that overloads two binary operators, the + and the -. The following program creates a class called ThreeD, which maintains the coordinates of an object in three-dimensional space. The overloaded + adds the individual coordinates of one ThreeD object to another. The overloaded - subtracts the coordinates of one object from the other.

```
// An example of operator overloading.

using System;

//A three-dimensional coordinate class.
class ThreeD 1
    int x, y, z; // 3-D coord: nates

    public ThreeD () { x = y = z - 0; }
    public ThreeD (int i, int j, int k) { x = i ; y = j; z = k; }

// Overload binary +,
public static ThreeD operator + (ThreeD opl, ThreeD op2)
{
    ThreeD result = new ThreeD();

    /* This adds together the coordinates of the two points
    and returns the result. */
    result. x = opl.x + op2.x; // These are integer additions
    result. y = opl.y + op2.y; // and the + retains its original
    result . z = opl . z + op2 . z; // meaning relative to them.

    return result;
}

// Overload binary -.
public static ThreeD operator -(ThreeD opl, ThreeD op2)
{
    ThreeD result = new ThreeD ();

    /* Notice the order of the operands, opl is the left
    operand and op2 is the right. */

    result.x - opl.x - op2. x; // these are integer subtractions
    result.y = opl-y - op2.y;
    result.z = opl.z - op2.z;

    return result;

    // Show X, Y, Z coordinates,
    public void Showf)
    {
        Console.WriteLine (x, ", " + y + ", " + z);
    }
}

class ThreeDDemo {
    static void Main{) {
        ThreeD a - new ThreeD(1, 2, 3);
        ThreeD b = new ThreeD(10, 10, 10);
        ThreeD c;

        Console.Write{"Here is a: " ) ;
        a.Show();
        Console.WriteLine();
        Console.Write("Here is b: ");
        b.Show();
        Console.WriteLine();
```

```
        c = a + b; // add a and b together
        Console.Wrile("Result of a + b: ");
        c.Show () ;
        Console.WriteLine{} ;

        c = a + b + c; // add a, b, and c together
        Console.Write("Result of a + b + c: ");
        c.Show() ;
        Console.WriteLine ();

        c = c - a; // subtract a
        Console.Write("Result of c - a: "};
        c.Show ();
        Console.WriteLine ();

        c = c - b; // subtract b
        Console.Write("Result of c - b: ");
        c.Show ();
        Console.WriteLine ();
    }
}
```

This program produces the following output:

```
Here is a: 1, 2, 3
Here is b: 10, 10, 10
Result of a + b: 11, 12, 13
Result of a + b + c: 22, 24, 26
Result of c - a: 21, 22, 23
Result of c - b; 11, 12, 13
```

Let's examine the preceding program carefully, beginning with the overloaded operator +. When two objects of type ThreeD are operated on by the + operator, the magnitudes of their respective coordinates are added together, as shown in operator+(). Notice, however, that this method does not modify the value of either operand. Instead, a new object of type ThreeD, which contains the result of the operation, is returned by the method. To understand why the + operation does not change the contents of either object, think about the standard arithmetic + operation as applied like this: 10 + 12. The outcome of this operation is 22, but neither 10 nor 12 is changed by it. Although no rule prevents an overloaded operator from altering the value of one of its operands, it is best for the actions of an overloaded operator to be consistent with its usual meaning.

Notice that operator+() returns an object of type ThreeD. Although the method could have returned any valid C# type, the fact that it returns a ThreeD object allows the + operator to be used in compound expressions, such as a+b+c. Here, a+b generates a result that is of type ThreeD. This value can then be added to c. Had any other type of value been generated by a+b, such an expression would not work.

Here is another important point: When the coordinates are added together inside operator+(), the addition of the individual coordinates results in an integer addition. This is because the individual coordinates, x, y, and z, are integer quantities. The fact that the + operator is overloaded for objects of type ThreeD has no effect on the + as it is applied to integer values.

Now, look at operator-(). The - operator works just like the + operator except that the order of the parameters is important. Recall that addition is commutative, but subtraction is not. (That is, A - B is not the same as B - A() For all binary operators, the first parameter to an operator method will contain the left operand. The second parameter will contain the one on the right. When implementing overloaded versions of the noncommutative operators, you must remember which operand is on the left and which is on the right.

## Overloading Unary Operators

The unary operators are overloaded just like the binary operators. The main difference, of course, is that there is only one operand. For example, here is a method that overloads the unary minus for the ThreeD class:

```
// Overleoad unar -;
public static ThreeD operator = {ThreeD op}
{
    ThreeD rcsulL = new ThreeD(};

    result.x = -op.x;
    result.y = -op.y;
    result.z = -op.z;

    return result;
}
```

Here, a new object is created that contains the negated fields of the operand. This object is then returned. Notice that the operand is unchanged. Again, this is in keeping with the usual meaning of the unary minus. For example, in an expression such as this,

```
a = -b
```

a receives the negation of b, but b is not changed.

In C#, overloading + + and - - is quite easy; simply return the incremented or decremented value, but don't change the invoking object. C# will automatically handle that for you, taking into account the difference between the prefix and postfix forms. For example, here is an operator + + <) method for the ThreeD class:

```
// Overload unary ++.
public static ThreeD operator ++(ThreeD op)
{

    ThreeD result. = new ThreeD () ;

    // Return the incremented result,
    reuslt.x = op.x + 1;
    result.y = op.y + 1;
    result.z = op.z + 1;

    return result;
}
```

Here is an expanded version of the previous example program that demonstrates the unary - and the + + operator;

```
// More operator overloading

using System;

// A three-dimensions1 coordinate class.
class ThreeD {
    int x, y, z;  // 3-D coordinates

    public ThreeD() { x = y = z = 0; }
    public ThreeD(int i, int j, int k) { x = i; y = j; z = k;}

// Overload binary +.
public static ThreeD operator +(ThreeD opl, ThreeD op2)
{
```

```
        ThreeD result = new ThreeDf);

        /* This adds Logether the coordinates of the two points
           and returns the result. */
        result.x = opl.x t op2.x;
        result.y = opl.y + op2.y;
        result.z = opl.z + op2.z;

        result result;
    }

    // Overload binary -
    public static ThreeD operator - (ThreeD opl, ThreeD op2)
    {
        ThreeD result = new ThreeDO;

        /* Notice the order of the operands, opl is the left
           operand and op2 is the right. */
           result.x = opl.x - op2.x;
           result.y = opl.y - op2.y;
           result.z = opl.z - op2.z;

           return result;
        }
        // Overload unary
        public static ThreeD operator -(ThreeD op)
        {
           ThreeD result - new ThreeDO;
           result.x =-op.x;
           result.y =-op.y;
           result.z =-op.z;
           return result;
        }

        // Overload unary ++.
        public static ThreeD operator ++(ThreeD op)
        {
           ThreeD result = new ThreeDO;

        // Return the incremented result.
           result.x = op.x + 1;
           result.y = op.y + 1;
           result.z = op.z + 1;

           return result;
        }

        // Show X, Y, Z coordinates.
        public void Show()
        {
           Console.WriteLine{x + " , " + y + " , " + z};
        }
    }

    class ThreeDDemo {
        static void MainO {
           ThreeD a = new ThreeD(1, 2, 3);
```

```
        ThreeD b = new ThreeD(10, 10, 10)
        ThreeD c = new ThreeDO;

        Console.Write("Here is a: ");
        a.Show();
        Console.WriteLine();

        Console.Write("Here is b: ");
        b.Show();
        Console.WriteLine();

        c = a + b; // add a and b together
        Console. Write ("Result of a + b: ");
        c . Show ( ) ;
        Console . WriteLine ( ) ;

        c = a + b + c; // add a, b, and c together
        Console.Write ("Result of a + b + c: ");
        c.Show () ;
        Console .WriteLine () ;

        c = c - a; // subtract a
        Console. Write ( "Resul t of c - a : ") ;
        c . Show ( ) ;
        Console. WrJ.LeLi.ne () ;

        c = c - b; // subtract b
        Console .Write ("Result of c - b: " ) ;
        c.Show ( ) ;
        Console.WriteLine {} ;

        c = -a; // assign -a to c
        Console .Write ( "Result of -a : ") ;
        c . Show ( ) ;
        Console .WriteLine ( ) ;

        c = a+ + ; // posL-inc;rement a
        Console.WriteLine ("Given c = a++") ;
        Console.Write ( "c is ") ;
        c . Show ( ) ;
        Console .Write ( "a is ");
        a. Show ( | ;

        // Reset a to 1, 2, 3
        a = new ThreeDfl, 2, 3);
        Console . Write ( "\nResetti ng a to " ) ;
        a . Show ( | ;

        c = ++ a; // pre-increment a
        Console.WriteLine ("\nGiven c = + + a" ) ;
        Console.Wri te ("c is " } ;
        c.Show() ;
        Console. Write ( "a is ") ;
        a.Show ();
    }
}
```

The output from the program is shown here:

```
Here is a: 1, 2, 3

Here is b: 10, 10, 10

Result of a + b: 11, 12, 13

Result of a + b + c: 22, 24, 26

Result of c - a: 21, 22, 23

Result of c - b: 11, 12, 13

Result of -a: -1, -2, -3

Given c = a++
c is 1, 2, 3
a is 2, 3, 4

Resetting a to 1, 2, 3

Given c = ++a
c is 2, 3, 4
a is 2, 3, 4
```

## Handling Operations on C# Built-in Types

For any given class and operator, an operator method can, itself, be overloaded. One of the most common reasons for this is to allow operations between a class type and other types of data, such as a built-in type. For example, once again consider the ThreeD class. To this point, you have seen how to overload the + so that it adds the coordinates of one ThreeD object to another. However, this is not the only way in which you might want to define addition for ThreeD. For example, it might be useful to add an integer value to each coordinate of a ThreeD object. Such an operation could be used to translate axes. To perform such an operation, you will need to overload + a second time, as shown here:

```
// Overload binary + for ThreeD + int
public static ThreeD operato + (ThreeD op1, int op2)
{
   ThreeD result = new ThreeD();

   result.x = op1.x + op2;
   result.y = op1.y + op2 ;
   result.z = op1.z + op2;

   return result;
}
```

Notice that the second parameter is of type int. Thus, the preceding method allows an integer value to be added to each field of a ThreeD object. This is permissible because, as explained earlier, when overloading a binary operator, one of the operands must be of the same type as the class for which the operator is being overloaded. However, the other operand can be of any other type.

Here is a version of ThreeD that has two overloaded + methods:

```
// Overload addition for ThreeD + ThreeD, and for ThreeD + int.

using System;

// A three-dimensional coordinate class.
```

```
class ThreeD {
    int x, y, z;  // 3D coordinates

    public ThreeD () ( x — y = z - 0; }
    public ThreeD (int i, int j , i nt k) { x = i ; y = j ; z = k; }

    /* This adds together the coordinates ol the two point
       and returns the result . */
    result.x = opl.x + op2.x;
    result.y = opl.y + op2.y;
    result.z = opl.z + op2.z;

    return result;
  }
  // Overload binary + for object + int.
  public static ThreeD operator + (ThreeD op1, int op2)
  {
    ThreeD result = new ThreeD();

    result.x = opl.x + op2;
    result.y = opl.y + op2;
    result.z = opl.z + op2;

    return result;
  }

    // Show X, Y, Z coordinates.
    public void Show()
    {
        Console.WriteLine(x + " , " + y + " , " + z);
    }
  }

  class ThreeDDemo {
    static void Main() {
        ThreeD a = new ThreeD(1, 2, 3);
        ThreeD b = new ThreeD(10, 10, 10)
        ThreeD c = new ThreeD ();

        Console.Write("Here is a: ");
        a,Show () ;
        Console.WriteLine();
        Console.Writc("Here is b: ");
        b.Show();
        Console.Wri teLine();

        c = a + b; // ThreeD + ThreeD
        Console.Write("Result of a + b: ");
        C.Show();
        Console.WriteLine();

        c =- b 4 10; // ThreeD + int
        Console.Write("Result of b + 10: ")
        c.Show() ;
    }
  }
```

The output from this program is shown here:

```
Here is a: 1, 2, 3

Here is b: 10, 10, 10

Result of a + b: 11, 12, 13

Result of b + 10: 20, 20, 20
```

As the output confirms, when the + is applied to two ThreeD objects, their coordinates are added together. When the + is applied to a ThreeD object and an integer, the coordinates are increased by the integer value.

While the overloading of + just shown certainly adds a useful capability to the ThreeD class, it does not quite finish the job. Here is why. The operator + fThreeD, int) method allows statements like this:

```
obi = ob2 + 10;
```

It does not, unfortunately, allow ones like this:

```
obl = 10 + ob2;
```

The reason is that the integer argument is the second argument, which is the right-hand operand, but the preceding statement puts the integer argument on the left. To allow both forms of statements, you will need to overload the + yet another time. This version must have its first parameter as type int and its second parameter as type ThreeD. One version of the operator + () method handles ThreeD + integer, and the other handles integer + ThreeD. Overloading the + (or any other binary operator) this way allows a built-in type to occur on the left or right side of the operator. Here is a version ThreeD that overloads the + operator as just described:

```
// Overload the + for ThreeD + ThreeD, ThreeD + int, and int + ThreeD.

using System;

//A three-dimensional coordinate class.
class ThreeD {
    int x, y, z; // 3-D coordinates
    public ThreeD() { x = y = z = 0; 1
    public ThreeD(int i, int j, int k) { x = i; y = j; z = k; }

    // Overload binary + for ThreeD + ThreeD.
    public static ThreeD operator +(ThreeD opl, ThreeD op2)
    {
        ThreeD result = new ThreeD();

        /* This adds together the coordinates of the two points
           and returns the result. */
        result.x = opl.x + op2.x;
        result.y = opl.y + op2,y;
        result.z = opl.z + op2.z;

        return result;
    }

    // Overload binary + for ThreeD + int.
    public static ThreeD operator +(ThreeD opl, int op2)
    {
        ThreeD result = new ThreeD ();

        result.x = opl.x + op2;
        result.y = opl.y + op2;
```

```
        result.z = opl.z + op2;
        return result;
    }

    // Overload binary + for int + ThreeD.
    public static ThreeD operator + (int opl, ThreeD op2)
    {
        ThreeD result = new ThreeD ();
        result.x = op2.x + opl;
        result.y = op2.y + opl;
        result.z = op2.z + opl;

        return result;
    }

    // Show X, Y, Z coordinates,
    public void Show()
    {
        Console.WriteLine(x + ", " + y + ", " + z);
    }
}

class ThreeDDemo {
    static void Mainf) {
        ThreeD a = new ThreeD(1, 2, 3);
        ThreeD b = new ThreeD(10, 10, 10);
        ThreeD c = new ThreeD();

        Console.Write ("Here is a: ");
        a.Show () ;
        Console.WriteLine ();
        Console.Write{"Here is b : ");
        b.Show() ;
        Console.WriteLine ();

        c = a + b; // ThreeD + ThreeD
        Console.Write("Result of a + b: ") ;
        c.Show();
        Console.WriteLine();

        c - b + 10; // ThreeD + int
        Console.Write("Result of b + 10: ")
        c.Show();
        Console.WriteLine() ;

        c = 15 + b; // int + ThreeD
        Console.Write("Result of 15 + b: ")
        c.Show () ;
    }
}
```

The output from this program is shown here:

```
Here is a: 1, 2, 3

Here is b: 10, 10, 10

Result of a + b: 11, 12, 13
```

```
Result of b + 10: 20, 20, 20

Result of 15 + b: 25, 25, 25
```

CHAPTER 4

## Overloading the Relational Operators

The relational operators, such as = = or <, can also be overloaded and the process is straightforward. Usually, an overloaded relational operator returns a true or false value. This i$ in keeping with the normal usage of these operators and allows the overloaded relational operators to be used in conditional expressions. If you return a different type result, then you are greatly restricting the operator's utility.

Here is a version of the ThreeD class that overloads the < and > operators. In this example, these operators compare ThreeD objects based on their distance from the origin. One object is greater than another if its distance from the origin is greater. One object is less than another if its distance from the origin is less than the other. Given two points, such an implementation could be used to determine which point lies on the larger sphere. If neither operator returns true, then the two points lie on the same sphere. Of course, other ordering schemes are possible.

```
// Overload < and >.

using System;

//A three-dimensional coordinate class.
class ThreeD (
    int x, y, z; // 3-D coordinates

    public ThreeD 0 { x = y - z = 0; }
    public ThreeD(int i, int j, int k} { x = i; y = j ; z = k; }

    // Overload <.
    public static bool operator < (ThreeD opl, ThreeD op2 }
    {
        if (Math. Sqrt (opl . x * op 1.x + opl.y * opl.y + opl.z * opl . z) <
            Math.Sqrt (op2.x * op2 . x + op2,y * op2 . y + op2 . z * op2.z))
        return true;
    else
        return false;
}

// Overload >.
public static bool operator > (ThreeD opl, ThreeD op2)
{
    if (Math.Sqrt (opl .x * opl.x + opl.y * opl.y + opl.z * opl.z) >
        Math.Sqrt (op2 .x * op2 . x + op2 . y * op2 . y + op2 . z * op2.z))
        return true;
    else
        return false;

    // Show X, Y, 2 coordinates.
    public void Show ( )
    {
        Console. WriteLine (x + ", " + y + ", " + z) ;
    }

    class ThreeDDemo {
        static void Mainf) (
            ThreeD a = new ThreeD (5, 6, 7);
            ThreeD b = new ThreeDflO, 10, 10)
```

```
        ThreeD c = new ThreeD (1, 2, 3);
        ThreeD d = new ThreeD (6, 7, 5);

        Console.Write("Here is a: ");
        a. Show{) ;
        Console-Write("Here is b: ");
        b.Show() ;
        Console-Write{"Here is c: "};
        c.Show() ;
        Console.Write("Here is d: ");
        d.Show() ;

    Console.WriteLine ();

    if(a > c) Console.WriteLine("a> c is true");
    if(a < c) Console.WriteLine ("a < c is true"};
    if(a > b) Console.WriteLine ("a > b is true");
    if(a < b) Console.WriteLine("a< b is true");
    if(a > d) Console.WriteLine("a > d is true");
    else if(a < d} Console.WriteLine("a < d is true");
    else Console.WriteLine("a and d are same distance from origin"};
  }
}
```

The output from this program is shown here:

```
Here is a: 5, 6, 7
Here is b: 10, 10, 10
Here is c: 1, 2, 3
Here is d: 6, 1, 5

a > c is true
a < b is true
a and d are same distance from origin
```

An important restriction applies to overloading the relational operators: You must overload them in pairs. For example, if you overload <, you must also overload >, and vice versa. The operator pairs are

```
==      !=
<       >
<=      >=
```

One other point: If you overload the = = and != operators, then you will usually need to override Object.Equals() and Object.GetHashCode().

## Overloading true and false

The keywords true and false can also be used as unary operators for the purposes of overloading. Overloaded versions of these operators provide custom determinations of true and false relative to classes that you create. Once true and false are overloaded for a class, you can use objects of that class to control the if, while, for, and do-while statements, or in a ? expression.

The true and false operators must be overloaded as a pair. You cannot overload just one. Both are unary operators and they have this general form:

```
public static bool operator tme(param-type operand)
{
    // return true or false
}
public static bool operator fa\se(param-type operand)
{
```

```
        // return true or false
    )
```

Notice that each returns a bool result.

The following example shows how true and false can be implemented for the ThreeD class. Each assumes that a ThreeD object is true if at least one coordinate is non-zero. If all three coordinates are zero, then the object is false. The decrement operator is also implemented for the purpose of illustration.

```
// Overload true and false for ThreeD.

using System;

//A three-dimensional coordinate class -
class ThreeD {
    int x, y, z; // 3-D coordinates

    public ThreeD {}  ( x - y - z = 0; {
    public ThreeD(int i, int j, int k) { x = i; y = j ; z = k; }

    // Overload true ,
    public static bool operator true (ThreeD op) {
        if(op.x != 0) || (op.y != 0) || (op.z != 0))
            return true; // at least one coordinate is non-zero
        else
            return false;
    }

    // Overload false .
    public static bool operator false (ThreeD op) {
        if((op.x == 0) && {op.y == 0) && (op.z == 0)
            return true; // all coordinates are zero
        else
            return false;
    }

    // Overload unary —.
    public static ThreeD operator —(ThreeD op)
    {
        ThreeD result = new ThreeD ();

        // Return the decremented result.
        result.x = op.x - 1;
        result.y = op.y - 1;
        result.z = op.z - 1;

        return result;
    }

    // Show X, Y, 2 coordinates.
    public void Show ( )
    {

    Console. WriteLine (x + ", " + y + ", " + 2}
    }
}

class TrueFalseDemo {
    static void Main() {
```

```
        ThreeD a = new ThreeD(5, 6, 7);
        ThreeD b = new ThreeD (10, 10, 10);
        ThreeD c = new ThreeD (0, 0, 0);

        Console.Write ("Here is a: ");
        a.Showf) ;
        Console .Write ("Here is b : " ) ;
        b.Show ( ) ;
        Console.Write ( "Here is c : " ) ;
        c.Show ( ) ;
        Console.WriteLine {() ;

        if (a) Console.WriteLine ("a is true . " ) ;
        else Console .WriteLine ("a is false . " } ;

        if (b) Console.WriteLine ("b is true . ") ;
        else Console. WriteLine ("b is false.");

        if (c) Console.WriteLine ("c is true.");
        else Console .WriteLine ( "c is false .");

        Console.WriteLine ( ) ;

        Console.WriteLine ("Control a loop using a ThreeD object.
        do {
            b.Show ( ) ;
            b–;
        } while (b) ;
    }
}
```

The output is shown here:

```
Here is a: 5, 6, 7
Here is b: 10, 10, 10
Here is c: 0, 0, 0

Control a loop using a ThreeD object.
10, 10, 10
9, 9, 9
8, 8, 8
7, 7, 7
6, 6, 6
5, 5, 5
4, 4, 4
3, 3, 3
2, 2, 2
1, 1, 1
```

Notice how the ThreeD objects are used to control if statements and a do-while loop. In the case of the if statements, the ThreeD object is evaluated using true. If the result of this operation is true, then the if statement succeeds. In the case of the do-while loop, each iteration of the loop decrements b. The loop repeats as long as b evaluates as true (that is, it contains at least one non-zero coordinate). When b contains all zero coordinates, it evaluates as false when the true operator is applied and the loop stops.

## Overloading the Logical Operators

As you know, C# defines the following logical operators: &, I,!, &&, and I I. Of these, only the &, I, and

! can be overloaded. By following certain rules, however, the benefits of the short-circuit && and I I can still be obtained. Each situation is examined here.



## A Simple Approach to Overloading the Logical Operators

Let's begin with the simplest situation. If you will not be making use of the short-circuit logical operators, then you can overload & and I as you would intuitively think, with each returning a bool result. An overloaded ! will also usually return a bool result.

Here is an example that overloads the !, &, and I logical operators for objects of type ThreeD. As before, each assumes that a ThreeD object is true if at least one coordinate is non-zero. If all three coordinates are zero, then the object is false.

```
// A simple way to overload !, I, and & for ThreeD.

using System;

//A three-dimensional coordinate class.
class ThreeD {
    int x, y, z; // 3-D coordinates

    public ThreeD() ( x = y = z - 0; }
    public ThreeD(int i, int j, int k) { x = i; y = j; z = k; }

    // Overload 1,
    public static bool operator I (ThreeD opl, ThreeD op2)
    {
        if( ((opl.x != 0) || (opl.y != 0} || (opl.z != 0)}
            ((op2.x != 0) II (op2.y != 0) || (op2.z != 0)} )
            return true;
        else
            return false;
    }

    // Overload &.
    public static bool operator & (ThreeD opl, ThreeD op2)
    {
        if( ((opl.x != 0) && (opl.y != 0) && (opl.z != 0)) &
            ((op2.x ! = 0} && (op2.y != 0) S.& (Op2.z != 0)) )
            return true;
        else
            return false;

    // Overload ! .
    public static bool operator ! (ThreeD op)
    {
        if(op.x != 0) || (op.y != 0) || (op.z != 0)
            return false;
        else
            return true;

    // Show X, Y, Z coordinates.
    public void Show ( )
    {
        Console.WriteLine (x + ", " + y + ", " + z) ;
    }

    class LogicalOpDemo )
```

```
    static void Main() {
        ThreeD a = new ThreeD (5, 6, 7);
        ThreeD b = new ThreeD (10, 10, 10);
        ThreeD c = new ThreeD(0, 0, 0) ;

        Console.Write ( "Here is a : " ) ;
        a.Show() ;
        Console .Write ("Here is b: ") ;
        b.Show ( ) ;
        Console.Write ("Here is c: ") ;
        c.Show() ;

        Console.WriteLine ( ) ;

        if(!a) Console. WriteLine ("a  is false.");
        if(!b) Console. WriteLine ("b  is false.");
        if(!c) Console. WriteLine ("c  is false.");

        Console .WriteLine ( ) ;

        if (a & b) Console. WriteLine ("a & b is true.");
        else Console.WriteLine ("a & b is false.");

        if(a & c) Console. WriteLine ("a & c is true.");
        else Console.WriteLine ("a S c is false .");

        if(a | b) Console. WriteLine ("a | b is true.");
        else Console.WriteLine ("a [ b is false .");

        if (a | c) Console.WriteLine ("a | c is true.");
        else Console .WriteLine ("a | c is false .");
    }
}
```

The output from the program is shown here:

```
Here is a: 5, 6, 7
Here is b: 10, 10, 10
Here is c: 0, 0, 0

c is false.

a & b is true.
a & c is false.
a | b is true.
a | c is true.
```

In this approach, the &, I, and ! operator methods each return a bool result. This is necessary if the operators are to be used in their normal manner (that is, in places that expect a bool result). Recall that for all built-in types, the outcome of a logical operation is a value of type bool. Thus, having the overloaded versions of these operators return type bool is a rational approach. Unfortunately, this approach works only if you will not be needing the short-circuit operators.

## Enabling the Short-Circuit Operators

To enable the use of the && and I I short-circuit operators, you must follow four rules. First, the class must overload & and I. Second, the return type of the overloaded & and I methods must be the same as the class for which the operators are being overloaded. Third, each parameter must be a reference to an

CHAPTER 4

object of the class for which the operator is being overloaded. Fourth, the true and false operators must be overloaded for the class. When these conditions have been met, the short-circuit operators automatically become available for use.

The following program shows how to properly implement the & and I for the ThreeD class so that the short-circuit operators && and I I are available.

```
/* A better way to overload !, I, and & for ThreeD.
   This version automatically enables the &s and || operators. */

using System;

// A Ihree-dimensional coordinate class,
class ThreeD {
    int x, y, z; // 3-D coordinates

    public ThreeD () { x - y = z - 0; }
    public ThreeD (int i, in I j , int k) { x •= i; y - j; z = k; }

    // Overload I for short-circuit evaluation.
    public static ThreeD operator I(ThreeD opl, ThreeD op2)
    {
        if{ ((opl.x !- 0) II (opl.y != 0) || (opl.z != 0)) |
              ((op2.x !- 0) || (op2.y != 0) || (op2.z != 0)) )
            return new ThreeD(1, 1, 1);
        else
            return new ThreeD(0, 0, 0);
    }

    // Overload & for short-circuit evaluation.
    public static ThreeD operator &(ThreeD opl, ThreeD op2)
    {
        if( ((opl.x !- 0) && (opl.y 1- 0) && (opl.z != 0)) &
              ((op2.x !- 0) && (op2.y != 0) && (op2.z != 0)))
            return new ThreeD(1, 1, 1) ;
        else
            return new ThreeD(G, 0, 0);

    // Overload true.
    public static bool operator true (ThreeD op) {
        if{op.x != 0) || (op.y != 0) || (op.z != 0})
            return true; // at least one coordinate is non-zero
        else
            return false;

    // Overload false .
    public static bool operator false {ThreeD op) (
        if((op.x == 0) && (op.y == 0) && (op.z == 0))
            return true; // all coordinates are zero
        else
            return false;

    // Show X, Y, Z coordinates.
    public vod Show()
    {
        Console.WriteLine(x + " , " + y " , " + z) ;
    }
}
```

```
class LoqicalOpDemo {
    static void Main() {
        ThreeD a - new ThreeD (5, 6, 7);
        ThreeD b = new ThreeD (10, 10, 10);
        ThreeD c = new ThreeD (0, 0, 0) ;

        Console.Write ("Here is a : " ) ;
        a.Show () ;
        Console.Write ("Here is b : " ) ;
        b.Showf) ;
        Console.Write ("Here is c: " ) ;
        c.Show() ;
        Console.WriteLine ( ) ;

    if(a)  Console.WriteLine ("a is true.");
    if(b)  Console.WriteLine ("b is true . " ) ;
    if(c)  Console.WriteLine ("c is true.");

    if ( ! a) Console.WriteLine ("a is false. ");
    if ( !b)  Console.WriteLine ("b is false .");
    if ( ! c) Console.WriteLine ("c is false. ");

    Console.WriteLine () ;

    Console.WriteLine ( "Use & and |");

    if (a & b} Console.WriteLine ( "a & b is true.");
    else Console.WriteLine { "a & b is false.");

    if (a & c) Console.WriteLine ( "a & c is true.");
    else Console.WriteLine ( "a & c is false . ") ;

    if (a | b} Console.WriteLine ( "a | b is true.");
    else Console.WriteLine ("a I b is false . "} ;

    if (a | c} Console.WriteLine ( "a | c is true.");
    else Console.WriteLine ( "a I

    Console.WriteLine | j ;

    // Now use short-circuit ops.
    Console.WriteLine ("Use short-circuit && and I I");
    if (a && b) Console.WriteLine ("a && b is true . "
    else Console .WriteLine ("a && b is false .");

    if (a && c) Console.WriteLine ("a && c is true . "
    else Console .WriteLine ("a &&• c is false .");

    if (a || b) Console.WriteLine ("a | | b is true."
    else Console .WriteLine ("a | | b is false .");

    if (a | | c} Console.WriteLine ("a || c is true."
    else Console .WriteLine ("a || c is false .");
    }
}
```

The output from the program is shown here:

```
Here is a: 5, 6, 7
```

```
Here is b: 10, 10, 10
Here is c: 0, 0, 0

a is true.
b is true.
c is false.

Use & and |
a & b is true.
a & c is false.
a | b is true.
a | c is true.

Use short-circuit && and ||
a && b is ture.
a && c is false.
a || b is true.
a || c is true.
```

Let's look closely at how the & and I are implemented. They are shown here:

```
// Overload | for short-circuit evaluation .
public static ThreeD operator | (ThreeD opl, ThreeD op2)
{
    if{ ((opl.x != 0) || (opl.y != 0) || (opl.z != 0)) {
        ((op2.x != 0) || (op2.y != 0} || (op2.z != 0)) )
        return new ThreeD (1, 1, 1 ) ;
    else
        return new ThreeD(0, 0, 0);
}

// Overload & for short-ci rcuit evaluation .
public static ThreeD operator 6 (ThreeD opl, ThreeD op2)
{
    if( ((opl.x != 0) && (opl.y != 0) && (opl.z != 0)} &
    ((op2.x != 0) && (op2.y !- 0) && (op2.z != 0)) )
        return new ThreeD (1, 1, "1 ) ;
    else
        return new ThreeD{0, 0, 0);
}
```

Notice first that both now return an object of type ThreeD. Pay attention to how this object is generated. If the outcome of the operation is true, then a true ThreeD object (one in which at least one coordinate is non-zero) is created and returned. If the outcome is false, then a false object is created and returned. Thus, in a statement like this

```
if (a & b) Console.WriteLine("a & b is true.");
else Console.WriteLine("a S b is false.");
```

the outcome of a & b is a ThreeD object, which in this case is a true object. Since the operators true and false are defined, this resulting object is subjected to the true operator, and a bool result is returned. In this case, the result is true and the if succeeds.

Because the necessary rules have been followed, the short-circuit operators are now available for use on ThreeD objects. They work like this. The first operand is tested by using operator true (for I I) or operator false (for &&). If it can determine the outcome of the operation, then the corresponding & or I is not evaluated.

Otherwise, the corresponding overloaded & or I is used to determine the result. Thus, using a && or I I causes the corresponding & or I to be invoked only when the first operand cannot determine the outcome of the expression. For example, consider this statement from the program:

```
if(a || c) Console.WriteLine("a || c is true,");
```

The true operator is first applied to a. Since a is true in this situation, there is no need to use the I operator method. However, if the statement were rewritten like this:

```
if{c || a) Console.WriteLine("c || a is true.");
```

then the true operator would first be applied to c, which in this case is false. Thus, the I operator method would be invoked to determine if a was true (which it is in this case). Although you might at first think that the technique used to enable the short-circuit operators is a bit convoluted, it makes sense if you think about it a bit. By overloading true and false for a class, you enable the compiler to utilize the short-circuit operators without having to explicitly overload either. Furthermore, you gain the ability to use objects in conditional expressions. In general, unless you need a very narrow implementation of & and I, you are better off creating a full implementation.

## Conversion Operators

In some situations, you will want to use an object of a class in an expression involving other types of data. Sometimes, overloading one or more operators can provide the means of doing this. However, in other cases, what you want is a simple type conversion from the class type to the target type. To handle these cases, C# allows you to create a special type of operator method called a conversion operator. A conversion operator converts an object of your class into another type. Conversion operators help fully integrate class types into the C# programming environment by allowing objects of a class to be freely mixed with other data types as long as a conversion to those other types is defined.

There are two forms of conversion operators, implicit and explicit. The general form for each is shown here:

public static operator implicit target-type(source-type v) { return value;}

public static operator explicit target-type($ource-type v) { return value;}

Here, target-type is the target type that you are converting to; source-type is the type you are converting from; and value is the value of the class after conversion. The conversion operators return data of type target-type, and no other return type specifier is allowed.

If the conversion operator specifies implicit, then the conversion is invoked automatically, such as when an object is used in an expression with the target type. When the conversion operator specifies explicit, the conversion is invoked when a cast is used. You cannot define both an implicit and explicit conversion operator for the same target and source types.

To illustrate a conversion operator, we will create one for the ThreeD class. Suppose you want to convert an object of type ThreeD into an integer so it can be used in an integer expression. Further, the conversion will take place by using the product of the three dimensions. To accomplish this, you will use an implicit conversion operator that looks like this:

```
public static implicit operator int(ThreeD opl)
{
    return opl.x * opl.y * opl.z;
}
```

Here is a program that illustrates this conversion operator:

```
// An example that uses an implicit conversion operator.

using System;

// a three-dimensional coordinate class.
```

```
class ThreeD {
    int x, y, z,  // 3-D coordinates

    public ThreeDf) { x = y ^ z ^ 0; }
    public ThreeD(int i, int j, int k) { x — i; y •= j; z = k; }

    // Overload binary +.
    public static ThreeD operator +(ThreeD opl, ThreeD op2)
    {
        ThreeD result = new ThreeDf);

        result.x = opl.x + op2.x;
        result.y = opl.y + op2.y;
        result.z = opl.z + op2.z;

        return result;
    }

    // An implicit conversion from ThreeD to int.
    public static implicit operator int(ThreeD opl}
    {
        return opl.x * opl.y * opl.z
    }

    // Show X, Y, Z coordinates,
    public void Show()
    {
        Console.WriteLine(x + ", " + y + " , " + z);
    }
}

class ThreeDDemo {
    static void Main() {
        ThreeD a = new ThreeD (1, 2, 3);
        ThreeD b = new ThreeD(10, 10, 10);
        ThreeD c = new ThreeD();
        int i;

        Console.Write("Here is a: ");
        a.Show();
        Console.WriteLine();
        Console.Write("Here is b: ");
        b.Show () ;
        Console.WriteLine{);

        c - a + b; // add a and b together
        Console.Write("Result of a + b: ");
        c.Show();

        Console.WriteLine{);

        i = a;     // convert to int
        Console.Write("Result of i = a: " + i);
        Console.WriteLine();

        i = a * 2- b; // convert to int
        Console.WriteLine("result of a * 2 - b: " + i);
```

```
    )
}
```

This program displays the output:

```
Here is a: 1, 2, 3

Here is b: 10, 10, 10

Result of a + b: 11, 12, 13

Result of i = a; 6

Result of a * 2 - b; -988
```

As the program illustrates, when a ThreeD object is used in an integer expression, such as i = a, the conversion is applied to the object. In this specific case, the conversion returns the value 6, which is the product of coordinates stored in a. However, when an expression does not require a conversion to int, the conversion operator is not called. This is why c = a + b does not invoke operator int().

Remember that you can create different conversion operators to meet different needs. You could define a second conversion operator that converts ThreeD to double, for example. Each conversion is applied automatically and independently.

An implicit conversion operator is applied automatically when a conversion is required in an expression, when passing an object to a method, in an assignment, and also when an explicit cast to the target type is used. Alternatively, you can create an explicit conversion operator, which is invoked only when an explicit cast is used. An explicit conversion operator is not invoked automatically. For example, here is the previous program reworked to use an explicit conversion to int:

```
// Use an explicit conversion.

using System;

// A three-dimensional coordinate class.
class ThreeD I
   int. x, y, z; // 3-D coordinates

   public ThreeD() { x = y = z = 0; }
   public ThreeD(int i, int j, int k) (x = i, y = j; z = k; }

   // Overload binary +.
   public static ThreeD operator 4 (ThreeD op1, ThreeD op2)
   {
      ThreeD result = new ThreeD();

      result.x = op1.x + op2.x;
      result.y = op1.y + op2.y;
      result.z = op1.z + op2.z;

      return result;
   }

   // This is now explicit .
   public static explicit operator int (ThreeD op1)
   {
      return op1.x ^ op1.y * op1.z;
   }

   // Show X, Y, Z coordinates .
```

```
    public void Show ( )
    {
        Console. WriteLine (x + " , " + y + " , " + z);
    }
}

class ThreeDDemo {
    static void Main{) {
        ThreeD a = new ThreeD(1, 2, 3);
        ThreeD b = new ThreeD (10, 10, 10);
        ThreeD c = new ThreeD();
        int i ;

        Console.Write("Here is a : ");
        a.Show ();
        Console.WriteLine ();
        Console.Write("Here is b: ");
        b.Show ();
        Console.WriteLine();

        c = a + b; // add a and b together
        Console.Write("Result of a + b: ");
        c.Show ();
        Console.WriteLine ();

        i = (int) a; // explicitly convert to int — cast required
        Console.WriteLine{"Result of i = a: " + i);
        Console.WriteLine() ;

        i = (int)a * 2 - (int)b; // casts required
        Console.WriteLine("result of a * 2 - b: " + i);
    }
}
```

Because the conversion operator is now marked as explicit, conversion to int must be explicitly cast. For example, in this line:

```
i = (i.nt) a; // explicitly convert to int — cast required
```

if you remove the cast, the program will not compile.

There are a few restrictions to conversion operators:

- Either the target type or the source type of the conversion must be the class in which the conversion is declared. You cannot, for example, redefine the conversion from double to int.
- You cannot define a conversion to or from object.
- You cannot define both an implicit and an explicit conversion for the same source and target types.
- You cannot define a conversion from a base class to a derived class.
- You cannot define a conversion from or to an interface.

In addition to these rules, there are suggestions that you should normally follow when choosing between implicit and explicit conversion operators. Although convenient, implicit conversions should be used only in situations in which the conversion is inherently error-free. To ensure this, implicit conversions should be created only when these two conditions are met: First, that no loss of information, such as truncation, overflow, or loss of sign, occurs, or that such loss of information is acceptable based on the circumstances. Second, that the conversion does not cause an exception. If the conversion cannot meet these two requirements, then you should use an explicit conversion.

## Operator Overloading Tips and Restrictions

The action of an overloaded operator as applied to the class for which it is defined need not bear any relationship to that operator's default usage, as applied to C#'s built-in types. However, for the purposes of the structure and readability of your code, an overloaded operator should reflect, when possible, the spirit of the operator's original use. For example, the + relative to ThreeD is conceptually similar to the + relative to integer types. There would be little benefit in defining the + operator relative to some class in such a way that it acts more the way you would expect the / operator to perform, for instance. The central concept is that while you can give an overloaded operator any meaning you like, for clarity it is best when its new meaning is related to its original meaning.

There are some restrictions to overloading operators. You cannot alter the precedence of any operator. You cannot alter the number of operands required by the operator, although your operator method could choose to ignore an operand. There are several operators that you cannot overload. Perhaps most significantly, you cannot overload any assignment operator, including the compound assignments, such as + =. Here are the other operators that cannot be overloaded. (This list includes several operators that are discussed later in this book.)

<table>
<tr><td>&&</td><td>()</td><td>.</td><td>?</td></tr>
<tr><td>??</td><td>[ ]</td><td>||</td><td>=</td></tr>
<tr><td>= =</td><td>-></td><td>as</td><td>checked</td></tr>
<tr><td>default</td><td>is</td><td>new</td><td>sizeof</td></tr>
<tr><td>typeof</td><td>unchecked</td><td></td><td></td></tr>
</table>

Although you cannot overload the cast operator () explicitly, you can create conversion operators, as shown earlier, that perform this function.

It may seem like a serious restriction that opera tors such as + = can't be overloaded, but it isn't. In general, if you have defined an operator, then if that operator is used ill a compound assignment, your overloaded operator method is invoked. Thus, + = automatically uses your-version of operator+ (). For example, assuming the ThreeD class, if you use a sequence like this:

```
ThreeD a = new ThreeD(1, 2, 3);
ThreeD b = new ThreeDf10, 10, 10);

b +- a; // add a and b together
```

ThreeD's operator+ () is automatically invoked, and b will contain the coordinate 11,12,13.

One last point: Although you cannot overload the [] array indexing operator using an operator method, you can create indexers, which are described in the next chapter.

## Another Example of Operator Overloading

Throughout this chapter we have been using the ThreeD class to demonstrate operator overloading, and in this regard it has served us well. Before concluding this chapter, however, it is useful to work through another example. Although the general principles of operator overloading are the same no matter what class is used, the following example helps show the power of operator overloading—especially where type extensibility is concerned.

This example develops a four-bit integer type and defines several operations for it. As you might know, in the early days of computing, the four-bit quantity was common because it represented half a byte. It is also large enough to hold one hexadecimal digit. Since four bits are half a byte, a four-bit quantity is sometimes referred to as a nybble. In the days of front-panel machines in which programmers entered code one nybble at a time, thinking in terms of nybbles was an everyday affair! Although not as common now, a four-bit type still makes an interesting addition to the other C# integers. Traditionally, a nybble is an unsigned value.

The following example uses the Nybble class to implement a nybble data type. It uses an int for its underlying storage, but it restricts the values that can be held to 0 through 15. It defines the following operators:

- Addition of a Nybble to a Nybble
- Addition of an int to a Nybble
- Addition of a Nybble to an int
- Greater than and less than
- The increment operator
- Conversion to Nybble from int
- Conversion to int from Nybble

These operations are sufficient to show how a class type can be fully integrated into the C# type system. However, for complete Nybble implementation, you will need to define all of the other operators. You might want to try adding these on your own.

The complete Nybble class is shown here along with a NybbleDemo, which demonstrates its use:

```
// Create a 4-bit type called Nybble.

using System;

// A 4-bit type.
class Nybble {
    int val; // underlying storage

    public Nybble() { val - 0; }
    public Nybble(int i) { val = i; val = val S OxF; // retain lower 4 bits
    }

    // Overload binary + for Nybble + Nybble.
    public static Nybble operator +(Nybble opl, Nybble op2)
    {
        Nybble result = new Nybble ();
        result.val = opl.val+ op2.val;
        result.val = result.val & OxF; // retain lower 4 bits

        return result;

    // Overload binary + for Nybble + int.
    public static Nybble operator + (Hybble opl, int op2)
    {
        Nybble result = new Nybblef);
        result.val = opl.val + op2;
        result.val = resuit.val & OxF; // retain lower 4 bits
        return result;
    }

    // Overload binary + for int + Nybble.
    public static Nybble operator +(int opl, Nybble Op2}
    {
        Nybble result = new Nybble();
        result.val = opl + op2.val;
```

```
        result.val = result.val & OxF; // retain lower 4 bits
        return result;
    }

    // Overload ++.
    public static Nybble operator ++ (Nybble op) {
    {
        Nybble result = new Nybble ();
        result.val = op.val + 1;
        result.val = result.val & OxF; // retain lower 4 bits
        return result;
    }

    // Overload >.
    public static bool operator > (Nybble opl, Nybble op2)
    {
        if(opl.val > op2.val) return true;
        else return false;
    }

    // Overload <.
    public static bool operator < {Nybble opl, Nybble op2)
    {
        if (opl .val < op2 .val) return true;
        else return false;
    }

    // Convert a Nybble into an int .
    public static implicit operator int (Nybble op)
    {
        return op. val;
    }

    // Convert an int into a Nybble.
    public static implicit operator Nybble (int op)
    {
        return new Nybble (op);
    }
}

class NybbleOemo (
    static void Main{) {
        Nybble a = new Nybble(1);
        Nybble b = new Nybble(10);
        Nybble c = new Nybbe () ;
        int t;

        Console.WriteLine("a; " + (int) a);
        Console.WriteLine("b; " + (int) b);

        // Use a Nybble in an if statement.
        if (a < b) Console.WriteLine("a is less than b\n");

        // Add two Nybbles together.
        c = a + b;
        Console.WriteLine ("c after c = a + b: " + (int) c]

        // Add an int to a Nybble.
```

CHAPTER 4

```
        a += 5;
        Console.WriteLine("a after a += 5: " + lint) a);

        Console.WriteT.ine () ;

        // Use a Nybble in an int expression,
        t = a * 2 + 3;
        Console.WrileLine("Result of a * 2 + 3: " + t);

        Console.WriteLine();

        // Illustrate int assignment and overflow.
        a = 19;
        Console.WriteLine("Result of a = 19: " + (int) a);

        Console.WriteLine();

        // Use a Nybble to control a loop.
        Console.WriteLine("Control a for loop with a Nybble.");
        for (a = 0; a < 10; a + + )
            Console.Write ( (inL) a + " ") ;
            Console.WriteLine ();
    }
}
```

The output from the program is shown here:

```
a: 1
b: 10
a is less than b
c after c = a + b; 11
a after a += 5; 6
Result of a * 2 + 3: 15
Result of a = 19: 3
Control a for loop with a Nybble.
0 1 2 3 4  5 6 7 8 9
```

Although most of the operation of Nybble should be easy to understand, there is one important point to make: The conversion operators play a large role in the integration of Nybble into the C# type system. Because conversions are defined from Nybble to int and from int to Nybble, a Nybble object can be freely mixed in arithmetic expressions. For example, consider this expression from the program:

```
t = a * 2 + 3;
```

Here, t is an int, as are 2 and 3, but a is a Nybble. These two types are compatible in the expression because of the implicit conversion of Nybble to int. In this case, since the rest of the expression is of type int, a is converted to int by its conversion method.

The conversion from int to Nybble allows a Nybble object to be assigned an int value. For example, in the program, the statement

```
a = 19;
```

works like this. The conversion operator from int to Nybble is executed. This causes a new Nybble object to be created that contains the low-order 4 bits of the value 19, which is 3 because 19 overflows the range of a Nybble. This object is then assigned to a. Without the conversion operators, such expressions would not be allowed. The conversion of Nybble to int is also used by the for loop. Without this conversion, it would not be possible to write the for loop in such a straightforward way.

CHAPTER 5

# String and Controls in C#

***In this chapter you will read about:***

- Concatenation Operator.
- Substring.
- Button Control.
- CheckedListBox Control.
- Sorting ComboBox.

## Introduction

Strings are the set of characters. C# provides lot of string related functions. You do not need to type many lines of code for performing string related operations.

## Concatenation Operator

It is used to join two or more strings or variables. For joining purpose you use plus sign (+).

The following code will demonstrate this properly.

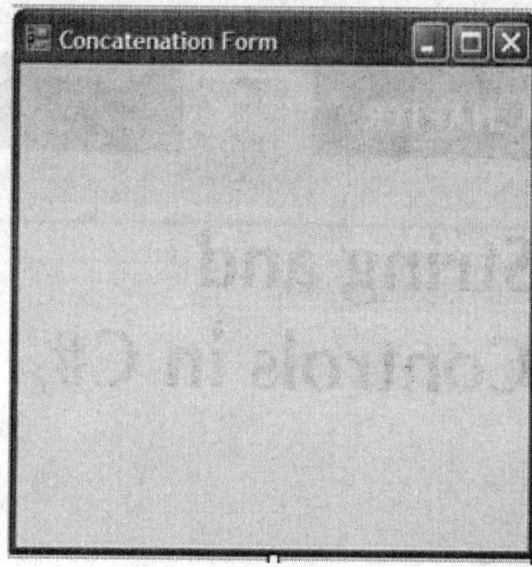


1. Click on File menu.
2. Click on New Project menu item.

   Or

   Use Shortcut key Ctrl + Shift + N
3. New Project dialog box will appear.
4. At the left side of dialog box, beneath Project Types, expand the C# by clicking + sign if not expanded.
5. Select Windows.
6. At the right side of dialog box beneath Templates: you can see several Visual Studio installed templates.
7. Select Windows Application.
8. In Name field type Stringconcatenation.
9. Click Ok.
10. In Solution Explorer click on the icon of Form1.cs for selection.
11. In the Properties window change the File Name property from Form1.cs to Concatenationform.cs.
12. Press Enter.
13. Click the form displayed in the Design window.
14. In the Properties window locate the Text property.
15. Type Concatenation Form.
16. Press Enter.
17. Notice the Title bar of the Form which is changed with the text you have recently typed in the Text property of the Form.
18. In the Properties window locate the Size field and type 400, 300 to specify the width and height of the form.
19. Press Enter.
20. Add Label control to the form.
21. Be sure that Label control is selected; if not then click it once for the selection.

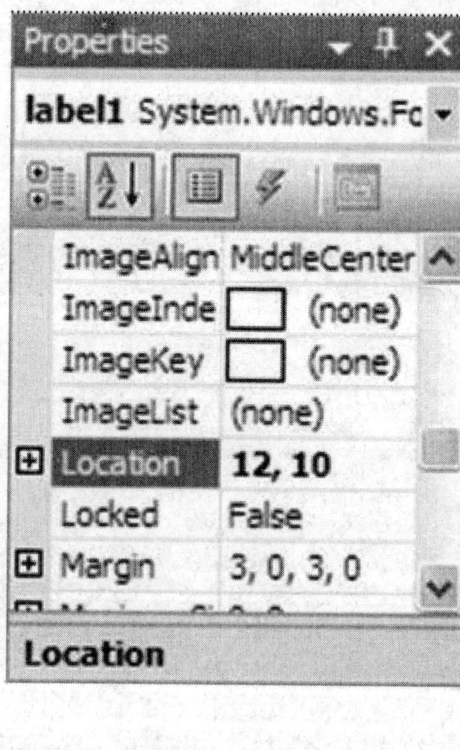

22. In Properties window locate the Text property.
23. Type, Please enter your name:.
24. In the Properties window locate the Location field and type 12, 10.
25. Add Textbox control to the form.
26. Be sure that Textbox control is selected; if not then click it once for the selection.
27. In Properties window locate the Name property and type txtusername.
28. Press Enter.
29. In the Properties window locate the Location field and type 140, 10.
30. Press Enter.
31. Add second Label control to the form.
32. Be sure that Label control is selected; if not then click it once for the selection.
33. In Properties window locate the Text property.
34. Type, Please enter your last name:.
35. In the Properties window locate the Location field and type 12, 71.
36. Add Textbox control to the form.
37. Be sure that Textbox control is selected; if not then click it once for the selection.
38. In Properties window locate the Name property and type txtuserlastname.
39. Press Enter.
40. In the Properties window locate the Location field and type 160, 70.
41. Press Enter to change the location of this Textbox control.
42. Add third Label control to the form.
43. Be sure that Label control is selected; if not then click it once for the selection.
44. In Properties window locate the Text property.
45. Type, Please click on the button below.
46. In the Properties window locate the Location field and type 125, 135.
47. Add Button control to the form.
48. Be sure that Button control is selected; if not then click it once for the selection.
49. In Properties window locate the Text property.
50. Type, Click me.
51. Press Enter.
52. Your form will now look like this:

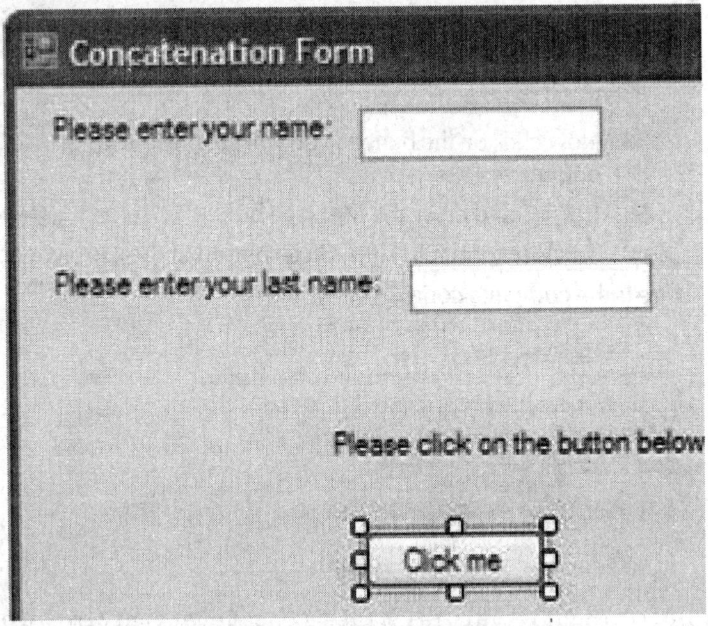


53. Double-click the button control to open the code window.

54. Add the following code to the procedure.

```
using System;
using System.Collections.Generic;
using System.ComponentModel;
using System.Data;
using System.Drawing;
using System.Text;
using System.Windows.Forms;

namespace Stringconcatenation
{
    public partial class Concatenationform : Form
    {
        public Concatenationform()
        {
            InitializeComponent();
        }

        private void button1_Click(object sender, EventArgs e)
        {
         String x;
         x = "Welcome: " ;
         x = x + txtusername.Text + " " ;
         x = x + txtuserlastname.Text;
        MessageBox.Show(x, "Displaying message");

        }
    }
}
```

55. Now this is the time to run the program. Click Start button on Toolbar.

    Or

    Press F5 key located on your keyboard.

56. In first Textbox type "Simran".
57. In second Textbox type "Ahuja".
58. Now click on the button. You will get the following output.
59. Click OK to close the Message box.
60. To close form, click the Close button at the top right corner of the form.

Here is the complete code:

```
– Concatenationform.cs –
using System;
using System.Collections.Generic;
using System.ComponentModel;
using System.Data;
using System.Drawing;
using System.Text;
using System.Windows.Forms;

namespace Stringconcatenation
{
    public partial class Concatenationform : Form
```

```
    {
        public Concatenationform()
        {
            InitializeComponent();
        }

        private void button1_Click(object sender, EventArgs e)
        {
         String x;
         x = "Welcome: " ;
         x = x + txtusername.Text + " " ;
         x = x + txtuserlastname.Text;
        MessageBox.Show(x, "Displaying message");

        }
    }
}
```

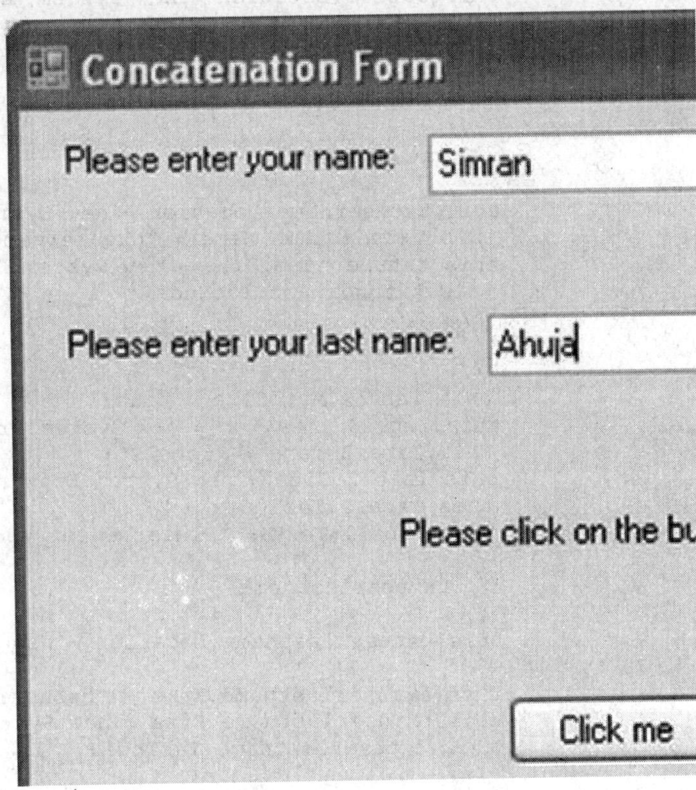


— Concatenationform.Designer.cs —

```
namespace
Stringconcatenation
{
    partial class
Concatenationform
    {
        /// <summary>
        /// Required
designer variable.
        /// </summary>
        private
System.ComponentModel.IContainer
components = null;

        /// <summary>
        /// Clean up any
resources being used.
        /// </summary>
        /// <param
name="disposing">true if
managed resources should
be disposed; otherwise, false.</param>
        protected override void Dispose(bool disposing)
        {
            if (disposing && (components != null))
            {
                components.Dispose();
            }
            base.Dispose(disposing);
        }

        #region Windows Form Designer generated code

        /// <summary>
        /// Required method for Designer support - do not modify
        /// the contents of this method with the code editor.
        /// </summary>
```

```
private void InitializeComponent()
{
    this.label1 = new System.Windows.Forms.Label();
    this.txtusername = new System.Windows.Forms.TextBox();
    this.label2 = new System.Windows.Forms.Label();
    this.txtuserlastname = new System.Windows.Forms.TextBox();
    this.label3 = new System.Windows.Forms.Label();
    this.button1 = new System.Windows.Forms.Button();
    this.SuspendLayout();
    //
    // label1
    //
    this.label1.AutoSize = true;
    this.label1.Location = new System.Drawing.Point(12, 10);
    this.label1.Name = "label1";
    this.label1.Size = new System.Drawing.Size(121, 13);
    this.label1.TabIndex = 0;
    this.label1.Text = "Please enter your name:";
    //
    // txtusername
    //
    this.txtusername.Location = new System.Drawing.Point(140, 10);
    this.txtusername.Name = "txtusername";
    this.txtusername.Size = new System.Drawing.Size(100, 20);
    this.txtusername.TabIndex = 1;
    //
    // label2
    //
    this.label2.AutoSize = true;
    this.label2.Location = new System.Drawing.Point(12, 71);
    this.label2.Name = "label2";
    this.label2.Size = new System.Drawing.Size(140, 13);
    this.label2.TabIndex = 2;
    this.label2.Text = "Please enter your last name:";
    //
    // txtuserlastname
    //
    this.txtuserlastname.Location = new System.Drawing.Point(160,
70);
    this.txtuserlastname.Name = "txtuserlastname";
    this.txtuserlastname.Size = new System.Drawing.Size(100, 20);
    this.txtuserlastname.TabIndex = 3;
    //
    // label3
    //
    this.label3.AutoSize = true;
    this.label3.Location = new System.Drawing.Point(125, 135);
    this.label3.Name = "label3";
    this.label3.Size = new System.Drawing.Size(161, 13);
    this.label3.TabIndex = 4;
    this.label3.Text = "Please click on the button below";
    //
    // button1
    //
    this.button1.Location = new System.Drawing.Point(140, 176);
    this.button1.Name = "button1";
    this.button1.Size = new System.Drawing.Size(75, 23);
    this.button1.TabIndex = 5;
```

```
            this.button1.Text = "Click me";
            this.button1.UseVisualStyleBackColor = true;
            this.button1.Click += new
System.EventHandler(this.button1_Click);
            //
            // Concatenationform
            //
            this.AutoScaleDimensions = new System.Drawing.SizeF(6F, 13F);
            this.AutoScaleMode = System.Windows.Forms.AutoScaleMode.Font;
            this.ClientSize = new System.Drawing.Size(392, 266);
            this.Controls.Add(this.button1);
            this.Controls.Add(this.label3);
            this.Controls.Add(this.txtuserlastname);
            this.Controls.Add(this.label2);
            this.Controls.Add(this.txtusername);
            this.Controls.Add(this.label1);
            this.Name = "Concatenationform";
            this.Text = "Concatenation Form";
            this.ResumeLayout(false);
            this.PerformLayout();

        }

        #endregion

        private System.Windows.Forms.Label label1;
        private System.Windows.Forms.TextBox txtusername;
        private System.Windows.Forms.Label label2;
        private System.Windows.Forms.TextBox txtuserlastname;
        private System.Windows.Forms.Label label3;
        private System.Windows.Forms.Button button1;
    }
}
```

## Calculating string length

While programming you often need to know the length of the string. You can calculate the string length. The following code will demonstrate this properly.

For this perform the following steps:

1. Click on File menu.
2. Click on New Project menu item.

   Or

   Use Shortcut key Ctrl + Shift + N
3. New Project dialog box will appear.
4. At the left side of dialog box, beneath Project Types, expand the C# by clicking + sign if not expanded.
5. Select Windows.
6. At the right side of dialog box beneath Templates: you can see several Visual Studio installed templates.
7. Select Windows Application.
8. In Name field type Stringlength.

9. Click Ok.
10. In Solution Explorer click on the icon of Form1.cs for selection.
11. In the Properties window change the File Name property from Form1.cs to Stringlengthform.cs.
12. Press Enter.
13. Click the form displayed in the Design window.
14. In the Properties window locate the Text property.
15. Type String Length Form.
16. Press Enter.
17. Notice the Title bar of the Form which is changed with the text you have recently typed in the Text property of the Form.
18. In the Properties window locate the Size field and type 400, 200 to specify the width and height of the form.
19. Press Enter.
20. Add Label control to the form.
21. Be sure that Label control is selected; if not then click it once for the selection.
22. In Properties window locate the Text property.
23. Type, Please enter any text:.
24. In the Properties window locate the Location field and type 109, 13.
25. Add Textbox control to the form.
26. Be sure that Textbox control is selected; if not then click it once for the selection.
27. In Properties window locate the Name property and type txttext.
28. Press Enter.
29. In the Properties window locate the Location field and type 177, 41.
30. Press Enter.
31. Add Button control to the form.
32. Be sure that Button control is selected; if not then click it once for the selection.
33. In Properties window locate the Text property.
34. Type, Count Length.
35. Press Enter.
36. In the Properties window locate the Location field and type 177, 103.
37. Press Enter
38. In the Properties window locate the Size field and type 100, 25.
39. Your form will now look like this:

40. Double-click the button control to open the code window.
41. Add the following code to the procedure.

```
using System;
using System.Collections.Generic;
```

CHAPTER 5

```
using System.ComponentModel;
using System.Data;
using System.Drawing;
using System.Text;
using System.Windows.Forms;

namespace Stringlength
{
    public partial class Stringlengthform : Form
    {
        public Stringlengthform()
        {
            InitializeComponent();
        }

        private void button1_Click(object sender, EventArgs e)
        {
        String x;
         x = txttext.Text;
        int y;
         y = x.Length;
          String lengthdisplay;
         lengthdisplay = "Length:= " + y;
        MessageBox.Show(lengthdisplay, "Displaying length");

          }
    }
}
```

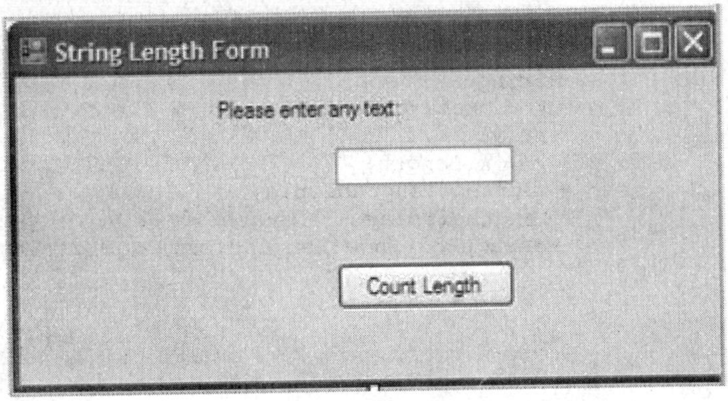


42. Now this is the time to run the program. Click Start button on Toolbar.

    Or

    Press F5 key located on your keyboard.
43. In the Textbox type "I Love India".
44. Now click on the button showing message Count Length.
45. You will get the following output.

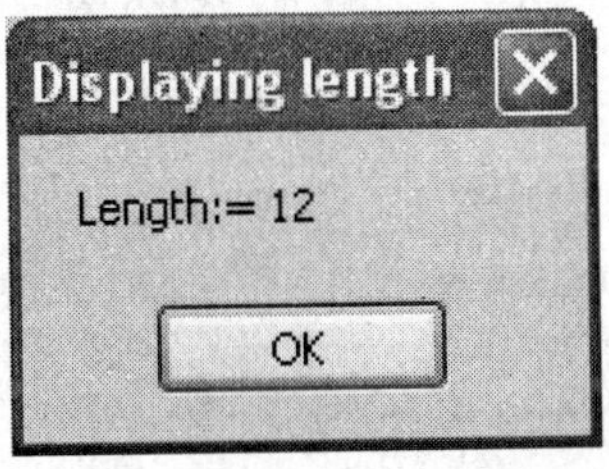


46. Click OK to close the Message box.
47. To close the form, click the Close button at the top right corner of the form.

Here is the complete code:

— Stringlengthform.cs —

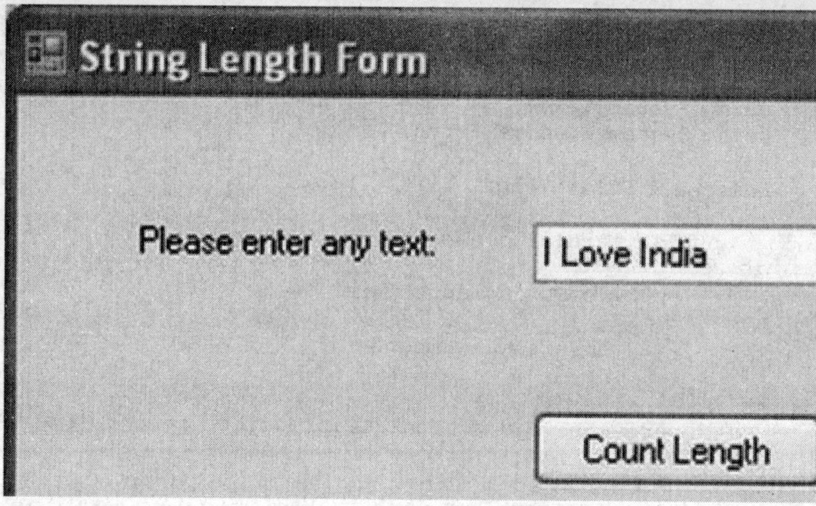


```
using System;
using
System.Collections.Generic;
using
System.ComponentModel;
using
System.Data;
using
System.Drawing;
using
System.Text;
using
System.Windows.Forms;

namespace
Stringlength
{
    public
partial class Stringlengthform : Form
    {
        public Stringlengthform()
         {
            InitializeComponent();
         }

        private void button1_Click(object sender, EventArgs e)
         {
        String x;
         x = txttext.Text;
        int y;
         y = x.Length;
          String lengthdisplay;
         lengthdisplay = "Length:= " + y;
        MessageBox.Show(lengthdisplay, "Displaying length");


         }
    }
}
```

— Stringlengthform.Designer.cs —

```
namespace Stringlength
{
    partial class Stringlengthform
    {
        /// <summary>
        /// Required designer variable.
        /// </summary>
       private System.ComponentModel.IContainer components = null;

        /// <summary>
        /// Clean up any resources being used.
        /// </summary>
       /// <param name="disposing">true if managed resources should be
disposed; otherwise, false.</param>
```

```
protected override void Dispose(bool disposing)
{
    if (disposing && (components != null))
    {
        components.Dispose();
    }
    base.Dispose(disposing);
}

#region Windows Form Designer generated code

/// <summary>
/// Required method for Designer support - do not modify
/// the contents of this method with the code editor.
/// </summary>
private void InitializeComponent()
{
    this.label1 = new System.Windows.Forms.Label();
    this.txttext = new System.Windows.Forms.TextBox();
    this.button1 = new System.Windows.Forms.Button();
    this.SuspendLayout();
    //
    // label1
    //
    this.label1.AutoSize = true;
    this.label1.Location = new System.Drawing.Point(109, 13);
    this.label1.Name = "label1";
    this.label1.Size = new System.Drawing.Size(109, 13);
    this.label1.TabIndex = 0;
    this.label1.Text = "Please enter any text:";
    //
    // txttext
    //
    this.txttext.Location = new System.Drawing.Point(177, 41);
    this.txttext.Name = "txttext";
    this.txttext.Size = new System.Drawing.Size(100, 20);
    this.txttext.TabIndex = 1;
    //
    // button1
    //
    this.button1.Location = new System.Drawing.Point(177, 103);
    this.button1.Name = "button1";
    this.button1.Size = new System.Drawing.Size(100, 25);
    this.button1.TabIndex = 2;
    this.button1.Text = "Count Length";
    this.button1.UseVisualStyleBackColor = true;
    this.button1.Click += new
System.EventHandler(this.button1_Click);
    //
    // Stringlengthform
    //
    this.AutoScaleDimensions = new System.Drawing.SizeF(6F, 13F);
    this.AutoScaleMode = System.Windows.Forms.AutoScaleMode.Font;
    this.ClientSize = new System.Drawing.Size(392, 166);
    this.Controls.Add(this.button1);
    this.Controls.Add(this.txttext);
    this.Controls.Add(this.label1);
    this.Name = "Stringlengthform";
```

```
            this.Text = "String Length Form";
            this.ResumeLayout(false);
            this.PerformLayout();

        }

        #endregion

        private System.Windows.Forms.Label label1;
        private System.Windows.Forms.TextBox txttext;
        private System.Windows.Forms.Button button1;
    }
}
```

## Substring

Using Substring you can extract the part of string from any given number.

The following code will demonstrate this properly.

For this perform the following steps:

1. Click on File menu.
2. Click on New Project menu item.

   Or

   Use Shortcut key Ctrl + Shift + N
3. New Project dialog box will appear.
4. At the left side of dialog box, beneath Project Types, expand the C# by clicking + sign if not expanded.
5. Select Windows.
6. At the right side of dialog box beneath Templates: you can see several Visual Studio installed templates.
7. Select Windows Application.
8. In Name field type stringsubstring.
9. Click Ok.
10. In Solution Explorer click on the icon of Form1.cs for selection.
11. In the Properties window change the File Name property from Form1.cs to Substringform.cs.
12. Press Enter.
13. Click the form displayed in the Design window.
14. In the Properties window locate the Text property.
15. Type Substring example form.
16. Press Enter.
17. Notice the Title bar of the Form which is changed with the text you have recently typed in the Text property of the Form.
18. In the Properties window locate the Size field and type 400, 300 to specify the width and height of the form.

19. Press Enter.
20. Add Label control to the form.
21. Be sure that Label control is selected; if not then click it once for the selection.
22. In Properties window locate the Text property.
23. Type, Please enter any text:.
24. In the Properties window locate the Location field and type 41, 40.
25. Add Textbox control to the form.
26. Be sure that Textbox control is selected; if not then click it once for the selection.
27. In Properties window locate the Name property and type txttext.
28. Press Enter.
29. In the Properties window locate the Location field and type 199, 38.
30. Press Enter.
31. Add Button control to the form.
32. Be sure that Button control is selected; if not then click it once for the selection.
33. In Properties window locate the Text property.
34. Type, Count from first character.
35. Press Enter.

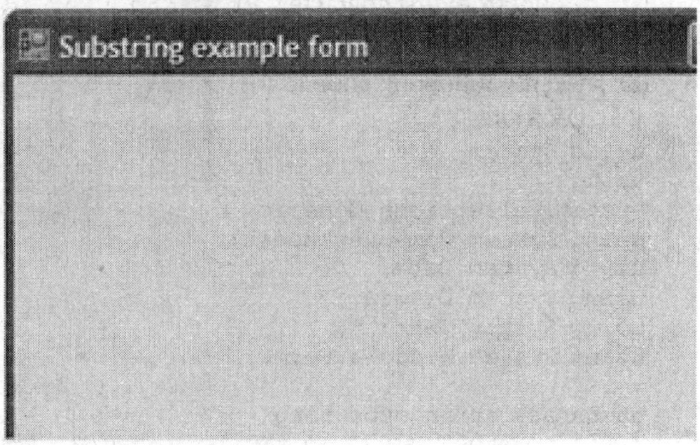


36. In the Properties window locate the Location field and type 166, 116.
37. Press Enter
38. In the Properties window locate the Size field and type 169, 23.
39. Press Enter.
40. Add second Button control to the form.
41. Be sure that Button control is selected; if not then click it once for the selection.
42. In Properties window locate the Text property.
43. Type, Count first four characters.
44. Press Enter.
45. In the Properties window locate the Location field and type 166, 170.
46. Press Enter
47. In the Properties window locate the Size field and type 169, 23.
48. Press Enter.
49. Add third Button control to the form.
50. Be sure that Button control is selected; if not then click it once for the selection.
51. In Properties window locate the Text property.
52. Type, Count last two characters.
53. Press Enter.

54. In the Properties window locate the Location field and type 166, 222.
55. Press Enter
56. In the Properties window locate the Size field and type 169, 23.
57. Press Enter.
58. Your form will now look like this:

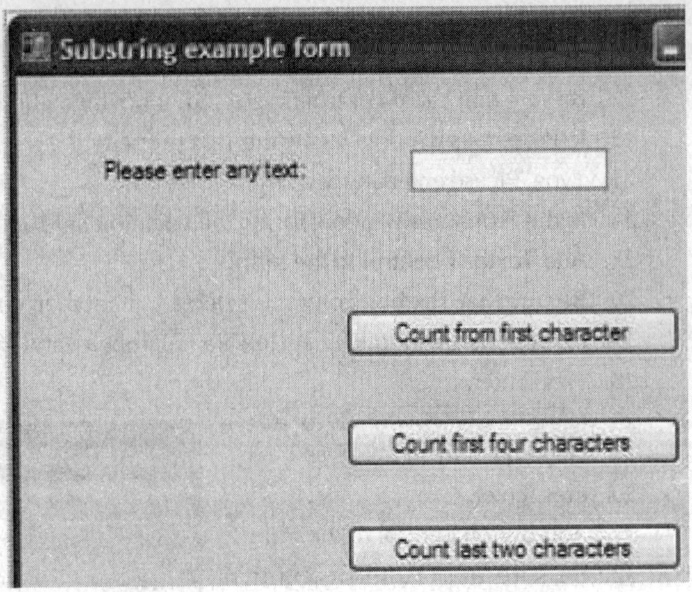


59. Double-click the first button control showing message "Count from first character" to open the code window.
60. Add the following code to the procedure.

```
using System;
using
System.Collections.Generic;
using System.ComponentModel;
using System.Data;
using System.Drawing;
using System.Text;
using System.Windows.Forms;

namespace stringsubstring
{
    public partial class Substringform : Form
    {
        public Substringform()
         {
             InitializeComponent();
         }

        private void button1_Click(object sender, EventArgs e)
         {
         String inputdata;
         inputdata = txttext.Text;
         String fromfirstchar;
        fromfirstchar = inputdata.Substring(0);
        MessageBox.Show(fromfirstchar, "From first character");

         }
    }
}
```

61. Now in Solution Explorer click on View Designer to again come back to Design view.
62. Double-click on second button showing message "Count first four characters" to open the code window.
63. Add the following code to the procedure.

```
private void button2_Click(object sender, EventArgs e)
        {
            String inputdata;
```

```
            inputdata = txttext.Text;
            int countlength;
            countlength = inputdata.Length;
           String firstfourtchars;
            if (countlength < 4)
            {
                MessageBox.Show("Please enter atleast 4 characters");
            }
            else
            {
                firstfourtchars = inputdata.Substring(0, 4);
                MessageBox.Show(firstfourtchars, "First four character");
            }

        }
```

64. Now in Solution Explorer click on View Designer to again come back to Design view.
65. Double-click on the third button showing message "Count last two characters" to open the code window.
66. Add the following code to the procedure.

```
private void button3_Click(object sender, EventArgs e)
        {
                        String inputdata;
            inputdata = txttext.Text;
            int countlength;
            countlength = inputdata.Length;
            String lasttwochars;
            if (countlength > 2)
            {
                lasttwochars = inputdata.Substring(countlength - 2);
           MessageBox.Show(lasttwochars, "Last two characters");

            }
            else
            {
                MessageBox.Show("Please enter string of more than 2 characters");
            }

        }
```

67. Now this is the time to run the program. Click Start button on Toolbar.

    Or

    Press F5 key located on your keyboard.
68. In the Textbox type "Visual Studio".
69. Click on the first button showing message "Count from first character".
70. You will receive following output.

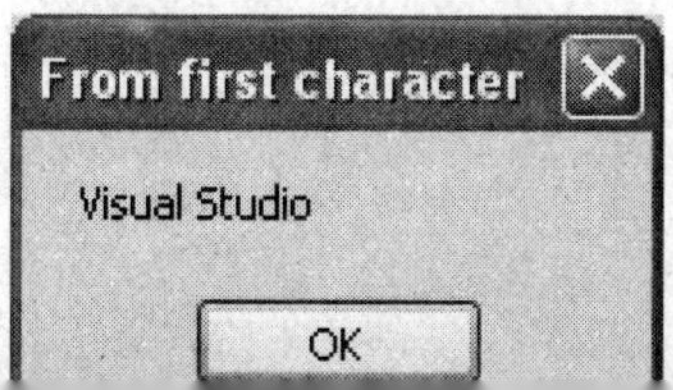

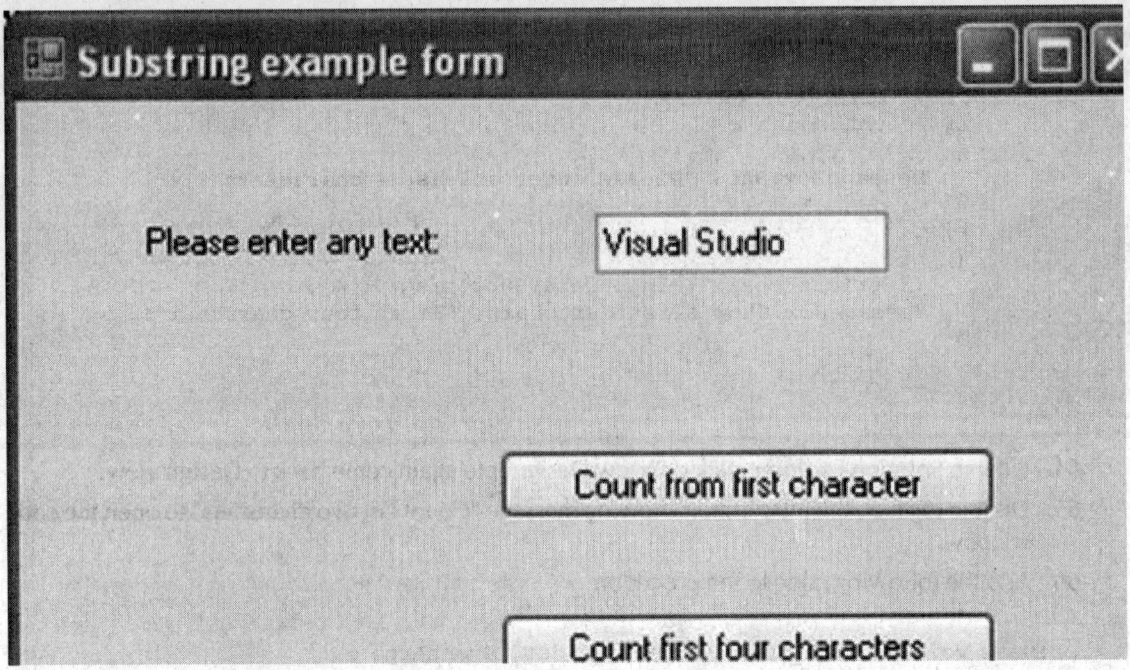


71. To close this message box click OK.
72. Now click on the second button showing message "Count first four characters"
73. You will receive the following output.

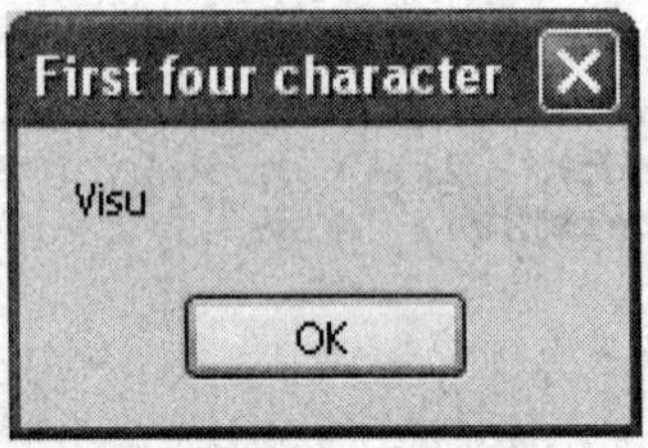


74. To close this message box click OK.
75. Now click on the third button showing message "Count last two characters"
76. You will receive the following output.

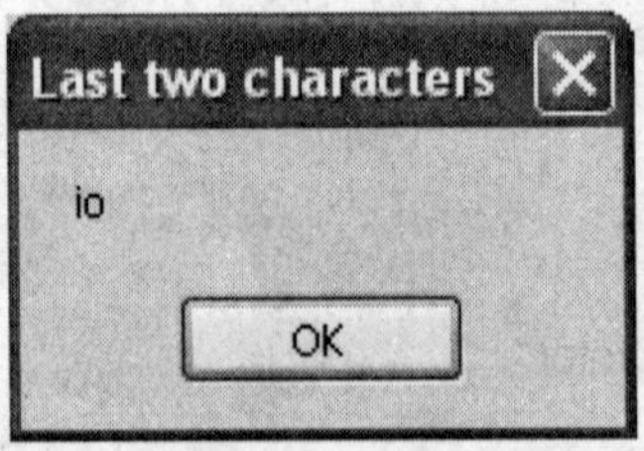


77. Click OK to close the Message box.
78. To close the form, click the Close button at the top right corner of the form.

Here is the complete code:

CHAPTER 5

— Substringform.cs —

```
using System;
using System.Collections.Generic;
using System.ComponentModel;
using System.Data;
using System.Drawing;
using System.Text;
using System.Windows.Forms;

namespace stringsubstring
{
    public partial class Substringform : Form
    {
        public Substringform()
        {
            InitializeComponent();
        }

        private void button1_Click(object sender, EventArgs e)
        {
        String inputdata;
        inputdata = txttext.Text;
        String fromfirstchar;
        fromfirstchar = inputdata.Substring(0);
        MessageBox.Show(fromfirstchar, "From first character");

        }

        private void button2_Click(object sender, EventArgs e)
        {
            String inputdata;
        inputdata = txttext.Text;
        int countlength;
        countlength = inputdata.Length;
        String firstfourtchars;
        if (countlength < 4)
        {
            MessageBox.Show("Please enter atleast 4 characters");
        }
        else
        {
            firstfourtchars = inputdata.Substring(0, 4);
            MessageBox.Show(firstfourtchars, "First four character");
        }

        }

        private void button3_Click(object sender, EventArgs e)
        {
                    String inputdata;
        inputdata = txttext.Text;
        int countlength;
        countlength = inputdata.Length;
        String lasttwochars;
        if (countlength > 2)
        {
            lasttwochars = inputdata.Substring(countlength - 2);
        MessageBox.Show(lasttwochars, "Last two characters");
```

CHAPTER 5

```
        }
        else
        {
            MessageBox.Show("Please enter string of more than 2 characters");
        }

        }
    }
}
```

— Substringform.Designer.cs —

```
namespace stringsubstring
{
    partial class Substringform
    {
        /// <summary>
        /// Required designer variable.
        /// </summary>
        private System.ComponentModel.IContainer components = null;

        /// <summary>
        /// Clean up any resources being used.
        /// </summary>
        /// <param name="disposing">true if managed resources should be
disposed; otherwise, false.</param>
        protected override void Dispose(bool disposing)
        {
            if (disposing && (components != null))
            {
                components.Dispose();
            }
            base.Dispose(disposing);
        }

        #region Windows Form Designer generated code

        /// <summary>
        /// Required method for Designer support - do not modify
        /// the contents of this method with the code editor.
        /// </summary>
        private void InitializeComponent()
        {
            this.label1 = new System.Windows.Forms.Label();
            this.txttext = new System.Windows.Forms.TextBox();
            this.button1 = new System.Windows.Forms.Button();
            this.button2 = new System.Windows.Forms.Button();
            this.button3 = new System.Windows.Forms.Button();
            this.SuspendLayout();
            //
            // label1
            //
            this.label1.AutoSize = true;
            this.label1.Location = new System.Drawing.Point(41, 40);
            this.label1.Name = "label1";
```

:

```
            this.label1.Size = new System.Drawing.Size(109, 13);
            this.label1.TabIndex = 0;
            this.label1.Text = "Please enter any text:";
            //
            // txttext
            //
            this.txttext.Location = new System.Drawing.Point(199, 38);
            this.txttext.Name = "txttext";
            this.txttext.Size = new System.Drawing.Size(100, 20);
            this.txttext.TabIndex = 1;
            //
            // button1
            //
            this.button1.Location = new System.Drawing.Point(166, 116);
            this.button1.Name = "button1";
            this.button1.Size = new System.Drawing.Size(169, 23);
            this.button1.TabIndex = 2;
            this.button1.Text = "Count from first character";
            this.button1.UseVisualStyleBackColor = true;
            this.button1.Click += new
System.EventHandler(this.button1_Click);
            //
            // button2
            //
            this.button2.Location = new System.Drawing.Point(166, 170);
            this.button2.Name = "button2";
            this.button2.Size = new System.Drawing.Size(169, 23);
            this.button2.TabIndex = 3;
            this.button2.Text = "Count first four characters";
            this.button2.UseVisualStyleBackColor = true;
            this.button2.Click += new
System.EventHandler(this.button2_Click);
            //
            // button3
            //
            this.button3.Location = new System.Drawing.Point(166, 222);
            this.button3.Name = "button3";
            this.button3.Size = new System.Drawing.Size(169, 23);
            this.button3.TabIndex = 4;
            this.button3.Text = "Count last two characters";
            this.button3.UseVisualStyleBackColor = true;
            this.button3.Click += new
System.EventHandler(this.button3_Click);
            //
            // Substringform
            //
            this.AutoScaleDimensions = new System.Drawing.SizeF(6F, 13F);
            this.AutoScaleMode = System.Windows.Forms.AutoScaleMode.Font;
            this.ClientSize = new System.Drawing.Size(392, 266);
            this.Controls.Add(this.button3);
            this.Controls.Add(this.button2);
            this.Controls.Add(this.button1);
            this.Controls.Add(this.txttext);
            this.Controls.Add(this.label1);
            this.Name = "Substringform";
            this.Text = "Substring example form";
            this.ResumeLayout(false);
            this.PerformLayout();
```

```
        }

        #endregion

        private System.Windows.Forms.Label label1;
        private System.Windows.Forms.TextBox txttext;
        private System.Windows.Forms.Button button1;
        private System.Windows.Forms.Button button2;
        private System.Windows.Forms.Button button3;
    }
}
```



Now we come to the various controls.

## Button Control

In a form user enters information in text boxes or select values from combo boxes or list boxes. Once he/she is done with the data inputs and selections, they generally click on button control for such confirmation.

In button control's event handler, programmer writes code to perform certain actions according to the business or client requirements.

*Button control plays vital role to finalize programming related tasks.*

You may say this that every form includes at least one button control although it is not compulsory but as habit user looks for button control in a form if he/she wants to confirm the task(S).

When user clicks the button, the button control looks that it is being pushed in and released and click event handler invokes that time. As I have described above that programmer writes codes in the click event handler of button control so you may write code there if you want to perform certain task(s).

Button control looks like this:

Button control can be selected in the following ways:

1. When the click event is invoked in code.
2. When a mouse is used to click the button.
3. When access key is pressed (ALT + the underlined letter) for the button.
4. When a TAB key is pressed to move the focus on button and pressing Spacebar or Enter key on keyboard for choosing button.
5. If the button control is the "cancel button and pressing Esc key on keyboard chooses the button.
6. It the button control is the "accept" button of the form and pressing Enter key on keyboard will choose it even if another control has the focus except this that other control is any other button or a multi-line text box or a custom control that traps the enter key.

You can find button control under Common controls in Toolbox.

There are two ways to add button control in design time:

1. Double-click on the button control in Toolbox.
2. Select the button control by clicking on it in Toolbox and then draw it in form.

Note: If Toolbox is not visible click View – Toolbox or use Alt + Ctrl + X shortcut key.

You may see this that by default Button1 text is displaying over the button. You can change this value by setting the text property of the button control.

```
button1.Text = "Something else";
```

To add the code in its event handler double-click the button control. Make sure that you are in design time, if not then click on the View Designer icon in Solution Explorer window.

```
using System;
using System.Collections.Generic;
using System.ComponentModel;
using System.Data;
using System.Drawing;
using System.Text;
using System.Windows.Forms;

namespace button
{
    public partial class Form1 : Form
    {
        public Form1()
        {
            InitializeComponent();
        }
        private void button1_Click(object sender, EventArgs e)
        {
            button1.Text = "Something else";
        }
    }
}
```

## Changing text of button control

By default Button1 text is displayed on button control. To change the text you can set the values in design time or run time. Better is to set this value in design time. Locate the text property in properties window and then set the desired value. I have inserted Click me. Button control will now looks like this:

To change the text in run time switch to code window and type the following code in form's load event:

```
button1.Text = "Click me";
```

Example:

```
using System;
using System.Collections.Generic;
using System.ComponentModel;
using System.Data;
using System.Drawing;
using System.Text;
using System.Windows.Forms;

namespace button
{
    public partial class Form1 : Form
    {
        public Form1()
        {
            InitializeComponent();
        }

        private void button1_Click(object sender, EventArgs e)
        {
            button1.Text = "Click Me";
```

```
            }
        }
    }
```



## Changing font of button control

To change the font of the button control in design time you can set its font property in properties window.

### Access Key

To invoke event handler of button control you generally clicks on it but if access key is defined then you can invoke the code by pressing Alt + (any defined key).

For ex: Alt + R

But remember this that you can not set access key for those controls which do not receive focus. Once the access key is defined then that letter will be shown as underlined. To define access key just include & (ampersand) before letter while setting the text property of control.

For example:

```
Control.text = "&Click me"
```

The following code will demonstrate this properly.

1. Add the button control on form.
2. Open the code window.
3. Write down the following code as shown below:

```
using System;
using System.Collections.Generic;
using System.ComponentModel;
using System.Data;
using System.Drawing;
using System.Text;
using System.Windows.Forms;

namespace button
{
    public partial class Form1 : Form
    {
        public Form1()
        {
            InitializeComponent();
        }

        private void button1_Click(object sender, EventArgs e)
        {
            MessageBox.Show("Button control has been clicked");

        }

        private void Form1_Load(object sender, EventArgs e)
        {
            button1.Text = "&Click Me";
        }
    }
```

```
}
```

4. Now run the program
5. Press Alt + C
6. You will find the following output because button controls event handler is invoked.

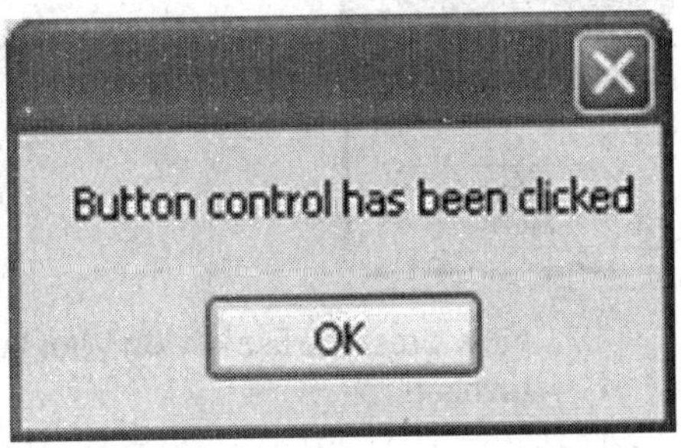


## Accept button

Suppose your form contains many buttons and now you want to fix one button as a default button so that whenever user presses Enter key the event handler of this button control should be invoked instead of any other button control even if any other such control contains the focus.

To define the button as default or accept button you have to set the forms AcceptButton property to the appropriate button control.

For example:

```
Form1.AcceptButton = Button2 ;
```

## Cancel button

Suppose user is filing its personal information in a form because this form is a registration form now in between user has canceled the idea for registration and like to exit the form at this stage. Generally for this user presses Esc key on keyboard. However on form you have already added the button control which performs such task but it will be invoked when user clicks on it. Now you have already written exit code in this button control so whenever user presses Esc key this button control should be invoked automatically. So for this purpose you have to set the CancelButton property of the form to this button control which contains the code to exit the form.

For example:

```
Form1.CancelButton = Buttonname;
```

The following code will demonstrate this properly.

1. Add two button controls on the form.
2. Your form should look like this:

3. Open the code window.
4. Type the following code.

```
using System;
using System.Collections.Generic;
using System.ComponentModel;
using System.Data;
using System.Drawing;
using System.Text;
using System.Windows.Forms;

namespace acceptcancel
{
```

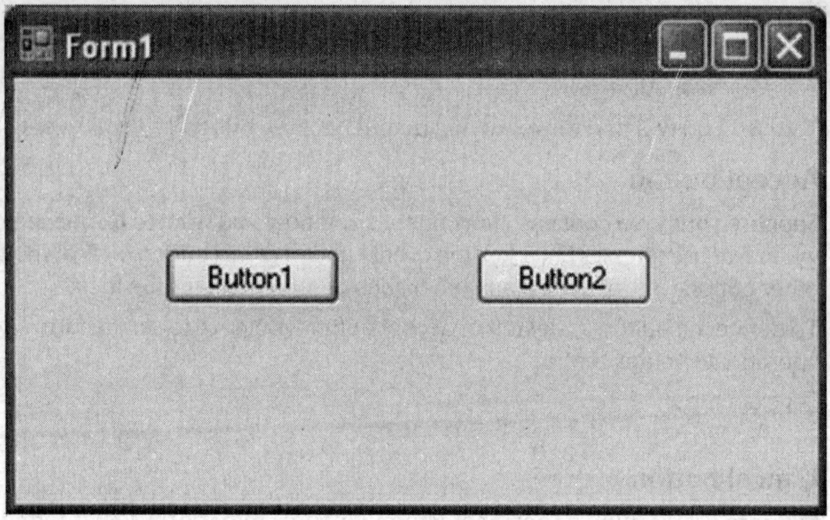


```
    public
partial class
Form1 : Form
    {
        public
Form1()
        {
    InitializeComponent();
        }

        private
void
button1_Click(object
sender, EventArgs
e)
        {
    MessageBox.Show("Button
1 is clicked");
        }

        private void button2_Click(object sender, EventArgs e)
        {
            this.Close();
        }

        private void Form1_Load(object sender, EventArgs e)
        {
            this.CancelButton = button2;
        }
    }
}
```

5. Now run the program by pressing F5 key on your keyboard.
6. Click on the first button it will display the message.

7. Now press the Esc key on your keyboard, automatically event handler of Button2 control will be invoked.

## Checkbox control

The checkbox control is useful when you want to give option to user to select multiple values in one time. For example in a registration form you want to provide facility to user to submit his hobbies now hobbies can be one, two or many.

For example: Sports, Music, Painting, Singing, Reading, Chatting etc.

Now you can design a form using check boxes like the one shown below.

Benefit is user can select multiple options by clicking on checkboxes.

If user selects the checkbox then particular checkbox contains the Checked value and if checkbox is not selected yet then this unselected checkbox contains the Unchecked value.

To access the True / False value of checkbox you can use Checked property. If you want to check this that particular checkbox is checked or unchecked then for this purpose you can use CheckState property.

The following code will demonstrate this properly.

1. Add six checkbox controls on a form with the following values:

| Control | Name property | Text property |
|---|---|---|
| Checkbox | chksports | Sports |
| Checkbox | chkpainting | Painting |
| Checkbox | chkreading | Reading |
| Checkbox | chkmusic | Music |
| Checkbox | chksinging | Singing |

2. Add two button controls on a form with the following values:

| Control | Name property | Text property |
|---|---|---|
| Button | Button1 | Check State (Music) |
| Button | Button2 | Set Checked (Painting) |

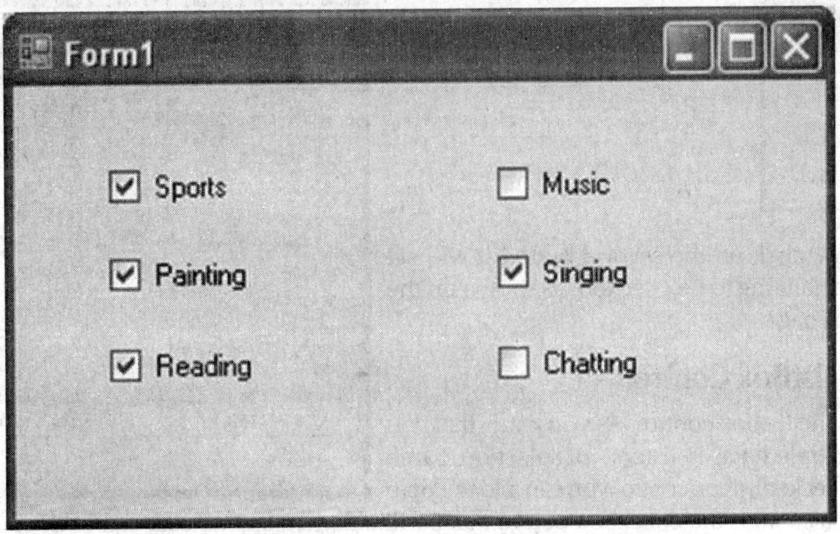


3. Your form should appear like the one shown next.
4. Now open the code window and write down the following code:

```
using System;
using System.Collections.Generic;
using System.ComponentModel;
using System.Data;
using System.Drawing;
using System.Text;
using System.Windows.Forms;

namespace checkbox
{
    public partial class Form1 : Form
```

```
    {
        public Form1()
        {
            InitializeComponent();
        }

        private void button1_Click(object sender, EventArgs e)
        {
            MessageBox.Show(chkmusic.CheckState.ToString());
        }

        private void button2_Click(object sender, EventArgs e)
        {
            chkpainting.Checked = true;
        }
    }
}
```

5. Now run the program by pressing F5 key on your keyboard.
6. Click on the first button. It will display Unchecked.

Note: When you get Unchecked then it means checkbox is not selected yet and when you receive Checked then it means checkbox is selected.

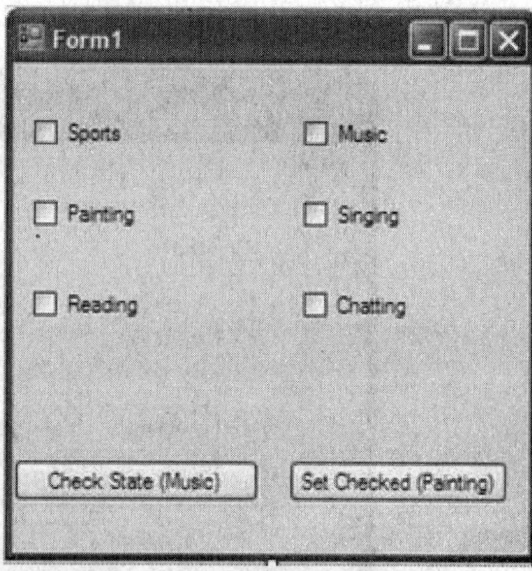


7. Now click on the second button it will set the Painting to be checked, as shown on the next page.

## CheckedListBox Control

It enhances the listbox control. As you know that you can add multiple items in listbox for selection. Same way using checkedlistbox control you can add multiple items but it also adds the checkbox before that particular item so that user can click on it for check or uncheck.

Checkedlistbox appears like this:

You may notice this that before Maharashtra item checkbox is visible.

Using its Checkeditems property you can find this that how many items are checked. Below code will demonstrate this:

1. Add Checkedlistbox control from Toolbox on form.
2. Add button control on form.

3. Set Text property of button control to "Show the checked values".

   Your form should appear like the one shown next.

4. Open the code window and type the following code:

```
using System;
using System.Collections.Generic;
using System.ComponentModel;
using System.Data;
using System.Drawing;
using System.Text;
using System.Windows.Forms;

namespace checkedlistbox
{
   public partial class Form1 : Form
```

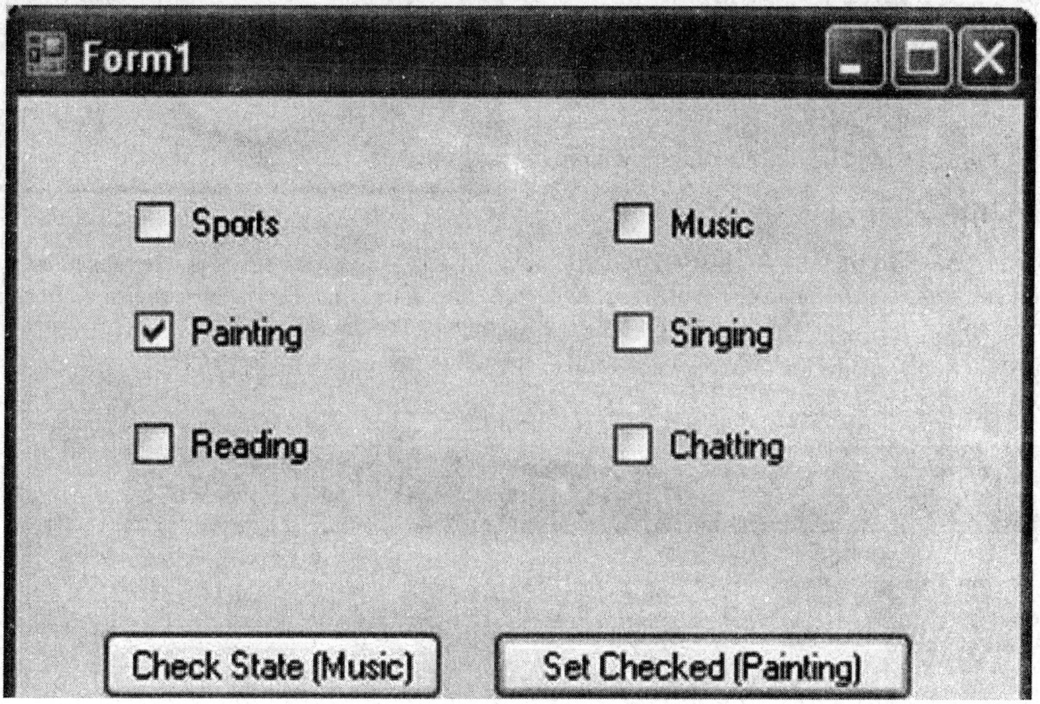


```
   {
      public Form1()
      {
         InitializeComponent();
      }

      private void Form1_Load(object sender, EventArgs e)
      {
      checkedListBox1.Items.Add("Maharashtra");
      checkedListBox1.Items.Add("Punjab");
      checkedListBox1.Items.Add("Madhya Pradesh");
      checkedListBox1.Items.Add("Gujrat");
      checkedListBox1.Items.Add("Karnatka");
      checkedListBox1.Items.Add("Goa");
      checkedListBox1.Items.Add("Jammu Kashmir");
      checkedListBox1.Items.Add("Haryana");

      }
```

```
        private void button1_Click(object sender, EventArgs e)
        {

        }
    }
}
```

In above code you will notice this that I'm filling listbox in form's load event. Although you can fill the items in design time using Items property of checkedlistbox control. You have to click on ellipse [...] for this. It will generate the String Collection Editor. Here you can specify the different items, as shown next.

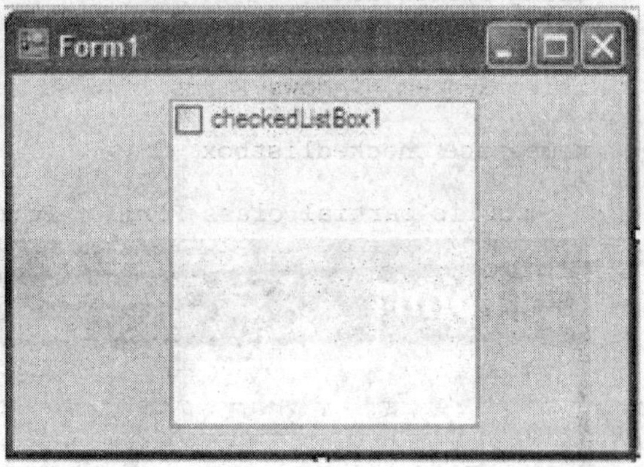


5. Now run the program by pressing F5 key on your keyboard.
6. Your form will look like the one shown next.
7. Check the multiple items, here I have checked Punjab and Gujrat.
8. Output would be like the one shown next.

## Combobox control

Combobox has two sections. In first section you have an access to type list items whereas in second section you can select value from list of items. Again we can say this that it enhances the listbox because listbox displays only data where as in combobox you can type the data too.

The first section contains the textbox where you can type the list items.

Combobox looks likes this:

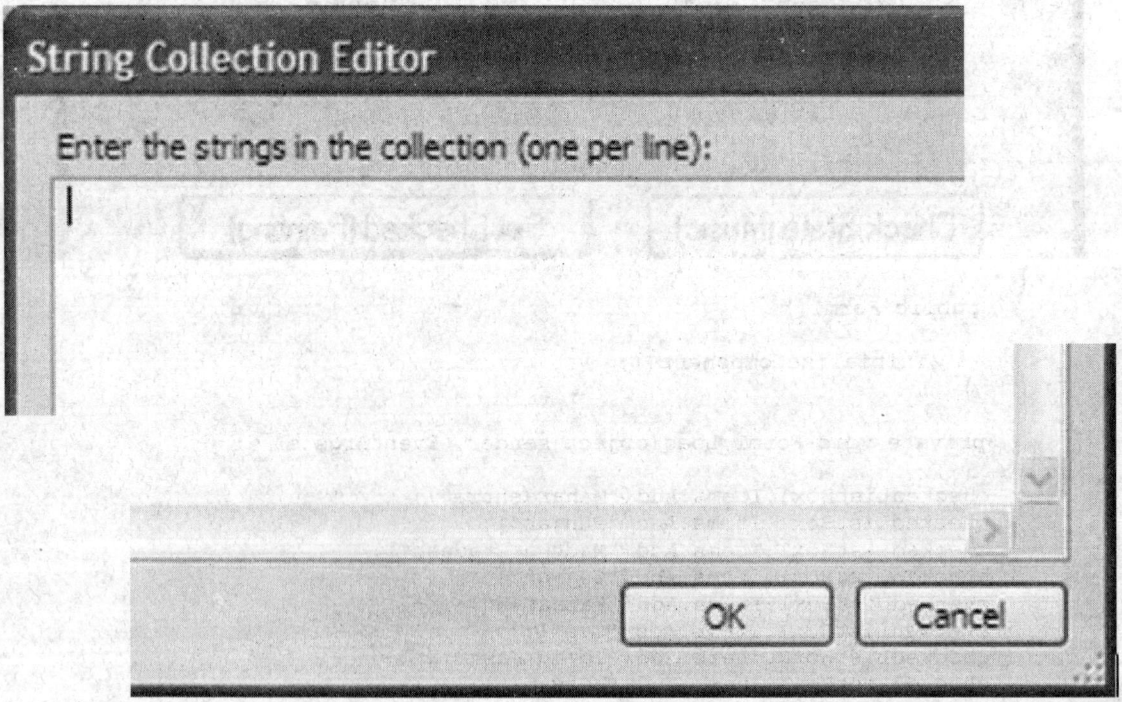

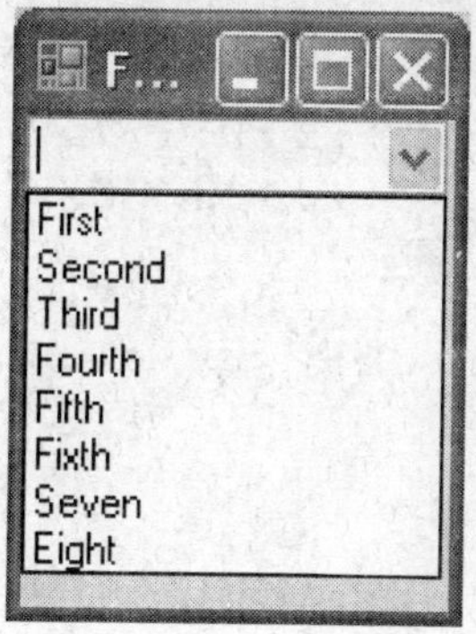


You can see here that First, Second, Third, Fourth etc are the list items where as above these you can find

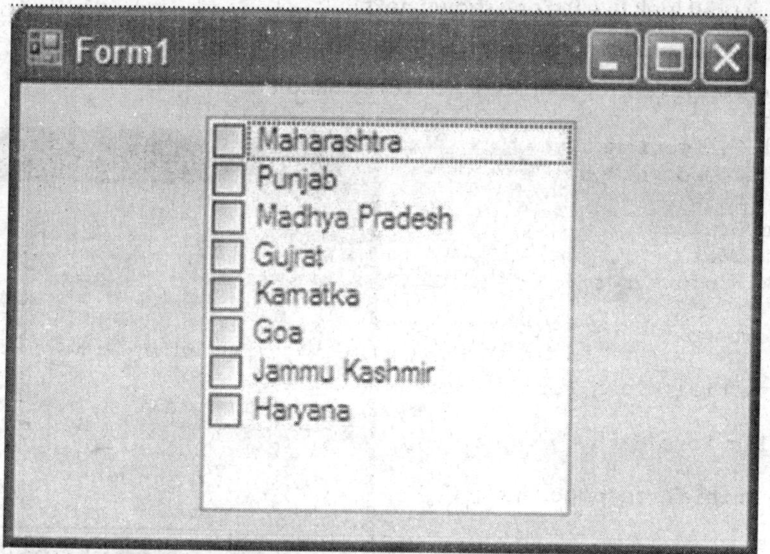


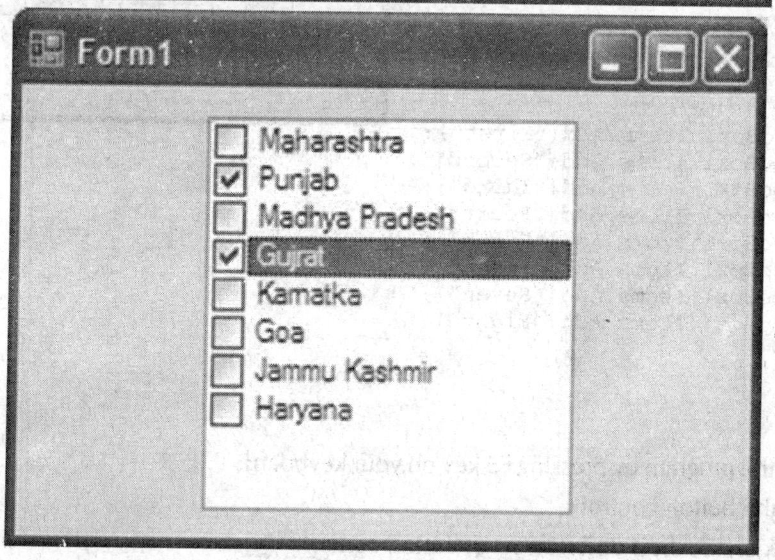

textbox where you can type desired list item for fast selection.

## Adding items



You can add items in combobox control through add method.

For example:

```
combobox1.items.add = "List item 1"
combobox1.items.add = "List item 2"
combobox1.items.add = "List item 3"
and so on .......
```

The following code will demonstrate this:

1. Add combobox control to your form.
2. Add button control to your form.
3. Set the text of button control to "Generate Combobox"
4. Your form should look like the one shown next.
5. Now double-click on button control it will open the code window.
6. Type the following code in button control's even handler:

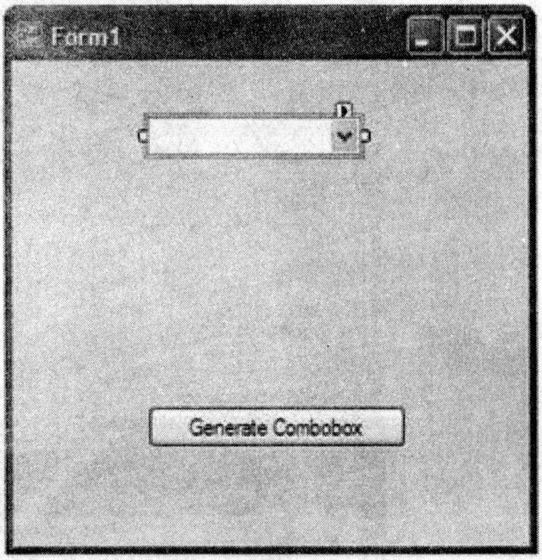


```
using System;
using System.Collections.Generic;
using System.ComponentModel;
using System.Data;
using System.Drawing;
using System.Text;
using System.Windows.Forms;

namespace combobox
{
    public partial class Form1 : Form
    {
        public Form1()
        {
            InitializeComponent();
        }

        private void
button1_Click(object sender, EventArgs
e)
        {
        comboBox1.Items.Add("First");
        comboBox1.Items.Add("Second");
        comboBox1.Items.Add("Third");
        comboBox1.Items.Add("Fourth");
        comboBox1.Items.Add("Fifth");
        comboBox1.Items.Add("Fixth");
        comboBox1.Items.Add("Seven");
        comboBox1.Items.Add("Eight");

        }
    }
}
```

7. Now run the program by pressing F5 key on your keyboard.
8. Click on the button control.
9. Now click on the drop-down arrow of button control.

10. You will find the following output.

## Removing Items

There can be a chance when you have to remove items from combobox control. You can remove by item name or index number. The first item receives the 0 index number, second 1 and so on.

To remove item by name you can use remove method.

For example:

```
combobox1.items.remove("First")
```

To remove item with index number you can use removeat method.

For example:

```
combobox1.items.removeat(2)
```

You can also remove selected item. For this use following code:

```
combobox1.items.remove(combobox1.items.selecteditem)
```

The following code will demonstrate this:

1. Add combobox control to your form.
2. Add three button controls to your form.

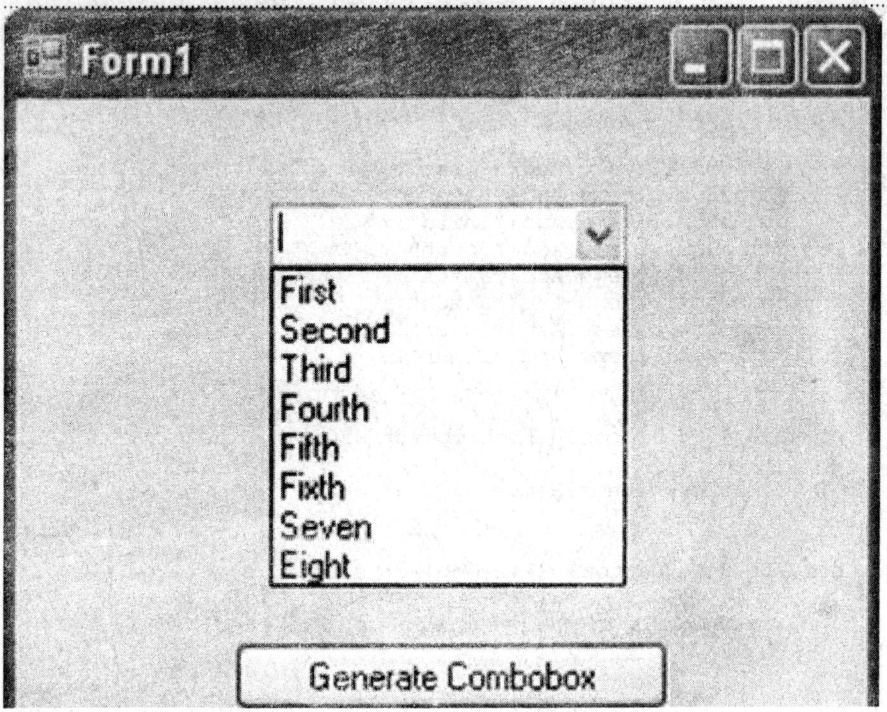


3. Set the text of first button control to "Remove Fourth item"
4. Set the text of second button control to "Remove item by index (0)"
5. Set the text of third button control to "Remove selected item"
6. Your form should look like the one shown next.
7. Now open the code window and type the following code:

```
using System;
using System.Collections.Generic;
```

```
using System.ComponentModel;
using System.Data;
using System.Drawing;
using System.Text;
using System.Windows.Forms;

namespace combobox
{
    public partial class Form1 :
Form
    {
        public Form1()
        {
            InitializeComponent();
        }

        private void
button1_Click(object sender,
EventArgs e)
        {
        comboBox1.Items.Remove("Fourth");

        }

        private void Form1_Load(object sender, EventArgs e)
        {
            comboBox1.Items.Add("First");
            comboBox1.Items.Add("Second");
            comboBox1.Items.Add("Third");
            comboBox1.Items.Add("Fourth");
            comboBox1.Items.Add("Fifth");
            comboBox1.Items.Add("Fixth");
            comboBox1.Items.Add("Seven");
            comboBox1.Items.Add("Eight");
        }

        private void button2_Click(object sender, EventArgs e)
        {
            comboBox1.Items.RemoveAt(0);
        }

        private void button3_Click(object sender, EventArgs e)
        {
           comboBox1.Items.Remove(comboBox1.SelectedItem);
        }
    }
}
```

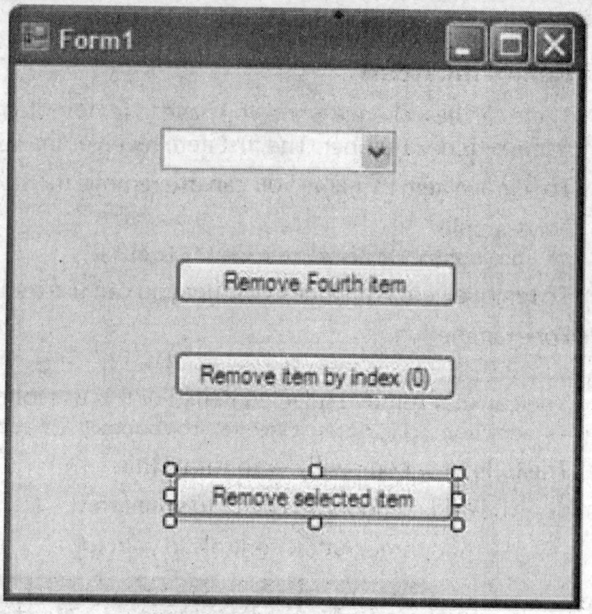


8. Now run the program by pressing F5 key on your keyboard.
9. Test the different remove operations by clicking on different buttons.

Here is the complete code of above program:

— Form1.cs —

```
using System;
using System.Collections.Generic;
using System.ComponentModel;
```

```
using System.Data;
using System.Drawing;
using System.Text;
using System.Windows.Forms;

namespace combobox
{
    public partial class Form1 : Form
    {
        public Form1()
        {
            InitializeComponent();
        }

        private void button1_Click(object sender, EventArgs e)
        {
            comboBox1.Items.Remove("Fourth");

        }

        private void Form1_Load(object sender, EventArgs e)
        {
            comboBox1.Items.Add("First");
            comboBox1.Items.Add("Second");
            comboBox1.Items.Add("Third");
            comboBox1.Items.Add("Fourth");
            comboBox1.Items.Add("Fifth");
            comboBox1.Items.Add("Fixth");
            comboBox1.Items.Add("Seven");
            comboBox1.Items.Add("Eight");
        }

        private void button2_Click(object sender, EventArgs e)
        {
            comboBox1.Items.RemoveAt(0);
        }

        private void button3_Click(object sender, EventArgs e)
        {
            comboBox1.Items.Remove(comboBox1.SelectedItem);
        }
    }
}
```

— Form1.Designer.cs —

```
namespace combobox
{
    partial class Form1
    {
        /// <summary>
        /// Required designer variable.
        /// </summary>
```

CHAPTER 5

```
        private System.ComponentModel.IContainer components = null;

        /// <summary>
        /// Clean up any resources being used.
        /// </summary>
        /// <param name="disposing">true if managed resources should be
disposed; otherwise, false.</param>
        protected override void Dispose(bool disposing)
        {
            if (disposing && (components != null))
            {
                components.Dispose();
            }
            base.Dispose(disposing);
        }

        #region Windows Form Designer generated code

        /// <summary>
        /// Required method for Designer support - do not modify
        /// the contents of this method with the code editor.
        /// </summary>
        private void InitializeComponent()
        {
            this.comboBox1 = new System.Windows.Forms.ComboBox();
            this.button1 = new System.Windows.Forms.Button();
            this.button2 = new System.Windows.Forms.Button();
            this.button3 = new System.Windows.Forms.Button();
            this.SuspendLayout();
            //
            // comboBox1
            //
            this.comboBox1.FormattingEnabled = true;
            this.comboBox1.Location = new System.Drawing.Point(76, 31);
            this.comboBox1.Name = "comboBox1";
            this.comboBox1.Size = new System.Drawing.Size(121, 21);
            this.comboBox1.TabIndex = 0;
            //
            // button1
            //
            this.button1.Location = new System.Drawing.Point(84, 96);
            this.button1.Name = "button1";
            this.button1.Size = new System.Drawing.Size(146, 23);
            this.button1.TabIndex = 1;
            this.button1.Text = "Remove Fourth item";
            this.button1.UseVisualStyleBackColor = true;
            this.button1.Click += new
System.EventHandler(this.button1_Click);
            //
            // button2
            //
            this.button2.Location = new System.Drawing.Point(84, 143);
            this.button2.Name = "button2";
```

```
            this.button2.Size = new System.Drawing.Size(146, 23);
            this.button2.TabIndex = 2;
            this.button2.Text = "Remove item by index (0)";
            this.button2.UseVisualStyleBackColor = true;
            this.button2.Click += new
System.EventHandler(this.button2_Click);
            //
            // button3
            //
            this.button3.Location = new System.Drawing.Point(84, 204);
            this.button3.Name = "button3";
            this.button3.Size = new System.Drawing.Size(146, 23);
            this.button3.TabIndex = 3;
            this.button3.Text = "Remove selected item";
            this.button3.UseVisualStyleBackColor = true;
            this.button3.Click += new
System.EventHandler(this.button3_Click);
            //
            // Form1
            //
            this.AutoScaleDimensions = new System.Drawing.SizeF(6F, 13F);
            this.AutoScaleMode = System.Windows.Forms.AutoScaleMode.Font;
            this.ClientSize = new System.Drawing.Size(292, 266);
            this.Controls.Add(this.button3);
            this.Controls.Add(this.button2);
            this.Controls.Add(this.button1);
            this.Controls.Add(this.comboBox1);
            this.Name = "Form1";
            this.Text = "Form1";
            this.Load += new System.EventHandler(this.Form1_Load);
            this.ResumeLayout(false);

        }

        #endregion

        private System.Windows.Forms.ComboBox comboBox1;
        private System.Windows.Forms.Button button1;
        private System.Windows.Forms.Button button2;
        private System.Windows.Forms.Button button3;
    }
}
```

## Sorting combobox

Sometimes you need to sort the combobox for better appearance at run time. C# provides you sorted property to accomplish such task.

You have to set the sorted property of desired combobox to True.

For example:

```
combobox1.sorted = True
```

The following code will demonstrate this:

1. Add the combobox control to your form.

2. Add button control to your form.
3. Set the text of button control to "Sort the combobox".
4. Your form should appear like this:
5. Open the code window.
6. Type the following code:

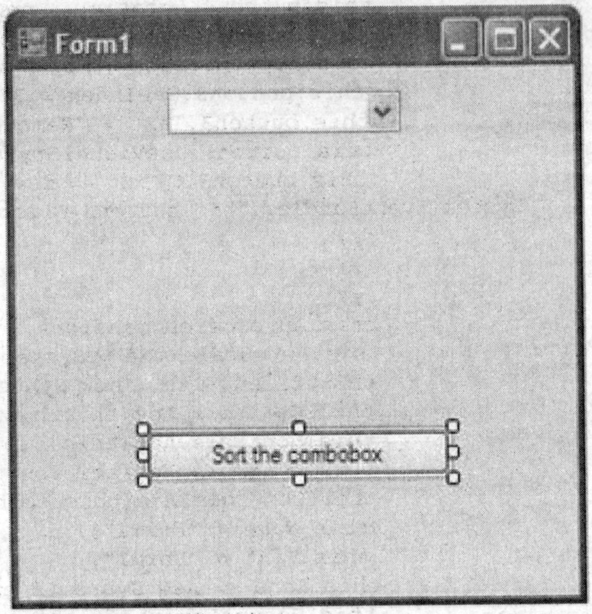


```
using System;
using System.Collections.Generic;
using System.ComponentModel;
using System.Data;
using System.Drawing;
using System.Text;
using System.Windows.Forms;

namespace comboboxsort
{
    public partial class Form1 :
Form
    {
        public Form1()
        {
            InitializeComponent();
        }

        private void
Form1_Load(object sender,
EventArgs e)
        {
        comboBox1.Items.Add("Z");
        comboBox1.Items.Add("C");
        comboBox1.Items.Add("M");
        comboBox1.Items.Add("N");
        comboBox1.Items.Add("T");
        comboBox1.Items.Add("A");
        comboBox1.Items.Add("G");

        }

        private void button1_Click(object sender, EventArgs e)
        {
            comboBox1.Sorted = true;
        }
    }
}
```

7. Now run the program by pressing F5 key on your keyboard.
8. Click on the button control it will sort the combobox items.

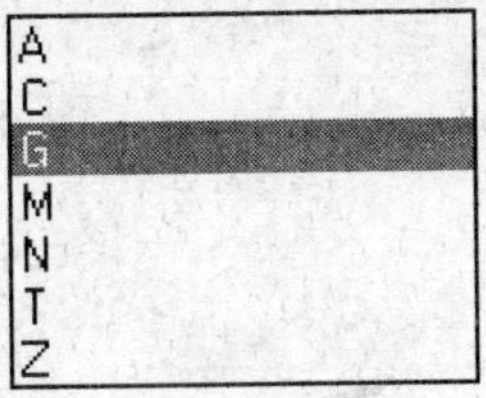


## Accessing Item

To access the item located inside combobox you need to write a little code. This is obvious that user will select the item in combobox and you have to fetch that selected item. For this purpose you can use Selecteditem property of combobox. Which will return you the string.

For example:

```
combobox1.selecteditem
```

The following example will demonstrate this:

1. Add combobox control to your form.
2. Add one button control to your form.
3. Set the text property of button control to "Show selection".
4. Your form should look like the one shown next.
5. Now open the code window.
6. Type the following code.

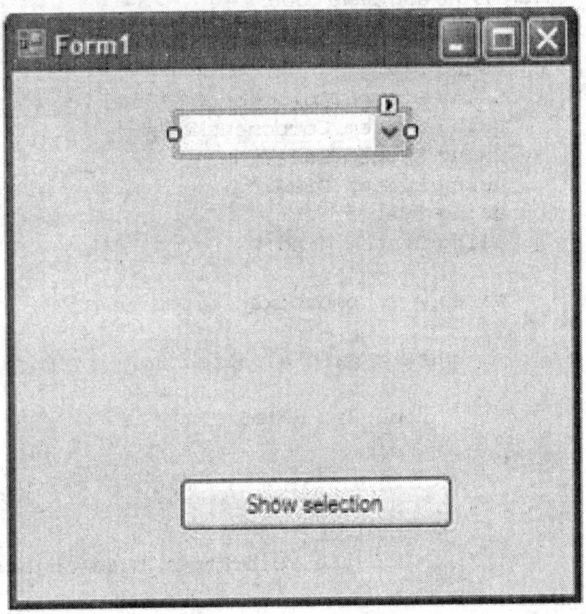


```
using System;
using System.Collections.Generic;
using System.ComponentModel;
using System.Data;
using System.Drawing;
using System.Text;
using System.Windows.Forms;

namespace comboboxselecteditem
{
    public partial class Form1 :
Form
     {
         public Form1()
          {
              InitializeComponent();
          }

         private void Form1_Load(object sender, EventArgs e)
          {
         comboBox1.Items.Add("C#");
         comboBox1.Items.Add("Java");
         comboBox1.Items.Add("SQL Server");
         comboBox1.Items.Add("Adobe Photoshop");

          }
```

```
        private void button1_Click(object sender, EventArgs e)
        {
            MessageBox.Show(comboBox1.SelectedItem.ToString());
        }
    }
}
```

7. Now run the program by pressing F5 key on your keyboard.
8. Select any item in combobox. I have selected here C#.
9. Click the button control.
10. You will get the following output.

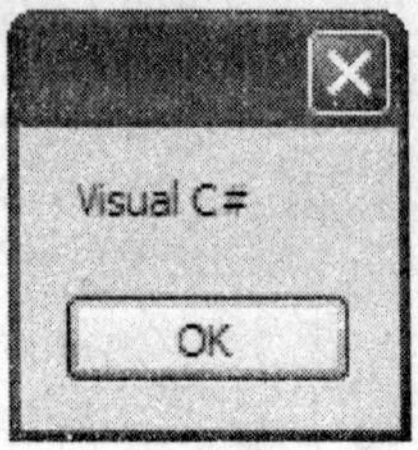


Here is the complete code:

— Form1.cs —

```
using System;
using System.Collections.Generic;
using System.ComponentModel;
using System.Data;
using System.Drawing;
using System.Text;
using System.Windows.Forms;

namespace comboboxselecteditem
{
    public partial class Form1 : Form
    {
        public Form1()
        {
            InitializeComponent();
        }

        private void Form1_Load(object sender, EventArgs e)
        {
        comboBox1.Items.Add("C#");
        comboBox1.Items.Add("Java");
        comboBox1.Items.Add("SQL Server");
        comboBox1.Items.Add("Adobe Photoshop");

        }

        private void button1_Click(object sender, EventArgs e)
        {
            MessageBox.Show(comboBox1.SelectedItem.ToString());
        }
```

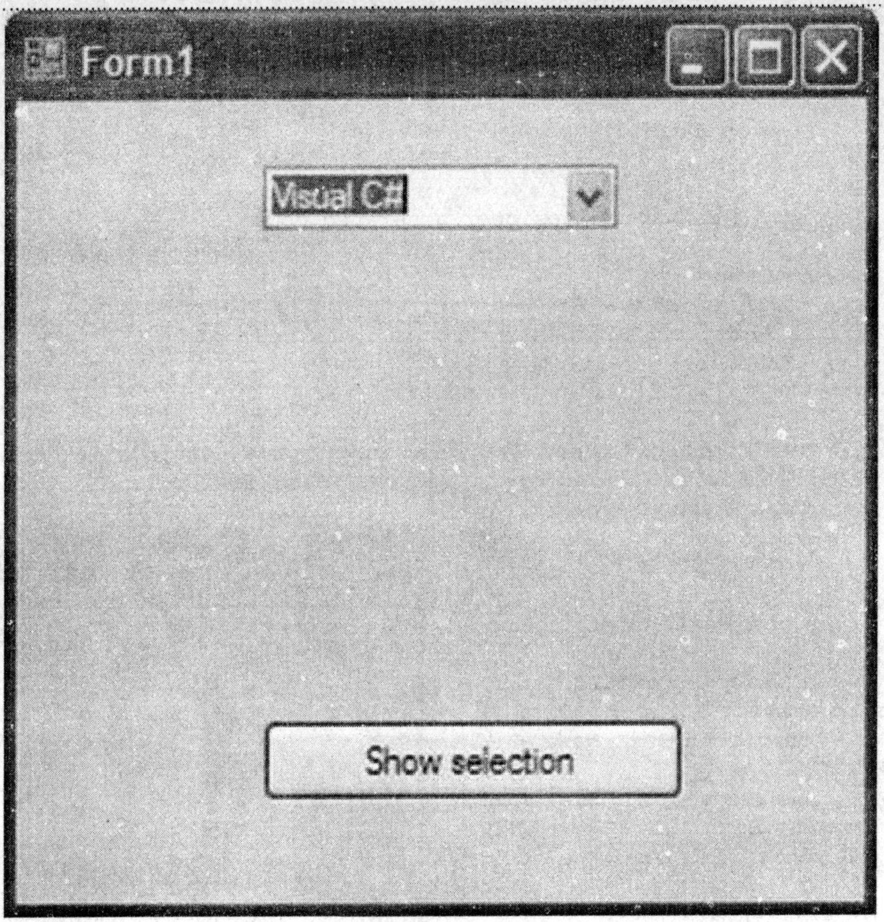


```
        }
    }
```

— Form1.Designer.cs —

```
namespace comboboxselecteditem
{
    partial class Form1
    {
        /// <summary>
        /// Required designer variable.
        /// </summary>
        private System.ComponentModel.IContainer components = null;

        /// <summary>
        /// Clean up any resources being used.
        /// </summary>
        /// <param name="disposing">true if managed resources should be
disposed; otherwise, false.</param>
        protected override void Dispose(bool disposing)
        {
```

```
            if (disposing && (components != null))
            {
                components.Dispose();
            }
            base.Dispose(disposing);
        }

        #region Windows Form Designer generated code

        /// <summary>
        /// Required method for Designer support - do not modify
        /// the contents of this method with the code editor.
        /// </summary>
        private void InitializeComponent()
        {
            this.comboBox1 = new System.Windows.Forms.ComboBox();
            this.button1 = new System.Windows.Forms.Button();
            this.SuspendLayout();
            //
            // comboBox1
            //
        this.comboBox1.FormattingEnabled
= true;
            this.comboBox1.Location =
new System.Drawing.Point(85, 22);
            this.comboBox1.Name =
"comboBox1";
            this.comboBox1.Size = new
System.Drawing.Size(121, 21);
            this.comboBox1.TabIndex =
0;
            //
            // button1
            //
            this.button1.Location =
new System.Drawing.Point(85, 205);
            this.button1.Name =
"button1";
            this.button1.Size = new System.Drawing.Size(144, 27);
            this.button1.TabIndex = 1;
            this.button1.Text = "Show selection";
            this.button1.UseVisualStyleBackColor = true;
            this.button1.Click += new
System.EventHandler(this.button1_Click);
            //
            // Form1
            //
            this.AutoScaleDimensions = new System.Drawing.SizeF(6F, 13F);
            this.AutoScaleMode = System.Windows.Forms.AutoScaleMode.Font;
            this.ClientSize = new System.Drawing.Size(292, 266);
            this.Controls.Add(this.button1);
            this.Controls.Add(this.comboBox1);
            this.Name = "Form1";
```

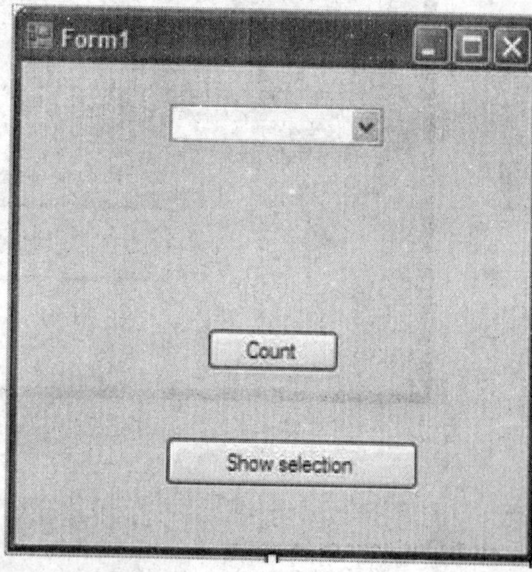

```
            this.Text = "Form1";
            this.Load += new System.EventHandler(this.Form1_Load);
            this.ResumeLayout(false);

        }

        #endregion

        private System.Windows.Forms.ComboBox comboBox1;
        private System.Windows.Forms.Button button1;
    }
}
```

## Count

You can count the number of items in the combobox using Count property.

For example:

```
comboBox1.Items.Count
```

To check this, add one more button control to the above demonstration to your form.

Your form should look like this:

Add the following procedure in code window:

```
using System;
using System.Collections.Generic;
using System.ComponentModel;
using System.Data;
using System.Drawing;
using System.Text;
using System.Windows.Forms;
namespace comboboxselecteditem
{
    public partial class Form1 : Form
    {
        public Form1()
        {
            InitializeComponent();
        }
        private void Form1_Load(object sender, EventArgs e)
        {
        comboBox1.Items.Add("C#");
        comboBox1.Items.Add("Java");
        comboBox1.Items.Add("SQL Server");
        comboBox1.Items.Add("Adobe Photoshop");
        }
        private void button1_Click(object sender, EventArgs e)
        {
            MessageBox.Show(comboBox1.SelectedItem.ToString());
        }

        private void button2_Click(object sender, EventArgs e)
        {
            MessageBox.Show(comboBox1.Items.Count.ToString());
        }
```

```
        }
    }
```



When you will run this program you will find the following output.

Here is the complete source code of above program:

— Form1.cs —

```
using System;
using System.Collections.Generic;
using System.ComponentModel;
using System.Data;
using System.Drawing;
using System.Text;
using System.Windows.Forms;
namespace comboboxselecteditem
{
    public partial class Form1 : Form
    {
        public Form1()
        {
            InitializeComponent();
        }
        private void Form1_Load(object sender, EventArgs e)
        {
        comboBox1.Items.Add("C#");
        comboBox1.Items.Add("Java");
        comboBox1.Items.Add("SQL Server");
        comboBox1.Items.Add("Adobe Photoshop");

        }
        private void button1_Click(object sender, EventArgs e)
        {
            MessageBox.Show(comboBox1.SelectedItem.ToString());
        }
        private void button2_Click(object sender, EventArgs e)
        {
            MessageBox.Show(comboBox1.Items.Count.ToString());
        }
    }
}
```

— Form1.Designer.cs —

```
namespace comboboxselecteditem
```

```
{
    partial class Form1
    {
        /// <summary>
        /// Required designer variable.
        /// </summary>
        private System.ComponentModel.IContainer components = null;
        /// <summary>
        /// Clean up any resources being used.
        /// </summary>
        /// <param name="disposing">true if managed resources should be
disposed; otherwise, false.</param>
        protected override void Dispose(bool disposing)
        {
            if (disposing && (components != null))
            {
                components.Dispose();
            }
            base.Dispose(disposing);
        }
        #region Windows Form Designer generated code

        /// <summary>
        /// Required method for Designer support - do not modify
        /// the contents of this method with the code editor.
        /// </summary>
        private void InitializeComponent()
        {
            this.comboBox1 = new System.Windows.Forms.ComboBox();
            this.button1 = new System.Windows.Forms.Button();
            this.button2 = new System.Windows.Forms.Button();
            this.SuspendLayout();
            //
            // comboBox1
            //
            this.comboBox1.FormattingEnabled = true;
            this.comboBox1.Location = new System.Drawing.Point(85, 22);
            this.comboBox1.Name = "comboBox1";
            this.comboBox1 Size = new System.Drawing.Size(121, 21);
            this.comboBox1.TabIndex = 0;
            //
            // button1
            //
            this.button1.Location = new System.Drawing.Point(85, 205);
            this.button1.Name = "button1";
            this.button1.Size = new System.Drawing.Size(144, 27);
            this.button1.TabIndex = 1;
            this.button1.Text = "Show selection";
            this.button1.UseVisualStyleBackColor = true;
            this.button1.Click += new

System.EventHandler(this.button1_Click);
            //
```

```
            // button2
            //
            this.button2.Location = new System.Drawing.Point(108, 145);
            this.button2.Name = "button2";
            this.button2.Size = new System.Drawing.Size(75, 23);
            this.button2.TabIndex = 2;
            this.button2.Text = "Count";
            this.button2.UseVisualStyleBackColor = true;
            this.button2.Click += new

System.EventHandler(this.button2_Click);
            //
            // Form1
            //
            this.AutoScaleDimensions = new System.Drawing.SizeF(6F, 13F);
            this.AutoScaleMode = System.Windows.Forms.AutoScaleMode.Font;
            this.ClientSize = new System.Drawing.Size(292, 266);
            this.Controls.Add(this.button2);
            this.Controls.Add(this.button1);
            this.Controls.Add(this.comboBox1);
            this.Name = "Form1";
            this.Text = "Form1";
            this.Load += new System.EventHandler(this.Form1_Load);
            this.ResumeLayout(false);

        }

        #endregion

        private System.Windows.Forms.ComboBox comboBox1;
        private System.Windows.Forms.Button button1;
        private System.Windows.Forms.Button button2;
    }
}
```

CHAPTER 6

# Inheritance

***In this chapter you will read about:***

- Inheritance Basics.
- Inheritance and Name Hiding.
- Abstract Classes.
- Object Class.
- Boxing and Unboxing.

CHAPTER 6

## Introduction

Inheritance is one of the three foundational principles of object-oriented programming because it allows the creation of hierarchical classifications. Using inheritance, you can create a general class that defines traits common to a set of related items. This class can then be inherited by other, more specific classes, each adding those things that are unique to it.

In the language of C#, a class that is inherited is called a *base class*. The class that does the inheriting is called a *derived class*. Therefore, a derived class is a specialized version of a base class. It inherits all of the variables, methods, properties, and indexers defined by the base class and adds its own unique elements.

## Inheritance Basics

C# supports inheritance by allowing one class to incorporate another class into its declaration. This is done by specifying a base class when a derived class is declared. Let's begin with an example. The following class called TwoDShape stores the width and height of a two-dimensional object, such as a square, rectangle, triangle, and so on.

```
// A class for two-dimensional objects.
class TwoDShape {
    public double Width;
    public double Heiqht;

    public void ShowDirn (I
    Console.WriteLine("Width and height are " +
        width + " and " + Height);
    }
}
```

**TwoDShape** can be used as a base class (that is, as a starting point) for classes that describe specific types of two-dimensional objects. For example, the following program uses **TwoDShape** to derive a class called Triangle. Pay close attention to the way that Triangle is declared.

```
//A simple class hierarchy,

using System;

// A class for two-dimensional objects.
class TwoDShape {
    public double Width;
    public double Height;

    public void ShowDimO {
        Console.WriteLine("Width and height are " +
                         Width + " and " + Height)

// Triangle is derived from TwoDShape.
class Triangle : TwoDShape {
    public string Style; // style of triangle

    // Return area of triangle.
    public double Area () {
        return Width * Height / 2;
```

```
    // Display a triangle's style.
    public void ShowStyle () {
        Console.WriteLine ("Triangle is " + Style);
    }
}

class Shapes {
    static void Main() {
    Triangle tl = new Triangle!) ;
    Triangle t2 = new Triangle ();

    tl.Width = 4.0;
    tl.Height = 4.0;
    tl.Style = "isosceles";

    tl.Width = 4.0;
    tl.Height = 4.0;
    tl.Style = "right";

    Console .WriteLine { " Info lor tl : " ) ;
    tl.ShowStyle () ;
    tl.ShowDim ( ) ;
    Console .WriteLine ("Area is " + tl .Area ( )

    Console .WriteLine () ;

    Console. WriLeLine ("Info for t2 : ");
    t2. ShowStyle () ;
    t2. ShowDim() ;
    Console.WriteLine("Area is " + I2.Area()
```

The output from this program is shown here:

```
Info for tl:
Triangle is isosceles
Width and height are 4 and 4
Area is 8

Info for t2:
Triangle is right
Width and height are 9 and 12
Area is 48
```

**The Triangle** class creates a specific type of **TwoDShape,** in this case, a triangle. The **Triangle** class includes all of **TwoDShape** and adds the field **Style,** the method **Area()**, and the method **ShowStyle()**. A description of the type of triangle is stored in Style; **Area()** computes and returns the area of the triangle; and **ShowStyle()** displays the triangle style.

Notice the syntax that **Triangle** uses to inherit **TwoDShape:**

This syntax can be generalized. Whenever one class inherits another, the base class name follows the name of the derived class, separated by a colon. In C#, the syntax for inheriting a class is remarkably simple and easy to use.

Because **Triangle** includes all of the members of its base class, **TwoDShape,** it can access **Width** and **Height** inside **Area().** Also, inside **Main()**, objects **tl** and t2 can refer to Width and Height directly, as if they were part of **Triangle.** Even though **TwoDShape** is a base for **Triangle,** it is also a completely independent, stand-alone class. Being a base class for a derived class does not mean that the base class cannot be used by itself. For example, the following is perfectly valid:

```
TwoDShape shape = new TwoDShape();

shape.Width = 10;
shape.Height = 20;

shape.ShowDim();
```

Of course, an object of **TwoDShape** has no knowledge of or access to any classes derived from **TwoDShape.**

The general form of a class declaration that inherits a base class is shown here:

```
class derived-class-ntmie : base-class-name {
    // body of class
}
```

You can specify only one base class for any derived class that you create. C# does not support the inheritance of multiple base classes into a single derived class. (This differs from C+ +, in which you can inherit multiple base classes, Be aware of this when converting C+ + code to C#.) You can, however, create a hierarchy of inheritance in which a derived class becomes a base class of another derived class. (Of course, no class can be a base class of itself, either directly or indirectly.) In all cases, a derived class inherits all of the members of its base class. This includes instance variables, methods, properties, and indexers.

A major advantage of inheritance is that once you have created a base class that defines the attributes common to a set of objects, it can be used to create any number of more specific derived classes. Each derived class can precisely tailor its own classification. For example, here is another class derived from **TwoDShape** that encapsulates rectangles:

```
// A derived class ol" TwoDShape for rectangles,
class Rectangle : TwoDShape {
    // Return true if the rectangle is square,
    public bool TsSquaref) (
        if (Width == Height) return true;
        return false;
    {

    // Return area of the rectangle.
    public double Area() {
        return Width + Height;
    }
}
```

The Rectangle class includes **TwoDShape** and adds the methods **IsSquare()**, which determines if the rectangle is square, and Area(), which computes the area of a rectangle.

## Member Access and Inheritance

Members of a class are often declared private to prevent their unauthorized use or tampering. Inheriting a class *does not* overrule the private access restriction. Thus, even though a derived class includes all of the members of its base class, it cannot access those members of the base class that are private. For example, if, as shown here, Width and Height are made private in TwoDShape, then Triangle will not be able to access them:

```
// Access to private members is not inherited.

//This example will not compile.
using System;

//A class for two-dimensional objects.
class TwoDShape {
    double Width;      // now private
    double Height;     // now private

    public void ShowDim() {
        Console.WriteLine("Width and height are " +
                          Width + " and " + Height);
    }
}

//Triangle is derived from TwoDShape.
class Triangle : TwoDShape {
    public string Style;        // style of triangle

    //Return area of a triangle.
    public double Area() {
    public Width + Height / 2; //Error, can't access private member
    }

    // Display a triangle's style.
    public void ShowStyle() {
        Console.WriteLine("Triangle is " + Sty;e);
    }
}
```

The Triangle class will not compile because the use of Width and Height inside the Area! ) method is illegal. Since Width and Height are now private, they are accessible only to other members of their own class. Derived classes have no access to them.

At first, you might think that it is a serious restriction that derived classes do not have access to the private members of base classes because it would prevent the use of private members in many situations. However, this is not true; C# provides various solutions. One is to use protected members, which is described in the next section. A second is to use public properties to provide access to private data.

As explained in the previous chapter, a property allows you to manage access to an instance variable. For example, you can enforce constraints on its values, or you can make the variable read-only. By making a property public, but declaring its underlying variable private, a derived class can still use the property, but it cannot directly access the underlying private variable.

Here is a rewrite of the TwoDShape class that makes Width and Height into properties. In the process, it ensures that the values of Width and Height will be positive. This would allow you, for example, to specify the Width and Height using the coordinates of the shape in any quadrant of the Cartesian plane without having to first obtain their absolute values.

```
// Use public properties to set and get private members.

using System;

    //A class for two-dimensional objects.
    class TwoDShape {
    double pri_width;           // now private
    double pri_height;          // now private
```

```
    // Properties tor widt.h and height,
    public double Width {
        get { return pri_width; }
        set { pri_widLh = value < 0 ? -value : value;
    }

    public void ShowDim() {
        Console.WriteLine("Width and height are " +
                          Width + " and " + Height);
    }
}

    //A derived class of TwoDShape for triangle
    class Triangle: TwoDShape {
        public string Style; // style of triangle

        // Return area of triangle.
        public double Area
            return Width * Height / 2;
        }

    // Displaya trnagle' style
    public void ShowStyle ()
        Console.WriteLine ("Triangle is " + Style)
    }
}

class Shapes2 {
    static void Main() (
        Triangle tl = new Triangle ()
        Triangle t2 = new Triangle ()

        tl.Width = 4.0;
        tl.Height = 4.0;
        tl.Style = "isosceles";

        t2.Width = 8.0;
        t2.Height = 12.0;
        t2.Style = "right";

        Console.WriteLine("Info for tl: ");
        tl.ShowStyle();
        tl.ShowDim();
        Console.WriteLine ("Area is " + tl.Area());

        Console.WriteLine ( Tnfo for t2: "I ;

        Console.WriteLine("Info for t2: ")
        t2.ShowStyle();
        t2.ShowDim();
        Console.WriteLine("Area is " + t2.Area()};
    }
}
```

In this version, the properties Width and Height provide access to the private members, pri_width and pri_height, which actually store the values. Therefore, even though pri_width and pri_height are private to TwoDShape, their values can still be set and obtained through their corresponding public properties.

When referring to base and derived classes, sometimes the terms *superclass* and *subclass* are used. These terms come from Java programming. What Java calls a superclass, C# calls a base class. What Java calls a subclass, C# calls a derived class. You will commonly hear both sets of terms applied to a class of either language, but this book will continue to use the standard C# terms. C++ also uses the base-class/derived-class terminology.



## Using Protected Access

As just explained, a private member of a base class is not accessible to a derived class. This would seem to imply that if you wanted a derived class to have access to some member in the base class, it would need to be public. Of course, making the member public also makes it available to all other code, which may not be desirable. Fortunately, this implication is untrue because C# allows you to create a *protected member.* A protected member is public within a class hierarchy, but private outside that hierarchy.

A protected member is created by using the protected access modifier. When a member of a class is declared as protected, that member is, with one important exception, private. The exception occurs when a protected member is inherited. Tn this case, a protected member of the base class becomes a protected member of the derived class and is, therefore, accessible to the derived class. Therefore, by using protected, you can create class members that are private to their class but that can still be inherited and accessed by a derived class.

Here is a simple example that uses protected:

```
// Demostrate protected.

using System;

class B {
   protected int i, j; // private to B, but accessible by D

   public void Set (int a, int b} {
      i = a;
      i = b;
   }

   public void Show() {
      Console.WriLeLine(i + " " + j);
   }
}
   class D : B {
      int k;     // private

   // D can access B's i and 1
   public void Setk()() {
      k = i * j;
   {

   public void Showk() {
      Console.WriteLine(k);
   }
}

   class ProtectedDemo {
      static void Main() {
         D ob = new D();

         ob.Set(2, 3);          // OK, known to D
```

```
        ob.Show();              // OK, known to D

        ob.Setk();              // OK, part of D
        ob.Showk();             // OK, part of D
    }
}
```

In this example, because B is inherited by D and because i and j are declared as protected in B, the Setk() method can access them. If i and j had been declared as private by B, then D would not have access to them, and the program would not compile.

Like public and private, protected status stays with a member no matter how many layers of inheritance are involved. Therefore, when a derived class is used as a base class for another derived class, any protected member of the initial base class that is inherited by the first derived class is also inherited as protected by a second derived class.

Although protected access is quite useful, it doesn't apply in all situations. For example, in the case of TwoDShape shown in the preceding section, we specifically want the Width and Height values to be publicly accessible. It's just that we want to manage the values they are assigned. Therefore, declaring them protected is not an option. In this case, the use of properties supplies the proper solution by controlling, rather than preventing, access. Remember, use protected when you want to create a member that is accessible throughout a class hierarchy, but otherwise private. To manage access to a value, use a property.

## Constructors and Inheritance

In a hierarchy, it is possible for both base classes and derived classes to have their own constructors. This raises an important question: What constructor is responsible for building an object of the derived class? The one in the base class, the one in the derived class, or both? Here is the answer: The constructor for the base class constructs the base class portion of the object, and the constructor for the derived class constructs the derived class part. This makes sense because the base class has no knowledge of or access to any element in a derived class. Thus, their construction must be separate. The preceding examples have relied upon the default constructors created automatically by C#, so this was not an issue. However, in practice, most classes will define constructors. Here you will see how to handle this situation.

When only the derived class defines a constructor, the process is straightforward: Simply construct the derived class object. The base class portion of the object is constructed automatically using its default constructor. For example, here is a reworked version of Triangle that defines a constructor. It also makes Style private since it is now set by the constructor.

```
// Add a construction is Triangle

using System;

// A class for tow-dimensional objects
class TwoDShape {
    double pri-width;
    double pri-height;
    // Properties for Width and Height;
    public double Width {
        get { return pri_width; }
        set { pri_width = value < 0 ? = value : value; }
    }

    public double Height {
```

```
        get { return pri_height; }
        set { pri_height = value < 0 ? = value : value; }
    }

    public void.ShowDim () {
        Console.WriteLine("Width and height are" =
                          Width + " and " + Height);
    }
}

    // A derived class ol TwoDShape for triangles.
    class Triangle : TwoDShape (
        string Style;

    //Constructor.
    public Triangle(string s, double w, double h) {
        Width = w;          // init the base class
        Heigth = h;         // int the base class

        Style = s;          // init the derived class
    }

    // Return area of triangle
    public double Area() {
        return Width * Height / 2;
    }

    // Display a trangle's style.
    public vod ShowStyle()  {
        Console.WriteLine("Trianle is " + Style);
    }
}

class Shapesj {
    static void Main() {
        Triangle tl = new Triangle("isosceles", 4.0, 4.0);
        Triangle t2 = new Triangle("right", 8.0, 12.0);
        Console.WriteLine("Area is " + tl.Area()

        Console.WriteLine()
        t1.ShowStyle();
        t2.ShowDim();
        Console.WriteLine("Area is " + t2.Area()));
    }
}
```

Here, **Triangle's** constructor initializes the members of **TwoDShape** that it inherits along with its own **Style** field. When both the base class and the derived class define constructors, the process is a bit more complicated because both the base class and derived class constructors must be executed. In this case, you must use another of C#'s keywords, **base,** which has two uses. The first use is to call a base class constructor. The second is to access a member of the base class that has been hidden by a member of a derived class. Here, we will look at its first use.

## Calling Base Class Constructors

A derived class can call a constructor defined in its base class by using an expanded form of the derived class' constructor declaration and the **base** keyword. The general form of this expanded declaration is shown here:

```
derived-constructor(parameter-Hst) : base(arg-list) {
   // body of constructor
}
```

Here, *arg-list* specifies any arguments needed by the constructor in the base class. Notice the placement of the colon.

To see how base is used, consider the version of **TwoDShape** in the following program. It defines a constructor that initializes the **Width and Height** properties. This constructor is then called by the Triangle constructor.

```
// Add constructor to TwoDShape.

using System;

// A class for two-dimensional objects.
class TwoDShape {
   double pri_width;
   double pri height;

   // Constructor for TwoDShape.
   public TwoDShape (double w, double h)
      Width = w;
      Height = h;
   }

   // Properties for Width and Height.
   public double Width {
      get { return pri_width; )
      set { pri_width = value < 0 ? -value : value;
   }

   public double Height I
      get { return pri_height; }
      set { pri__height = value < 0 ? -value : value; }
   }

   public void ShowDimO {
      Console .WriteLine {"Width and height are " +
         Width + " and " + Height);
   }
}

//A derived class of TwoDShape for triangles.
class Triangle : TwoDShape {
   string Style;

   // Call the base class constructor .
   public Triangle (string s, double w, double h) : base (w, h)
      Style = s;
   }

   // Return area of triangle.
   public double Area () {
      return Width * Height / 2;
   }
```

```
    // Display a triangle's style.
    public void ShowStyle() {
        Console.WriteLine ("Triangle is " + Style);
    }
}

class Shapes4 {
    static void Main() {
        Triangle tl = new Triangle("isosceles", 4.0, 4.0)
        Triangle t2 = new Triangle("right", 8.0, 12.0);

        Console.WriteLine("Info for tl: ");
        tl.ShowStyle();
        tl.ShowDimf) ;
        Console.WriteLine("Area is " + tl.Area());

        Console.WriteLine();
        Console.WriteLine("Info for t2: ");
        t2.ShowStyle();
        t2.ShowDim();
        Console.WriteLine("Area is " + t2.Area()};
    }
}
```

Notice that the **Triangle** constructor is now declared as shown here.

```
public Triangle(string s, double w, double h) : base(w, h) {
```

In this version, **Triangle()** calls base with the parameters w and h. This causes the **TwoDShape()** constructor to be called, which initializes **Width** and **Height** using these values. **Triangle** no longer initializes these values itself. It need only initialize the value unique to it: **Style.** This leaves **TwoDShape** free to construct its subobject in any manner that it chooses. Furthermore, **TwoDShape** can add functionality about which existing derived classes have no knowledge, thus preventing existing code from breaking.

Any form of constructor defined by the base class can be called by **base.** The constructor executed will be the one that matches the arguments. For example, here are expanded versions of both **TwoDShape and Triangle** that include default constructors and constructors that take one argument.

```
// Add more constructors to TwoDShape.

using System;

class TwoDShape {
    double pri_width;
    double pri_height;

    // Default constructor.
    public TwoDShape() {
        Width = Height = 0.0;
    }

    // Constructor for TwoDShape.
    public TwoDShape (double w, double h) {
        Width = w;
        Height = h;
    }

    // Construct object with equal width and height.
    public TwoDShape (double x) {
```

```
        Width = Height = x;
    }

    // Properties for Width and Height.
    public double Width {
        get { return pri_width; }
        set { pri_width = value < 0 ? -value : value; }
    }

    public double Height {
        get { return pri_height; }
        set { pri_height = value < 0 ? -value : value; }
    }

    public void ShowDim() {
        Console.WriteLine("Width and height are " +
                    Width + " and " + Height);
    }
}

// A derived class of TwoDShape for triangles.
class Triangle : TwoDShape {
    string Style;
}

    /* A default constructor. This automatically invokes
       the default constructor of TwoDShape. */
    public Triangle () {
        Style = "null" ;
    }

    // Constructor that takes three arguments.
    public Triangle (string s, double w, double h) : base (w, h) {
        Style = s;
    }

    // Construct an isosceles triangle.
    public Triangle (double x) : base{x) {
        Style = "isosceles";
    }

    // Return area of triangle.
    public double Area ( ) {
        return Width * Height / 2;
    }

    // Display a triangle's style,
    public void ShowStyle0 (
        Console.WriteLine("Triangle is " + Style);
    }
}

class ShapesS {
    static void Main() {
        Triangle tl = new Triangle!);
        Triangle t2 = new Triangle("right", 8.0, 12.0)
        Triangle t3 = new Triangle(4.0);
```

```
        tl - t2;

        Console.WriteLine("Info for tl: ");
        tl.showStyle(};
        tl.ShowDim();
        Console.WriteLine ("Area is " + tl.AreaO);

        Console.Write Line (} ;

        Console.WriteLine("Info for t2 : ") ;
        t2.ShowStyle() ;
        t2.ShowDimf);
        Console.WriteLine("Area is " I t2.Area(});

        Console.WriLeLine() ;

        Console.WriteLine("Info for t3: ");
        t3.ShowStyle();
        t3.ShowDim();
        Console.WriteLine("Area is " + t3.Area());

        Console.WriteLine();
    }
}
```

Here is the output from this version:

```
Info for tl:
Triangle is right
Width and height are 8 and 12
Area is 48

Info for t2:
Triang]e is right
Width and height are 8 and 12
Area is 48

Info for t3:
Triangle is isosceles
Width and height are 4 and 4
Area is 8
```

Let's review the key concepts behind base. When a derived class specifies a base clause, it is calling the constructor of its immediate base class. Ihus, base always refers to the base class immediately above the calling class. This is true even in a multileveled hierarchy. You pass arguments to the base constructor by specifying them as arguments to base. If no base clause is present, then the base class' default constructor is called automatically.

## Inheritance and Name Hiding

It is possible for a derived class to define a member that has the same name as a member in its base class. When this happens, the member in the base class is hidden within the derived class. While this is not technically an error in C#, the compiler will issue a warning message. This warning alerts you to the fact that a name is being hidden. If your intent is to hide a base class member, then to prevent this warning, the derived class member must be preceded by the new keyword. Understand that this use of new is separate and distinct from its use when creating an object instance.

Here is an example of name hiding:

```
// An example of inheritance-related name hiding.

using System;

class & {
    public int i = 0;
}

// Create a derived class.
class B : A {
    new int. i;   // this i hides the i in A

    public void Show() {
        i = b;      // i in B

    public void.Show() {
        Console.WriteLine("i in derived class: " + i);
    }
}

class NameHiding {
    static void Main() {
        B ob = new B(2);

        on.Show();
    }
}
```

First, notice the use of new in this line.

```
new int i; // this i hides the i in A
```

In essence, it tells the compiler that you know a new variable called i is being created that hides the i in the base class A. If you leave new out, a warning is generated. The output produced by this program is shown here:

```
i in derived class: 2
```

Since B defines its own instance variable called i, it hides the i in A. Therefore, when Show() is invoked on an object of type B, the value of i as defined by B is displayed—not the one defined in A.

## Using base to Access a Hidden Name

There is a second form of base that acts somewhat like this, except that it always refers to the base class of the derived class in which it is used. This usage has the following general form:

```
base, member
```

Here, *member* can be either a method or an instance variable. This form of base is most applicable to situations in which member names of a derived class hide members by the same name in the base class. Consider this version of the class hierarchy from the preceding example:

```
// Using base to overcome name hiding.

using System;

class A {
    public int i = 0;
}
```

```
// Create a derived class .
class B : A {
    new int i; // this i hides the i in A

    public B (int a, int b) {
        base.i = a;                 // this uncovers the i in A
        i = b;                      // i in B
    }

    public void Show () (
        // This displays the i in A,
        Console.WriteLine{"i in base class: " + base.i)

        // This displays the i in B.
        Console.WriteLine("i in derived class: " + i);
    }
}

class UncoverName {
    static void Main() {
        B ob = new B (1, 2);

        ob.Show();
    }
}
```

This program displays the following:

```
i in base class: 1
i in derived class: 2
```

Although the instance variable i in B hides the i in A, **base** allows access to the i defined in the base class. Hidden methods can also be called through the use of **base.** For example, in the following code, class B inherits class A, and both A and B declare a method called **ShowO.** Inside, **B's Show()**, the version of **Show()** defined by A is called through the use of **base.**

```
// Call a hidden method.

using System;

class A {

    public int i = 0;

    // Show() in A
    public void Show() {
        Console.WriteLine("i in base class: " + i);
    }
}

// Create a derived class.
class B : A {
    new int i;          // this i hides the i in A

    public B(int a, intb) {
    base.i = a;         // this uncovers the i in A
        i - b;          // i in B
    }
```

```
    // This hides Show() in A. Notice the use of new,
    new public void Show() {
        base.Show();  // this calls Show ( ) in A

    // this displays the i in B
    Console.WriteLine("i in derived class : " + i) ;
    }
}

class UncoverName {
    static void Main{) {
        B ob - new B(1, 2) ;

        ob.Show();
    }
}
```

The output from the program is shown here:

```
i in base class; 1
i in derived clas: 2
```

As you can see, **base.Show()** calls the base class version of **Show{).**

One other point: Notice that **new** is used in this program to tell the compiler that you know a new method called **Show{**) is being declared that hides the **Show() in A.**

## Creating a Multilevel Hierarchy

Up to this point, we have been using simple class hierarchies consisting of only a base class and a derived class. However, you can build hierarchies that contain as many layers of inheritance as you like. As mentioned, it is perfectly acceptable to use a derived class as a base class of another. For example, given three classes called A, B, and C, C can be derived from B, which can be derived from A. When this type of situation occurs, each derived class inherits all of the traits found in all of its base classes. In this case, C inherits all aspects of B and A.

To see how a multilevel hierarchy can be useful, consider the following program. In it, the derived class **Triangle** is used as a base class to create the derived class called **ColorTriangle. ColorTriangle** inherits all of the traits of **Triangle and TwoDShape** and adds a field called **color,** which holds the color of the triangle.

```
// A multilevel hierarchy.

using System;

class TwoDShape {
    double pri_width;
    double pri_height;

// Default constructor,
public TwoDShape() {
    Width = Height =0.0;
}

// Constructor for TwoDShape .
public TwoDShape (double w, double h} (
    Width = w; Height = h;
}
```

```
// Construct object with equal width and height,
public TwoDShape (double x) {
    Width = Height = x;
}

// Properties for Width and Height.
public double Width {
    get { return pri_width; }
    set { pri_width = value < 0 ? -value : value; }
}

public double Height {
    get { return pri_height; }
    set ( pri_height = value < 0 ? -value : value; }
}

public void ShowDim ( ) {
    Console.WriteLine ("Width and height are " +
                       Width + " and " + Height) ;
    }
}

    // A derived class of TwoDShape for triangles.
    class Triangle : TwoDShape {
        string Style; // private

    /* A default constructor. This invokes the default
    constructor of TwoDShape. */
    public Triangle() {
        Style = "null";
    }

    // Constructor.
    public Triangle(sting s, double w, double h;) : base(w, h) {
        Style = s;
    }

    // Construct an issosceles triangle.
    public Triangle(double x) : base(x) {
        Style = "isosceless"
    }

    // Return area of triangle.
    public double Area() }
        return Width * Height / 2;
    }

    // Display a triangle's style.
    public vod ShowStyle() {
        Console.WriteLine("Triangle is " + Style);
    }
}

// Extend Triangle.
class ColorTriangle : Triangle {
    string color;
```

```
        public ColorTriangle(string c, string s,
                                   double w, double h) : base(s, w, h) {
        color = n;
    }

    // Display the color.
    public void ShowColor() {
        Console.WriteLine)"Color is " + color);
    }
}

class Shapes6 {
    static void Hain() {
        ColorTriangle tl -
            new ColorTriangle("Blue", "right", 8.0, 12.0);
        ColorTriangle t? =
            new ColorTri angle("Red", "isosceles", 2.0, 2.0);

        Console.WriteLine ("Info for tl : ") ;
        tl.ShowStyle();
        tl.ShowDim();
        tl.ShowColor();
        Console.WriteLine("Area is " + tl.Area()) ;

        Console.WriteLine("info for t2:");
        t2.ShowStyle();
        t2.ShowDim();
        t2.ShowColor();

        Console.WriteLine("Area is " + t2.Area()}'
    }
}
```

The output of this program is shown here:

```
Info for tl:
Triangle is right
Width and height are 8 and 12
Color is Blue
Area is 48

info for t2:
Triangle is isosceles
Width and height are 2 and 2
Color is Red
Area is 2
```

Because of inheritance, ColorTriangle can make use of the previously defined classes of Triangle and TwoDShape, adding only the extra information it needs for its own, specific application. This is part of the value of inheritance; it allows the reuse of code.

This example illustrates one other important point: base always refers to the constructor in the closest base class. The base in ColorTriangle calls the constructor in Triangle. The base in Triangle calls the constructor in TwoDShape. In a class hierarchy, if a base class constructor requires parameters, then all derived classes must pass those parameters "up the line." This is true whether or not a derived class needs parameters of its own.

## When Are Constructors Called?

Tn the foregoing discussion of inheritance and class hierarchies, an important question may have occurred to you: When a derived class object is created, whose constructor is executed first? The one in the derived class or the one defined by the base class? For example, given a derived class called B and a base class called A, is A's constructor called before B's, or vice versa? The answer is that in a class hierarchy, constructors are called in order of derivation, from base class to derived class. Furthermore, this order is the same whether or not base is used. If base is not used, then the default (parameterless) constructor of each base class will be executed. The following program illustrates the order of constructor execution:

```
// Demonstrate when constructors are called.

using System;

// Create a base class.
class A {
    public A() {
        Console.WriteLine("Constructing A.");
    }
}

// Create a class derived from A.
class B : A{

    public B() {
    Console.WriteLine("Constructing B, ")
    }
}

    // Create a class derived B.
    class C : B {
        public C() {
            Console.WriteLine("Constructing C,")
    }
}

class OrderOfConstruction {
    static void Main() {
        C c = new C();
    }
}
```

The output from this problem is shown here.

```
Constructing A.
Constructing B.
Constructing C.
```

As you can see, the constructors are called in order of derivation.

If you think about it, it makes sense that constructors are executed in order of derivation. Because a base class has no knowledge of any derived class, any initialization it needs to perform is separate from and possibly prerequisite to any initialization performed by the derived class. Therefore, it must be executed first.

## Base Class References and Derived Objects

As you know, C# is a strongly typed language. Aside from the standard conversions and automatic promotions that apply to its value types, type compatibility is strictly enforced. Therefore, a reference variable for one class type cannot normally refer to an object of another class type. For example, consider the following program that declares two classes that are identical in their composition:

```
// This program will not compiie.

class X {
    int a;

    public s(int i) { a = i; )
}

class Y {
    int a;

    public Y(inl i) { a = i; }
}

class IncompatibleRef {
    static void Main() {
    X x = new X(10);
    Y x2;
    Y y = new Y(5);

    x2 = x;        // OK, both of same type
    x2 = y;        // Error, not of same type
    }
}
```

Here, even though class X and class Y are physically the same, it is not possible to assign a reference of type Y to a variable of type X because they have different types. Therefore, this line is incorrect because it causes a compile-time type mismatch:

In general, an object reference variable can refer only to objects of its type.

There is, however, an important exception to C#'s strict type enforcement. A reference variable of a base class can be assigned a reference to an object of any class derived from that base class. This is legal because an instance of a derived type encapsulates an instance of the base type. Thus, a base class reference can refer to it. Here is an example:

```
// A base class refernce can refer to a desired class object.

using System;

class X {
    public int a;

    public X(int i) {
        a = i
    }
}

class Y : X {
    public int b;

    public Y(int i, intj( : base(j) {
        b = i;
    }
}
```

```
class BaseRef {
    static void Main () {
        X x = new X (10);
        X x2;
        Y y - new Y (5, 6) ;

        x2 = x;         // OK, both of ssame type
        Console.WriteLine("x2.a: " + x2.a)

        x2 = y;         // OK, because Y is derived from X
        Console.WriteLine ("x2.a: " + x2.a);

        // X reference know only about X members
        x2.a = 19,          //OR
        x2.b = 2;           // Error, X doesn't have a b member
    }
}
```

In this program, Y is derived from X. Now, the assignment

is permissible because a base class reference, x2 in this case, can refer to a derived class object (which is the object referred to by y).

It is important to understand that it is the type of the reference variable—not the type of the object that it refers *to*—that determines what members can be accessed. That is, when a reference to a derived class object is assigned to a base class reference variable, you will have access only to those parts of the object defined by the base class. This is why x2 can't access b even when it refers to a Y object. This makes sense because the base class has no knowledge of what a derived class adds to it. This is why the last line of code in the program is commented out.

Although the preceding discussion may seem a bit esoteric, it has some important practical applications. One is described here. The other is discussed later in this chapter, when virtual methods are covered.

An important place where derived class references are assigned to base class variables is when constructors are called in a class hierarchy. As you know, it is common for a class to define a constructor that takes an object of its class as a parameter. This allows the class to construct a copy of an object. Classes derived from such a class can take advantage of this feature. For example, consider the following versions of **TwoDShape** and **Triangle.** Both add constructors that take an object as a parameter.

```
// Pass a derived class refernce to a base class refernce

using System;

class TwoDShape {
    double pri_width;
    double pri_height;

    // Default constructor
    public TwoDShaper() {
        Width = Height =0,0;
    }

    // Constructor for TwoDShape.
    public TwoDShape(double w, double h) {
        Width = w;
        Height = h;
    }
```

```
    // Construct object with equal width and height.
    public TwoDShape(double x) {
        Width = Height = x;
    }

    // Construct a copy of a TwoDShape object.
    public TwoDShape{TwoDShape ob) {
        Width = ob.Width;
        Height = ob.Height;

    // Properties for Width and Height,
    public double Width j
        get { return pri_width; }
        set { pri_width = value < 0 ? -value : value; }
    }

    // Properties double Height,
        get { return  pri_height; }
        set { pri_height = value < 0 ? -value : value; }
    }

    public void ShowDim() {
        Console.WriteLine ("Width and height are " +
                           Width + " and " + Height);
    }
}

// A derived class of TwoDShape for triangles.
class Triangle : TwoDShape {
    string Style;

    // A default constructor.
    public Triangle() {
        Style = "null";
    }

    // Construct an isosceles triangle.
    public Triangle(double x) : base(x) {
        Style = "isosceles";
    }

    // Construct a copy of a Triangle object.
    public Triangle(Triangle ob) : base(ob) {
        Style = ob.Style;
    }

    // Return ara of triangle.
    public double Area() {
        return Width * Height / 2;
    }

    // Display a triangle's style.
    public void ShowStyle() {
        Console.WriteLine("Triangle is " + Style);
    }
}
```

```
class Shapes7 {
  static void Main() {
    Triangle t1 = new Triangle("right", 8.0, 12.0);

    // Make a copy of t1.
    Triangle t2 = new Triangle(t1);

    Console.WriteLine("Info for t1; ");
    t1.ShowStyle();
    t1.ShowDim();
    Console.WriteLine("Area is " + t1.Area());

    Console.WriteLine();

    Console.WriteLine("Info for t2: ");
    t2.ShowStyle();
    t2.ShowDim();
    Console.WriteLine("Area is " + t2.Area());
    }
  }
```

In this program, *t2* is constructed from t1 and is, thus, identical. The output is shown here;

```
Info for 1;
Triangle is right
Width and height are 8 and 12
Area is 48

Info for t2:
Triangle is right
Width and height are 8 and 12
Area is 48
```

Pay special attention to this Triangle constructor:

```
public Triange(Triangle ob) : base(ob) {
    Style = ob.Style;
}
```

It receives an object of type **Triangle,** and it passes that object (through base) to this **TwoDShape** constructor:

```
public TwoDShape(TwoDShape ob) {
    Width = ob.Width;
    Height = ob.Height;
}
```

The key point is that TwoDShape() is expecting a TwoDShape object. However, Triangle() passes it a Triangle object. As explained, the reason this works is because a base class reference can refer to a derived class object. Thus, it is perfectly acceptable to pass TwoDShapet) a reference to an object of a class derived from TwoDShape. Because the TwoDShape() constructor is initializing only those portions of the derived class object that are members of TwoDShape, it doesn't matter that the object might also contain other members added by derived classes.

## Virtual Methods and Overriding

A *virtual method* is a method that is declared as virtual in a base class. The defining characteristic of a virtual method is that it can be redefined in one or more derived classes. Thus, each derived class can have its own version of a virtual method. Virtual methods are interesting because of what happens when one is called through a base class reference. In this situation, C# determines which version of the method to call based upon the *type* of the object *referred to* by the reference—and this determination is made *at runtime*. Thus, when different objects are referred to, different versions of the virtual method are executed, hi other words, it is the type of the object being referred to (not the type of the reference) that determines which version of the virtual method will be executed. Therefore, if a base class contains a virtual method and classes are derived from that base class, then when different types of objects are referred to through a base class reference, different versions of the virtual method can be executed.

You declare a method as virtual inside a base class by preceding its declaration with the keyword virtual. When a virtual method is redefined by a derived class, the override modifier is used. Thus, the process of redefining a virtual method inside a derived class is called *method overriding*. When overriding a method, the name, return type, and signature of the overriding method must be the same as the virtual method that is being overridden. Also, a virtual method cannot be specified as static or abstract (discussed later in this chapter).

Method overriding forms the basis for one of C#'s most powerful concepts: *dynamic method dispatch*. Dynamic method dispatch is the mechanism by which a call to an overridden method is resolved at runtime, rather than compile time. Dynamic method dispatch is important because this is how C# implements runtime polymorphism.

Here is an example that illustrates virtual methods and overriding:

```
// Create virtual method.

using System;

class Base {
    //Create virtual methd in the base class.
    public virutal void Who() {
    }
}

class Derived : Base {
    // Override Who(] in a derived class,
    public override void Who() (
        Console.WriteLine("Who() in Derivedl");
    }
}

class Derived2 : Base {
    // Override Who() again in another derived class,
    public override void Whof) {
        Console.WriteLine("Who() in Derived2");
class OverrideDemo { static void Main()
    }
}

class overrideDemo {
    static void Main() {
        Base baseOb = new Base();
        Derived1 dOb1 = new Derived1();
        Derived2 dOb2 = new Derived2();

        Base baseRef;              // a base class reference

        baseRef = baseOb;
        baseRef.who();
```

```
        baseRef = dObl;
        baseRef.Who() ;

        baseRef = dOb2;
        baseRef.Who();
    }
}
```

The output from the program is shown here:

```
Who (} in Base
Who () in Derivedl
Who() in Derived2
```

This program creates a base class called **Base** and two derived classes, called **Derivedl and Derived2. Base** declares a method called **Who<**), and the derived classes override it. Inside the **Main()** method, objects of type **Base, Derivedl, and Derived2** are declared. Also, a reference of type **Base,** called **baseRef,** is declared. The program then assigns a reference to each type of object to **baseRef** and uses that reference to call **Who().** As the output shows, the version of **Who() executed is determined by the type of object** being referred to at the time of the call, not by the class type of **baseRef.**

It is not necessary to override a virtual method. If a derived class does not provide its own version of a virtual method, then the one in the base class is used. For example:

```
/* When a virtual method is not overridden,
   the base class method is used. */

using System;

class Base {
// Create virtual method in the base class.
public virtual void Who() {
   Console.WriteLine("Who() in Base");
   }
}

class Derived2 : Base {
   // Override Who() again in another derived class
   public override void Who() {
      Console.WriteLine("Who() in Derived2");
   }
}

class Derived2 : Base {
   // This class does not override Who().
}

class NoOverrideDemo {
   static void Main() {
      Base baseOb = new Base();
      Derivedl dObl = new Derivedlf);
      Derived2 dOb2 - new Derived2();

      baseRef = baseOb;
      baseRef.Who();

      baseRef = dObl;
      baseRet.Who();
```

```
        baseRef = dOb2;
        baseRef.Who();                  // calls Base's Who()
    }
}
```

The output from the program is shown here:

```
Who()  in Base
Who()  in Derivedl
Who()  in Derived2
```

This program creates a base class called **Base** and two derived classes, called **Derivedl and Derived2. Base** declares a method called **Who()**, and the derived classes override it. Inside the **Main()** method, objects of type **Base, Derivedl, and Derived2** are declared. Also, a reference of type **Base,** called **baseRef,** is declared. The program then assigns a reference to each type of object to **baseRef** and uses that reference to call **Who()**. As the output shows, the version of **Who()** executed is determined by the type of object being referred to at the time of the call, not by the class type of **baseRef.**

It is not necessary to override a virtual method. If a derived class does not provide its own version of a virtual method, then the one in the base class is used. For example:

```
/* When a virtual method is not overridden,
   the base class method is used. */

using System;

class Base {
   // Create virtual method in the base class.
   public virtual void Who() {
      Console.WriteLine("Who() in Base");
   }
}

class Derivedl : Base {
   // Override Who() in a derived class,
   public override void Who() {
      Console.WriteLine("Who() in Derivedl") ;
   }
}

class Derived2 : Base {
   // This class also does not override Who()
}

class NoOverrideDemo2 {
static void Main ( ) {
   Base baseOb new Base();
   Derivedl dObl = new Derivedl();
   Derived2 dOb2 = new Derived2();

   Base baseRef;         // a base class reference

   baseRef = baseOb;
   baseRef.Who();

   baseRef = dObl;
   baseRef.Who();
```

```
    baseRef = dOb2
    baseRef.Who();    // calls Base's Who()
    }
}
```

The output is shown here:

```
Who() in Base
Who() in Derivedl
Who() in Base
```

Here Derived2 does not override Who(). Thus, whern Who() is called on a Derived2 object, the Who() in Base is executed.

In the case of a multilevel hierarchy, if a derived class does not override a virtual method, then, while moving up the hierarchy, the first override of the method that is encountered is the one executed. For example.

```
/* In a multilevel hierarchy, the first override of a virtual
   method that is found while moving up the hierarchy is the
   one executed. */

using System;

class Base {
   // Create virtual mehtod in the base class.
   public virual void Who() {
      Console.WriteLine("Who() in Base");
   }
}

class Derived1 : Base {
   // Override Who() in a derived class.
   public override void Who() {
      Console.WriteLine{"Who() in Derived1"};
   }
}

class Derived2 : Derived1 {
   // This class does not override Who().
}

class Derived3 : Derived2 {
   // This class does not override Who().
}

class NoOverrideDemo3 {
   static void Main() {
      Derived3 dOb = new Derived3();
      Base baseRef;    // a base class reference

      baseRef = dOb;
      baseRef.Who()    // calls Derived1's Who()
   }
}
```

The output is shown here:

```
Who() in Derived1
```

Here, Derived3 inherits Derived2, which inherits Derivedl, which inherits Base. As the output verifies, since Who( ) is not overridden by either DerivedS or Derived2, it is the override of Who( ) in Derivedl that is executed, since it is the first version of Who( ) that is found.

One other point: Properties can also be modified by the virtual keyword and overridden using override. The same is true for indexers.

## Why Overridden Methods?

Overridden methods allow C# to support runtime polymorphism. Polymorphism is essential to object-oriented programming for one reason: It allows a general class to specify methods that will be common to all of its derivatives, while allowing derived classes to define the specific implementation of some or all of those methods. Overridden methods are another way that C# implements the "one interface, multiple methods" aspect of polymorphism.

Part of the key to applying polymorphism successfully is understanding that the base classes and derived classes form a hierarchy that moves from lesser to greater specialization. Used correctly, the base class provides all elements that a derived class can use directly. Through virtual methods, it also defines those methods that the derived class can implement on its own. This allows the derived class flexibility, yet still enforces a consistent interface. Thus, by combining inheritance with overridden methods, a base class can define the general form of the methods that will be used by all of its derived classes.

## Applying Virtual Methods

To better understand the power of virtual methods, we will apply them to the **TwoDShape** class. In the preceding examples, each class derived from **TwoDShape** defines a method called **Area()**. This suggests that it might be better to make **Area()** a virtual method of the **TwoDShape** class, allowing each derived class to override it, defining how the area is calculated for the type of shape that the class encapsulates. The following program docs this. For convenience, it also adds a name property to **TwoDShape.** (This makes it easier to demonstrate the classes.)

```
// Use virtual methods and polymorphism.

using System;

class TwoDShape {
    double pri_width;
    double pri_height;

    // A default constructor.
    public TwoDShape () {
        Width - Height - 0.0;
        name = "null" ;
    }

    // Parameterized constructor .
    public TwoDShape (double w, double h, string n) {
        Width = w;
        Height = h;
        name = n ;
    }

    // Construct object with equal width and height,
    public TwoDShape(double x, string n) {
        Width = Height = x;
        name - n;
    }
```

```
    // Construct a copy of a TwoDShape object.
    public TwoDShape(TwoDShape ob) {
        Width = ob.Width;
        Height = ob.Height;
        name = ob.name;
    }

    // Properies for Width and Height.
        public double Width {
            get { return pri_width; {
            set { pri_width = value < 0 ? -value : value; }
    }


    public double Height {
        get { return pri^height; }
        set { pri_heighL = value < 0 ? -value : value; }
    }

    public string name } ge; set; }

    public void ShowDim() {
        Console.WriteLine("Width and height are " +
                        Width + " and " + Height);
    }

    public virtual double Area() {
        Console.WriteLine("Area() must be overridden");
        return 0,0;
    }
}

// A derived class of TwoDShape for tirangles.
class Triangle : TwoDShape {
    string Style;

    // A default constructor.
    public Triangle() {
        Style = "null";
    }

    // Constructor for Triangle.
    public Triangle(string s, double w, double h);
        base (w, h, "triangle") {
        Style = s;
    }

    // Constructor for isosceles triangle.
    public Triangle(double x) : base(x, "triangle"); {
        Style = isosceles";
    }

    // Construct a copy of a Triangle object.
    public Triangle(Triangle ob) : base(ob) {();
        Style = ob.Style;
    }

    // Override Area() for Rectangle.
```

```
    public override double Area)) {
        return Width * Height / 2;
    }

    // ODisplay a triangle's style.
    public void ShowStyle() {
        Console.WriteLine("Triangle is " + Style);
    }
}

// A derived class of TwoDShape for rectangle.
class Rectangle : TwoDShape {

    // Constructor for Rectangle/
    public Rectangle(double w, double h);
        base(w, h, "rectangle") { }

    // Construct a square.
    public Rectangle(double x) ;
        base(x, "rectangle") { }

    //Construct a copy of a Rectangle object.
    public bool IsSquare() {
        if(Width == Height) return true;
        return false;
    }

    //Override Area() for Rectangle.
    public override double Aras() {
        return Width * Height;
    }
}

class DynShapes {
    static void Main() {
        TwoDShape[] shapes = new TwoDShape [5];

        shapesTO] = new Triangle("right", 8,0, 12,0);
        shapes[1] = new Rectangle(10);
        shapes[2] = new Rectangle(10, 4);
        shapes[3] = new TriangleP.0);
        shapes[4] = new TwoDShape (10, 20, "generic");

        for(int i-0; i < shapes.Length; i++) {
            Console.WriteLine("object is " + shapes[i].name)
            Console.WriteLine("Area is " + shapes[i].Area())

            Console.WriteLine() ;
        }
    }
}
```

The output from the program is shown here:

```
object is rectangle
Area is 48

object is rectangle
```

```
Area is 100

object is rectangle
Area is 40

object is rectangle
Area is 24.5

object is generic
Area() must be overridden
Area is 0
```

Let's examine this program closely. First, as explained, **Area()** is declared as **virtual** in the **TwoDShape** class and is overridden by **Triangle** and Rectangle. Inside **TwoDShape,** Area() is given a placeholder implementation that simply informs the user that this method must be overridden by a derived class. Fach override of **Area()** supplies an implementation that is suitable for the type of object encapsulated by the derived class. Thus, if you were to implement an ellipse class, for example, then **Area()** would need to compute the area of an ellipse.

There is one other important feature in the preceding program. Notice in Main() that shapes is declared as an array of **TwoDShape** objects. However, the elements of this array are assigned **Triangle, Rectangle,** and **TwoDShape** references. This is valid because a base class reference can refer to a derived class object. The program then cycles through the array, displaying information about each object. Although quite simple, this illustrates the power of both inheritance and method overriding. The type of object stored in a base class reference variable is determined at runtime and acted on accordingly. If an object is derived from **TwoDShape,** then its area can be obtained by calling **Area().** The interface to this operation is the same no matter what type of shape is being used.

## Using Abstract Classes

Sometimes you will want to create a base class that defines only a generalized form that will be shared by all of its derived classes, leaving it to each derived class to fill in the details. Such a class determines the nature of the methods that the derived classes must implement, but does not, itself, provide an implementation of one or more of these methods. One way this situation can occur is when a base class is unable to create a meaningful implementation for a method. This is the case with the version of TwoDShape used in the preceding example. The definition of Area{) is simply a placeholder. It will not compute and display the area of any type of object.

You will see as you create your own class libraries that it is not uncommon for a method to have no meaningful definition in the context of its base class. You can handle this situation two ways. One way, as shown in the previous example, is to simply have it report a warning message. Although this approach can be useful in certain situations—such as debugging—it is not usually appropriate. You may have methods that must be overridden by the derived class in order for the derived class to have any meaning. Consider the class **Triangle.** It is incomplete if Area() is not defined. In such a case, you want some way to ensure that a derived class does, indeed, override all necessary methods. C#'s solution to this problem is the *abstract method.*

An abstract method is created by specifying the **abstract** type modifier. An abstract method contains no body and is, therefore, not implemented by the base class. Thus, a derived class must override it—it cannot simply use the version defined in the base class. As you can probably guess, an abstract method is automatically virtual, and there is no need to use the virtual modifier. In fact, it is an error to use **virtual** and **abstract** together.

CHAPTER 6

To declare an abstract method, use this general form;

```
abstract type namc' (pammeter-Ust');
```

As you can see, no method body is present. The **abstract** modifier can be used only on instance methods. It cannot be applied to **static** methods. Properties and indexers can also be abstract.

A class that contains one or more abstract methods must also be declared as abstract by preceding its class declaration with the abstract specifier. Since an abstract class does not define a complete implementation, there can be no objects of an abstract class. Thus, attempting to create an object of an abstract class by using new will result in a compile-time error.

When a derived class inherits an abstract class, it must implement all of the abstract methods in the base class. If it doesn't, then the derived class must also be specified as abstract. Thus, the abstract attribute is inherited until such time as a complete implementation is achieved.

Using an abstract class, you can improve the TwoDShape class. Since there is no meaningful concept of area for an undefined two-dimensional figure, the following version of the preceding program declares Area() as abstract inside TwoDShape and TwoDShape as abstract. This, of course, means that all classes derived from TwoDShape must override Area().

```
// Create an abstract class.

using System;

abstract class TwoDShape {
    double pri_width;
    double pri_height;

    // A default constructor.
    public TwoDShape() {
        Width = Height = 0.0;
        name = n;
    }

    // Parameterized constructor.
    public TwoDShape(double w, double h, string n) {
        Width = w; Height = h;
        name - n;
    }

    // Construct object with equal width and height,
    public TwoDShape(double x, string n) {
        Width = Height = x;
        name = n;
    }

    // Construct a copy of a TwoDShape object.
    public TwoDShape(TwoDShape ob) {
        Width = ob.Width;
        Height = ob.Height;
        name = ob.name;
    }

    // Properties for Width and Height,
    public double Width {
        get ( return pri_width; }
        set { pri_width = value < 0 ? -value : value; }
    }
```

```
public double Height {
   get { return pri_height; }
   set { pri_height = value < 0 ? -value : value; }
}

public string name { get; set; }

public void ShowDim!) {
   Console.WriteLine("Width and height are " +
                     Width + " and " + Height);
}

// Now, Area() is abstract.
public abstract double Areaf);

// A derived class of TwoDShape for triangles
class Triangle : TwoDShape {
string Style;
}

// A default constructor.
public Triangle () (
   Style = "null";
}

// Constructor for Triangle.
public Triangle (string s, double w, double h)
base (w, h, "triangle" ) {
   Style = s;
}

// Construct an isosceles triangle.
public Triangle (double x) : base(x, "triangle") {
   Style = "isosceles";
}

// Construct a copy of a Triangle object.
public Triangle(Triangle ob) : base(ob) {
   Style = ob.Style;
}

// Override Area() for Triangle.
public override double Area() {
   return Width * Height / 2;
}

// Display a triangle's style,
public void ShowStyle() I
   Console.WriteLine("Triangle is " + Style);
}
}

// A derived class of TwoDShape for rectangles.
class Rectangle : TwoDShape {

//Constructor for Rectangle.
public Rectangle(double w, double h);
   base(w, h, "rectangle") { }
```

```
    //Construct a square.
    public Rectangle(double x);
        base(x, "rectangle") { }

    //Construct a copy of a Rectangle object,
    public Rectangle(Rectangle ob) : base fob) {

    //Return true if the rectangle is square.
    public bool IsSquare() {
        if(Width -= Height) return true;
        return false;
    }

    // Override Area() lor Rectangle.
    public override double Area() {
        return Width * Height;
    }
}

class AbsShape {
    static void Main() {
        TwoDShape[] shapes = new TwoDShape[4];

        shapes[0]  =  new Triangle("right", 8.0, 12.0};
        shapes[1]  =  new Rectangle(10};
        shapes(2]  -  new Rectangle(10, 4);
        shapes[3]  =  new Triangle (7.0);

        forfint i=0; i < shapes.Length; i++) {
            Console.WriteLine("object is " + shapes[i].name}
            Console.WriteLine("Area is " + shapes[i].Area())

            Console.WriteLine();
        }
    }
}
```

As-the program illustrates, all derived classes *must* override **Area()** (or also be declared abstract). To prove this to yourself, try creating a derived class that does not override Area(). You will receive a compile-time error. Of course, it is still possible to create an object reference of type **TwoDShape,** which the program does. However, it is no longer possible to declare objects of type **TwoDShape.** Because of this, in **Main() the shapes** array has been shortened to 4, and a generic **TwoDShape** object is no longer created.

One other point: Notice that **TwoDShape** still includes the **ShowDim()** method and that it is not modified by **abstract** It is perfectly acceptable—indeed, quite common—for an abstract class to contain concrete methods that a derived class is free to use as-is. Only those methods declared as **abstract** must be overridden by derived classes.

## Using sealed to Prevent Inheritance

As powerful and useful as inheritance is, sometimes you will want to prevent it. For example, you might have a class that encapsulates the initialization sequence of some specialized hardware device, such as a medical monitor. In this case, you don't want users of your class to be able to change the way the monitor is initialized, possibly setting the device incorrectly. Whatever the reason, in C# it is easy to prevent a class from being inherited by using the keyword **sealed.**

To prevent a class from being inherited, precede its declaration with **sealed.** As you might expect, it is illegal to declare a class as both **abstract and sealed** because an abstract class is incomplete by itself and relies upon its derived classes to provide complete implementations.

Here is an example of a **sealed** class:

```
sealed class A {
    //
}

// The following class is illegal.
class B : A { // ERROR! Can't derive from class A
    //
}
```

As the comments imply, it is illegal for B to inherit A because A is declared as **sealed.**

One other point: **sealed** can also be used on virtual methods to prevent further overrrides. For example, assume a base class called B and a derived class called D. A method declared **virtual** in **B** can be declared **sealed** by **D.** This would prevent any class that inherits D from overriding the method. This situation is illustrated by the following:

```
class B |
    public virtual void MyMethod() { /* ... */ }
}

class D : B {
    // This seals MyMethod() and prevents further overrides.
    sealed public override void MyMethod0 { /* ... */ }
}

class X : D {
    // Error! MyMethod{) is sealed!
    public override void MyMethod() ( /* ... */ }
}
```

Because **MyMethod()** is sealed by D, it can't be overridden by X.

## The object Class

C# defines one special class called **object** that is an implicit base class of all other classes and for all other types (including the value types), hi other words, all other types are derived from **object.** This means that a reference variable of type **object** can refer to an object of any

other type. Also, since arrays are implemented as objects, a variable of type object can also refer to any array. Technically, the C# name object is just another name for System.Object, which is part of the .NET Framework class library.

The object class defines the methods shown in follwoing Table, which means that they are available in every object.

A few of these methods warrant some additional explanation. By default, the Equals(object) method determines if the invoking object refers to the same object as the one referred to by the argument. (That is, it determines if the two references are the same.) It returns true if the objects are the same, and false otherwise. You can override this method in classes that you create. Doing so allows you to define what equality means relative to a class. For example, you could define Equals(object) so that it compares the contents of two objects for equality.

The GetHashCode() method returns a hash code associated with the invoking object. A hash code is needed by any algorithm that employs hashing as a means of accessing stored objects. It is important to understand that the default implementation of GetHashCode() will not be adequate for all uses.

If you overload the = = operator, then you will usually need to override Equals(object) and GetHashCode() because most of the time you will want the = = operator and the Equals(object) methods to function the same. When Equalsf) is overridden, you often need to override GetHashCode(), so that the two methods are compatible.

The ToString() method returns a string that contains'a description of the object on which it is called. Also, this method is automatically called when an object is output using

| **Method** | **Purpose** |
|---|---|
| public virtual bool Equals(object *obj)* | Determines whether the invoking object is the same as the one referred to by *obj*. |
| public static bool Equalsfobject *objA*, object *objB)* | Determines whether *objA* is the same as *objB*. |
| protected virtual Finalize{) | Performs shutdown actions prior to garbage collection. In C#, **Finallze()** is accessed through a destructor. |
| public virtual int GetHashCode{) | Returns the hash code associated with the invoking object. |
| public Type GetType() | Obtains the type of an object at runtime. |
| protected object MemberwiseCloneO | Makes a "shallow copy" of the object. This is one in which the members are copied, but objects referred to by members are not. |
| public static bool ReferenceEquals(object *objA*, object *objB)* | Determines whether *objA* and *objB* refer to the same object. |
| public virtual string ToString() | Returns a string that describes the object. |

**Methods of the object Class**

**WriteLine()**. Many classes override this method. Doing so allows them to tailor a description specifically for the types of objects that they create. For example:

```
// Demonstrate ToString()

using System;

class MyClass {
   static int count = 0;
   int id;

   public MyClass() {
      id = count;
      count++;
   }

   public override string ToString() {
      return "MyClass object #" + id;
```

```
    }
}

class Test (
    static void Main() {
    MyClass obl = new MyClass()
    MyClass ob2 = new MyClass()
    MyClass ob3 = new MyClass()

    Console.WriteLine(ob1);
    Console.WriteLine(ob2);
    Console.WriteLine(ob3);
    }
}
```

The output from the program is shown here:

```
MyClass object #0
MyClass object #1
MyClass object #2
```

## Boxing and Unboxing

As explained, all C# types, including the value types, are derived from **object.** Thus, a reference of type **object** can be used to refer to any other type, including value types. When an **object** reference refers to a value type, a process known as *boxing* occurs. Boxing causes the value of a value type to be stored in an object instance. Thus, a value type is "boxed" inside an object. This object can then be used like any other object, hi all cases, boxing occurs automatically. You simply assign a value to an **object** reference. C# handles the rest.

*Unboxing* is the process of retrieving a value from a boxed object. This action is performed using an explicit cast from the **object** reference to its corresponding value type. Attempting to unbox an object into a different type will result in a runtime error.

Here is a simple example that illustrates boxing and unboxing:

```
//A simple boxing/unboxing example.

using System;

class BoxingDemo {
    static void Main() {
    int x;
    object obj;

    x = 10;

    int y = (int)obj ;   // unbox obi i nto an int
    Console.WriteLine (y);
    }
}
```

This program displays the value 10. Notice that the value in x is boxed simply by assigning it to obj, which is an **object** reference. The integer value in obj is retrieved by casting obj to int.

Here is another, more interesting example of boxing. In this case, an int is passed as an argument to the **Sqr()** method, which uses an **object** parameter.

```
//Boxing also occurs when passing values.

using System;

class BoxingDemo {
    static void Main() {
        int x;

        x = 10;
        Console.WriteLine("How is x: " + x);

        // x is automatically boxed when passed to Sqr().
        x = BoxingDemo.Sqr(x);
        Console.WriteLine("Here is a x squared; " + x);
    }

    static int sqr(object o) {
        return (int)o * (int)o;
    }
}
```

The output from the program is shown here:

```
Here is x: 10
Here is x squared: 100
```

Here, the value of x is automatically boxed when it is passed to **Sqr()**.

Boxing and unboxing allow C#'s type system to be fully unified. All types derive from **object,** A reference to any type can be assigned to a variable of type **object.** Boxing and unboxing automatically handle the details for the value types. Furthermore, because all types are derived from object, they all have access to **object's** methods. For example, consider the following rather surprising program:

```
// Boxing makes it possible to call methods on a value!

using System;

class MathOnValue {
    static void Main () {

    Console.WiiLeLine(10.ToString()};
    }
}
```

This program displays 10. The reason is that the **ToString()** method returns a string representation of the object on which it is called. In this case, the string representation of 10 is 10!

## Is object a Universal Data Type?

Given that **object** is a base class for all other types and that boxing of the value types takes place automatically, it is possible to use **object** as a "universal" data type. For example, consider the following program that creates an array of **object** and then assigns various other types of data to its elements:

```
//Use object to create a "generic" array.

using System;

class GenericDemo {
    static void Main() {
        object() ga = new object(10);

      // Store ints.
      for(int i = 0; i < 3; i++);
          ga(i) = i;

      // Store double
      for(int i = 3; i < 6; i++)
          ga(i) = (double) 1 / 2;


      // Store two stri ngs, a bool, and a char.
      ga[6j = "Hello";
      ga[7] = true;
      ga[8] = 'X';
      ga[9] = "end";

      for (int i = 0; i < ga.Length; i++)
          Console.WriteLine("ga(" + i + ")" " + ga(i) + " ");
      }
}
```

The output is shown here:

```
ga[0]  0
ga[1]  1
ga[2]  2
ga[3]  1.5
ga[4]  2
```

The output is shown here:

```
ga[0]: 0
qa[1]: 1
qa[2]: 2
ga[3]: 1.5
ga[4]: 2
ga[5]: 2.5
qa[6]: Hello
qa[7]: True
```

```
ga[8]: X
ga[9]: end
```



As this program illustrates, because an object reference can hold a reference to any other type of data, it is possible to use an object reference to refer to any type of data. Thus, an array of object as used by the program can store any type of data. Expanding on this concept, it is easy to see how you could construct a stack class, for example, that stored object references. This would enable the stack to store any type of data.

Although the universal-type feature of object is powerful and can be used quite effectively in some situations, it is a mistake to think that you should use object as a way around C#'s otherwise strong type checking. In general, when you need to store an int, use an int variable; when you need to store a string, use a string reference; and so on.

More importantly, since version 2.0, true generic types are available to the C# programmer. Generics enable you to easily define classes and algorithms that automatically work with different types of data in a type-safe manner. Because of generics, you will normally not need to use object as a universal type when creating new code. Today, it's best to reserve object's universal nature for specialized situations.

CHAPTER 7

# Exception Handling

***In this chapter you will read about:***

- The System.Exception Class.
- Exception-Handling Fundamentals.
- Multiple catch Clauses.
- Nesting try Blocks.
- Exception Classes.

## Introduction

An *exception* is an error that occurs at runtime. Using C#'s exception-handling subsystem, you can, in a structured and controlled manner, handle runtime errors. A principal advantage of exception handling is that it automates much of the error-handling code that previously had to be entered "by hand" into any large program. For example, in a computer language without exception handling, error codes must be returned when a method fails, and these values must be checked manually each time the method is called. This approach is both tedious and error-prone. Exception handling streamlines error-handling by allowing your program to define a block of code, called an *exception handler,* that is executed automatically when an error occurs. It is not necessary to manually check the success or failure of each specific operation or method call. If an error occurs, it will be processed by the exception handler.

Exception handling is also important because C# defines standard exceptions for common program errors, such as divide-by-zero or index-out-of-range. To respond to these errors, your program must watch for and handle these exceptions. In the final analysis, to be a successful C# programmer means that you are fully capable of navigating C#'s exception-handling subsystem.

## The System.Exception Class

In C#, exceptions are represented by classes. All exception classes must be derived from the built-in exception class Exception, which is part of the System namespace. Thus, all exceptions are subclasses of Exception.

One very important subclass of Exception is SystemException. This is the exception class from which all exceptions generated by the C# runtime system (that is, the CLR) are derived. SystemException does not add anything to Exception. It simply defines the top of the standard exceptions hierarchy.

The .NET Framework defines several built-in exceptions that are derived from SystemException. For example, when a division-by-zero is attempted, a DivideByZeroException exception is generated. As you will see later in this chapter, you can create your own exception classes by deriving them from Exception.

## Exception-Handling Fundamentals

C# exception handling is managed via four keywords: try, catch, throw, and finally. They form an interrelated subsystem in which the use of one implies the use of another. Throughout the course of this chapter, each keyword is examined in detail. However, it is useful at the outset to have a general understanding of the role each plays in exception handling. Briefly, here is how they work.

Program statements that you want to monitor for exceptions are contained within a try block. If an exception occurs within the try block, it is *thrown.* Your code can catch this exception using catch and handle it in some rational manner. System-generated exceptions are automatically thrown by the runtime system. To manually throw an exception, use the keyword throw. Any code that absolutely must be executed upon exiting from a try block is put in a finally block.

## Using try and catch

At the core of exception handling are try and catch. These keywords work together, and you can't have a catch without a try. Here is the general form of the try/catch exception-handling blocks:

```
try{
    // block of code to monitor for errors
}

catch(ExccpTypcl exOb) {
    // handler for ExcepTypel
}
```

```
catch(ExcepType1 exOb) {
    // handler for ExcepType2
}
:
:
```

Here, *ExcepType* is the type of exception that has occurred. When an exception is thrown, it is caught by its corresponding catch clause, which then processes the exception. As the general form shows, more than one catch clause can be associated with a try. The type of the exception determines which catch is executed. That is, if the exception type specified by a catch matches that of the exception, then that catch is executed (and all others are bypassed). When an exception is caught, the exception variable *exOb* will receive its value.

Actually, specifying *exOb* is optional. If the exception handler does not need access to the exception object (as is often the case), there is no need to specify *exOb*. The exception type alone is sufficient. For this reason, many of the examples in this chapter will not specify *exOb*.

Here is an important point: If no exception is thrown, then a try block ends normally, and all of its catch clauses are bypassed. Execution resumes with the first statement following the last catch. Thus, a catch is executed only if an exception is thrown.

## A Simple Exception Example

Here is a simple example that illustrates how to watch for and catch an exception. As you know, it is an error to attempt to index an array beyond its boundaries. When this error occurs, the CLR throws an IndexOutOfRangeException, which is a standard exception defined by the .NET Framework. The following program purposely generates such an exception and then catches it:

```
// Demonstrat exception handling.

using System;
class ExcDemo1 {
    static void Main() {
        int{} nums = new int{4};

        try {
            Console.WriteLine("Befor exception is generated.");

            // Generate an index out-of -bounds exception.
            for (inL i=0; i < 10; i++) {
                nums [il = i;
                Console.WriteLine("nums ({ 0}]:{1}", i, nums (i);
            }

            Console.WriteLine("this won't be displayed");
        }
        catch (indexOutOfRangeException) {
            // Catch the exception.
            console.WriteLine("index out-of-bounds!");
        }
        console.WriteLine("After catch block,");
    }
}
```

This program displays the following output:

```
Before exception is generated
nums[0]: 0
```

```
nums[1]: 1
nums[2]: 2
nums[3]: 3
Index out-of-bounds!
After catch block.
```



Notice that nums is an int array of four elements. However, the for loop tries to index nums from 0 to 9, which causes an IndexOutOfKangeException to occur when an index value of 4 is tried.

Although quite short, the preceding program illustrates several key points about exception handling. First, the code that you want to monitor for errors is contained within a try block. Second, when an exception occurs (in this case, because of the attempt to index nums beyond its bounds inside the for loop), the exception is thrown out of the try block and caught by the catch. At this point, control passes to the catch block, and the try block is terminated. That is, catch is *not* called. Rather, program execution is transferred to it. Thus, the WriteLinel ) statement following the out-of-bounds index will never execute. After the catch block executes, program control continues with the statements following the catch. Thus, it is the job of your exception handler to remedy the problem that caused the exception so program execution can continue normally.

Notice that no exception variable is specified in the **catch** clause. Instead, only the type of the exception **(IndexOutOfRangeException** in this case) is required. As mentioned, an exception variable is needed only when access to the exception object is required. Tn some cases, the value of the exception object can be used by the exception handler to obtain additional information about the error, but in many cases, it is sufficient to simply know that an exception occurred. Thus, it is not unusual for the **catch** variable to be absent in the exception handler, as is the case in the preceding program.

As explained, if no exception is thrown by a try block, no **catch** will be executed and program control resumes after the **catch.** To confirm this, in the preceding program, change the for loop from

```
for(int i=0; i < 10; i++) {
```

to

```
for(int i=0; i < nums.Length; i++) {
```

Now, the loop does not overrun **minis'** boundary. Thus, no exception is generated, and the **catch** block is not executed.

## A Second Exception Example

It is important to understand that all code executed within a try block is monitored for exceptions. This includes exceptions that might be generated by a method called from within the try block. An exception thrown by a method called from within a try block can be caught by that try block, assuming, of course, that the method itself did not catch the exception.

For example, consider the following program. **Main()** establishes a try block from which the method **GenExceptionO** is called. Inside **GenExceptionO, an IndexOutOfRangeException** is generated. This exception is not caught by **GenExceptionO.** However, since **GenExceptionO** was called from within a try block in MainO, the exception is caught by the **catch** statement associated with that try.

```
/* An exception can be generated by one method and caught by another. */

using System;

class ExecText {
   // Generate an exception.
   public static void GenException() {
      int {} nums = new int(4);
```

```
        Console.WriteLine("Before exception is generated.");

        // Generate an index out-of-bounds exception,
        forfint i=0; i < 10; i++) {
            nums [i] = i;
            Console.HriteLine("nums[{0}J : (1}", i, nums[i]);
        }

        Console.WriteLine("this won't be displayed");
    }
}

class ExcDemo2 {
    static void Main() {

        try {
            ExcTest .GenException () ;
        }
        catch (IndexOutOfRangeException) {
            // Catch the exception.
            Console.WriteLine("Index out-of-bounds!");
        }
        Console. WriteLine ("After catch block.");
    }
}
```

This program produces the following output, which is the same as that produced by the first version of the program shown earlier:

```
Before exception is generated.
nums[0]: 0
nums[1]: 1
nums[2]: 2
nums[3]: 3
Index out-of-bounds!
After catch block.
```

As explained, because GenException() is called from within a try block, the exception that it generates (and does not catch) is caught by the catch in Main(). Understand, however, that if GenException() had caught the exception, then it never would have been passed back to Main().

## The Consequences of an Uncaught Exception

Catching one of the standard exceptions, as the preceding program does, has a side benefit: It prevents abnormal program termination. When an exception is thrown, it must be caught by some piece of code, somewhere. In general, if your program does not catch an exception, it will be caught by the runtime system. The trouble is that the runtime system will report an error and terminate the program. For instance, in this example, the index out-of-bounds exception is not caught by the program:

```
// Let the C# runtime system handle the error,

using System;

class NotHandled {
    static void Main() {
        int[1 nums = new int [4];
        Console.WriLeLine("Before exception is generated."};
```

```
        // Generate an index out-of-bounds exception.
        for(int i-O; i < 10; i++) {
            nums[i] - i;
            Console.WriteLine("nums[0}] : (1)", i, nums[i]) ;
        }
    }
}
```

When the array index error occurs, execution is halted and the following error message is displayed:

```
Unhandled Exception: System,IndexOuLGfRanqeException:
        Index was outside the bounds of the array.
    at NotHandled.Main()
```

Although such a message is useful while debugging, you would not want others to see it, to say the least! This is why it is important for your program to handle exceptions itself.

As mentioned earlier, the type of the exception must match the type specified in a catch. If it doesn't, the exception won't be caught. For example, the following program tries to catch an array boundary error with a catch for a DivideByZeroException (another built-in exception). When the array boundary is overrun, an IndexOutOfRangeException is generated, but it won't be caught by the catch. This results in abnormal program termination.

```
// This won't work!

using System;

class ExcTypeMismatch {
    static void Main() {
        int [ ] nums = new int [4] ;

        try {
        Console .WriteLine { "Before exception is generated. ") ;

        // Generate an index out-of-bounds exception.
        forfint i-O; i < 10; i++) {
            nums [ i] = i ;
            Console.WriteLine ( "nums [{0}]: {1}", i, nums [i]);
        }

        Console .WriLeLine ("this won't be displayed")
    }

    /* Can't catch an array boundary error with a
        DivideByZeroException. */
    catch (DivideByZeroException} {
        // Catch the exception.
        Console.Wri teLine("Index out-of-bounds!");
    }

        Console.WriteLine("After catch block.")
    }
}
```

The output is shown here:

```
Before exception is generated.
nums [0] : 0
nums [1] : 1
nums [2] : 2
nums [3] : 3
```

```
Unhandled Exception : System. IndexOutOfRangeException :
     Index was outside the bounds of the array.
   at ExcTypeMismatch .Main {}
```

As the output demonstrates, a catch for DivideByZeroException won't catch an IndexOutOfRangeException.

## Exceptions Let You Handle Errors Gracefully

One of the key benefits of exception handling is that it enables your program to respond to an error and then continue running. For example, consider the following example that divides the elements of one array by the elements of another. If a division-by-zero occurs, a **DivideByZeroException** is generated, hi the program, this exception is handled by reporting the error and then continuing with execution. Thus, attempting to divide by zero does not cause an abrupt runtime error resulting in the termination of the program. Instead, it is handled gracefully, allowing program execution to continue.

```
// Handle error gracefully and continue.

using System;

class ExcDemoS (
    static void Main() {
        int[] numer = { 4, 8, 16, 32, 64, 128 } ;
        int[] denom ={2, 0, 4, 4, 0, 8};

        for(int i=0; i < numer . Length; {
            try {
                Console .WriteLine (numer [i] + " / " +
                                    denom[i] + " is " +
                                    numer [i] /denom[i] );
            }
            catch (DivideByZeroException) {
                // Catch the exception.
                Console.WriteLine ("Can't divide by Zero!");
            }
        }
    }
}
```

The output from the program is shown here:

```
4 / 2 is 2
Can't divide by Zero!
16 / 4 is 4
32 / 4 io 8
Can't divide by Zero!
128 / 8 is 16
```

This example makes another important point: Once an exception has been handled, it is removed from the system. Therefore, in the program, each pass through the loop enters the try block anew—any prior exceptions have been handled. This enables your program to handle repeated errors.

## Using Multiple catch Clauses

You can associate more than one **catch** clause with a try. In fact, it is common to do so. However, each catch must catch a different type of exception. For example, the program shown here catches both array boundary and divide-by-zero errors:

```
// Use multiple catch clauses,
```

```
using System;

class ExcDemo4 {
    static void Main() {
        // Here, numer is longer than denom.
        intf] numer = { 4, 8, 16, 32, 64, 128, 256, 512 };
        int[] denom ={2, 0, 4, 4, 0, 8);

        forfint i=0; i < numer.Length; i++) {
            try {
                Console.WriLeLine(numer[i] + " / " +
                                  denom[i] + " is " +
                                  numer[i]/denom[i]};
            }
            catch {DivideByZeroException} {
                Consolc.WriteLine("Can't divide by Zero!");
            }
            catch (IndexOutOfRangeException} {
                Console.WriteLine("No matching element found.");
                }
            }
    }
}
```

This program produces the following output:

```
4 / 2 is 2
Can't divide by Zero!
16 / 4 is 4
32 / 4 is 8
Can't divide by Zero!
128 / 8 is 16
No matching element found.
No matching element found.
```

As the output confirms, each **catch** clause responds only to its own type of exception.

In general, catch clauses are checked in the order in which they occur in a program. Only the first matching clause is executed. All other **catch** blocks are ignored.

## Catching All Exceptions

Occasionally, you might want to catch all exceptions, no matter the type. To do this, use a **catch** clause that specifies no exception type or variable. It has this general form:

```
catch (
// handle exceptions
}
```

This creates a "catch all" handler that ensures that all exceptions are caught by your program.

Here is an example of a "catch all" exception handler. Notice that it catches both the **IndexOutOfRangeException** and the **DivideByZeroException** generated by the program:

```
// Use the "catch all" catch.

using System;

class ExcDemo5 {
    static void Main() {
        // Here, numer is longer than denom.
        int[] numer = { 4, 8, 16, 32, 64, 128, 256, 512 } ;
        int[] denom =12, 0, 4, A, 0, 8 };
```

```
        for (int i=0 ; i < numer. Length;
            try {
                Console.WriteLine (numer [i] + " / " +
                                  denom [ i] + " is " +
                                  numer [i] / denom [i]);
            }
            catch { //A "catch-all" catch .
                Console.WriteLine ("Some exception occurred.");
            }
        }
    }
```

The output is shown here:

```
4 / 2 is 2
Some exception occurred.
16 / 4 is 4
32 / 4 is 8
Some exception occurred.
128 / 8 is 16
Some exception occurred.
Some exception occurred.
```

There is one point to remember about using a catch-all catch: It must be the **last** catch clause in the catch sequence.

## Nesting try Blocks

One try block can be nested within another. An exception generated within the inner try block **that is** not caught by a catch associated with that try is propagated to the outer try block. For example, here the IndexOutOfRangeException is not caught by the inner try block, but by the 0uter try:

```
// Use a nested try block,

using System;

class NestTrys {
    static void MainO {
        // Here, numer is longer than denom.
        int[] numer = { 4, 8, 16, 32, 64, 128, 256, 512 };
        int[] denom = { 2, 0, 4, A, 0, 8 };

        try { // outer try
            for (int i=0; i < numer , Length; i++) {
                try { // nested try
                    Console.Write Line(numer [i] + " / " +
                                      denom[i] + " is " +
                                      numer [il /denom [i] ) ;
                }
                catch (DivldeByZeroException) {
                    Console. WriteLine ("Can't divide by Zero !");
                }
            }
        }
        catch { IndexOutOfRangeException) {
            Console.WriteLine {" No matching element found. " } ;
            Console.WriteLine ("Fatal error — program terminated.");
        }
    }
}
```

The output **from** the program is shown here:

```
4 / 2 is 2
Can't divide by Zero!
16 / 4 is 4
32 / 4 is 8
Can't divide by Zero!
128 / 8 is 16
No matching element found.
Fatal error – program terminated.
```

In this example, an exception that can be handled by the inner try—in this case a divide-by-zero error—allows the program to continue. However, an array boundary error is caught by the outer try, which causes the program to terminate.

Although certainly not the only reason for nested try statements, the preceding program makes an important point that can be generalized. Often, nested try blocks are used to allow different categories of errors to be handled in different ways. Some types of errors are catastrophic and cannot be fixed. Some are minor and can be handled immediately. Many programmers use an outer try block to catch the most severe errors, allowing inner try blocks to handle less serious ones. You can also use an outer try block as a "catch all" block for those errors that are not handled by the inner block.

## Throwing an Exception

The preceding examples have been catching exceptions generated automatically by the runtime system. However, it is possible to throw an exception manually by using the **throw** statement. Its general form is shown here;

```
throw exceptOb;
```

The *exceptOb* must be an object of an exception class derived from **Exception.**

Here is an example that illustrates the throw statement by manually throwing a **DivideByZero Exception:**

```
// Manually throw an exception.

using System;

class ThrowDemo {
   static void Main() {
      try {
         Console.WriteLine("Before throw.");
         throw new DivideByZeroException();
      }
      catch (DivideByZeroException) {
         Console.WriteLine("Exception caught.");
      }
      Console.WriteLine("After try/catch statement.");
   }
}
```

The output from the program is shown here:

```
Before throw.
Exception caught.
After try/catch statement.
```

Notice how the **DivideByZeroException** was created using **new** in the **throw** statement Remember, **throw** throws an object. Thus, you must create an object for it to throw. That is, you can't just throw a type. In this case, the default constructor is used to create a **DivideByZeroException** object, but other constructors are available for exceptions.

Most often, exceptions that you throw will be instances of exception classes that you created. As you will see later in this chapter, creating your own exception classes allows you to handle errors in your code as part of your program's overall exception-handling strategy.

## Rethrowing an Exception

An exception caught by one **catch** can be rethrown so that it can be caught by an outer **catch.** The most likely reason for rethrowing an exception is to allow multiple handlers access to the exception. For example, perhaps one exception handler manages one aspect of an exception, and a second handler copes with another aspect. To rethrow an exception, you simply specify **throw,** without specifying an expression. That is, you use this form of **throw:**

```
throw ;
```

Remember, when you rethrow an exception, it will not be recaught by the same **catch** clause. Instead, it will propagate to an outer **catch.**

The following program illustrates rethrowing an exception. In this case, it rethrows an **IndexOutOf RangeException .**

```
// Rethrow an exception.

using System;

class Rethrow {
    public static void GenException {} {
        // Here, numer is longer than denom,
        int[] numer = { 4, 8, 16, 32, 64, 128, 256, 512 } ;
        int[] denom = { 2, 0, 4, 4, 0, 8);

        for (int i = 0; i<numer. Length; i++) }
            try {
                Console.WriteLine (numer [i] + " / " +
                                   denom[i] + " is " +
                                   numer [i] /denom [i] ) ;
        }
        catch (DivideByZeroException) {
            Console.WriteLine ( "Can't divide by Zero ! ") ; "
        }
        catch (IndexOutOfRangeException) {
            Console.WriteLine ("No matching element found."}
            throw; // rethrow the exception
            }
        }
    }
}

class RethrowDemo {
    static void Main() {
        try {
        Rethrow. GenException () ;
        }
        catch ( TndexOutOf RarigeException) (
            // re catch exception
            Console . WrïteLine ( "Fatal error — " + "program terminated.");
        }
    }
}
```

In this program, divide-by-zero errors are handled locally, by **GenException()**, but an array boundary error is rethrown. In this case, the **IndexOutOfRangeException** is handled by **Main().**



## Using finally

Sometimes you will want to define a block of code that will execute when a **try/catch** block is left. For example, an exception might cause an error that terminates the current method, causing its premature return. However, that method may have opened a file or a network connection that needs to be closed. Such types of circumstances are common in programming, and C# provides a convenient way to handle them: **finally.**

To specify a block of code to execute when a **try/catch** block is exited, include a **finally** block at the end of a **try/ catch** sequence. The general form of a **try/catch** that includes **finally** is shown here:

```
try{
    // block of code to monitor for errors
}

catch (ExcepTypel exOb) {
    // handler for ExcepTypel
}

catch (ExcepType2 exOb) {
    // handler for ExcepTypeZ
}
:
:
finally {
    // finally code
}
```

**The finally** block will be executed whenever execution leaves a **try/catch** block, no matter what conditions cause it. That is, whether the try block ends normally, or because of an exception, the last code executed is that defined by **finally. The finally** block is also executed if any code within the try block or any of its **catch** blocks returns from the method.

Here is an example of **finally:**

```
// Use finally,

usinq System;

class UseFinally {
    public static void GenException(int what) {
        int t;
        int[] nums = new int[2];

    Console.Write Line ("Receiving " + what);
    try {
        switch (what) {
            case 0 :
                t = 10 / what;    // generate div-by-zero error break;
            case 1 :
                nums [4] = 4;     // generate array index error break;
            case 2:
                return;           // return from try block
```

```
            }
        }
        catch (DivideByZeroException) {
            Console, WriteLine {"Can¹ t divide by Zero!");
            return; // return from catch } catch (IndexOutOfRangeException)
        {
        Console .WriteLine ( "No matching element found."}
        }
        finally {
            Console .WriteLine ("Leaving try . ") ;
            }
        }
    }

    class Final lyDemo {
        static void Mainf)

        for(int i=0; i < 3; i++) {
            UseFinally.GenException (i)
            Console .WriteLine ( ) ;
            }
        }
    }
```

Here is the output produced by the program:

```
Receiving 0
Can ' t divide by Zero !
Leaving try,

Receiving 1
No matching element found.
Leaving try.

Receiving 2
Leaving try.
```

As the output shows, no matter how the try block is exited, the **finally** block is executed.

One other point: Syntactically, when a **finally** block follows a try block, no **catch** clauses are technically required. Thus, you can have a try followed by a **finally** with no **catch** clauses. In this case, the **finally** block is executed when the try exits, but no exceptions are handled.

## A Closer Look at the Exception Class

Up to this point, we have beeii catching exceptions, but we haven't been doing anything with the exception object itself. As explained earlier, a catch clause allows you to specify an exception type *and* a i ariable. The variable receives a reference to the exception object. Since all exceptions are derived from **Exception,** all exceptions support the members defined by **Exception,** Here v-e will examine several of its most useful members and constructors, and put the exception variable to use.

**Exception** defines several properties. Three of the most interesting are **Message, StackTrace, a-id TargetSite.** All are read-only. **Message** contains a string that describes the nature of the irror. **StackTrace** contains a string that contains the stack of calls that lead to the exception. **TargetSite** obtains an object that specifies the method that generated the exception.

**Exception** also defines several methods. One that you will often use is **ToString()**, which returns a string that describes the exception. **ToString()** is automatically called when an exception is displayed via **WrlteLine()**, for example.

The following program demonstrates these properties and this method:

```
// Using Exception members.

using System;

class ExcTest {
    public static void GenException () {
        int [] nums = new int [4];

        Console.WriteLine("Before exception is generated.");

        // Generate an index out-of-bounds exception.
            for(int i-O; i < 10; i+t) {
                nums [i] = i;
                Console.WriteLine ("nums [{0}]: {1( ",1,nums [i]);
            }

        Console.WriteLine ( "this won't be displayed");
    }
}

class UseExcept {
    static void Main() {

        try {
            ExcTest.GenException();
        }
        catch (IndexOutOfRangeException exc) {

            Console.Writ eLine ("Standard message is : ") ;
            Console.WriteLine (exc) ;  // calls ToString()
            Console.WriteLine ("Stack trace: " + exc . StackTrace) ;
            Console.WriteLine ("Message : " + exc. Mess age) ;
            Console.WriteLine ( "Target Site : " + exc .Target Site);)
        }
        Console. WriteLine ("After catch block. ") ;
    }
}
```

CHAPTER 7

The output from this program is shown here:

```
Before exception is generated.
nums [0] : 0
nums [1] : 1
nums [2] : 2
nums [3] : 3
Standard message is:
System. IndexOutOfRangeException : Index was outside the bounds of the array.
   at ExcTest .GenException ()
   at UseExcept .Main ()
Stack trace:  at ExcTest . GenException ()
   at UseExcept. Main ()
Message : Index was outside the bounds of the array.
TargetSite: Void GenException ()
After catch block.
```

**Exception** defines the following four constructors:

public Exception( )
public Exception(string *message)*
public Exceptionfstring *message,* Exception *innerExceptiori)*
protected Exception( System.Runtime.Serialization.Serializationlnfo *info,*
System.Runtime.Serialization.StreamingContext confer)

The first is the default constructor. The second specifies the string associated with the **Message** property associated with the exception. The third specifies what is called an *inner exception.* It is used when one exception gives rise to another. In this case, *innerException* specifies the first exception, which will be null if no inner exception exists. (The inner exception, if it exists, can be obtained from the **InnerException** property defined by **Exception.)** The last constructor handles exceptions that occur remotely and require deserialization.

One other point: In the fourth **Exception** constructor shown above, notice that the types **Serializationlnfo and StreamingContext** are contained in the **System.Runtime. Serialization** namespace.

## Commonly Used Exceptions

**The System** namespace defines several standard, built-in exceptions. All are derived (either directly or indirectly) from **SystemException** since they are generated by the CLR when runtime errors occur. Several of the more commonly used standard exceptions are shown in following Table.

**Commonly Used Exceptions Defined Within the System Namespace**

| Exception | Meaning |
|---|---|
| Array TypeMismatch Exception | Type of value being stored is incompatible with the type of the array. |
| DivideByZeroException | Division by zero attempted. |
| IndexOutOfRangeException | Array index is out-of-bounds. |
| InvalidCastException | A runtime cast is invalid. |
| OutOf Memory Exception | Insufficient free memory exists to continue program execution. For example, this exception will be thrown if there is not sufficient free memory to create an object via **new.** |
| Overflow Exception | An arithmetic overflow occurred. |
| NullReferenceException | An attempt was made to operate on a null reference—that is, a reference that does not refer to an object |

Most of the exceptions in the Table are self-explanatory, with the possible exception of NullReferenceException. This exception is thrown when there is an attempt to use a null reference as if it referred to an object — for example, if you attempt to call a method on a null reference. A *null reference* is a reference that does not point to any object. One way to create a null reference is to explicitly assign it the value null by using the keyword null- Null references can also occur in other ways that are less obvious. Here is a program that demonstrates the NullRef erenceException :

```
// Use the NullReferenceException.

using System;

class X {
    int x;
    public X(int a) {
        x = a;
    }

    public int Add(X o) {
        return x + o .x;
    }
}

// Demonstrate NullReferenceException.
class NREDemo {
    static void Main() (
        X p = new X(10);
        X q = null; // q is explicitly assigned null
        int val;
    try {
        val = p.Add(q); // this will lead to an exception
    } catch (NullReferenceException) {
        Console.WriteLine("NullReferenceException!");
        Console.WriteLine ("fixing. . An") ;

        // Now, fix it.
        q = new X(9);
        val = p.Add(q);
    }

    Console.WriLeLine{"val is {0}", val);
    )
}
```

The output from the program is shown here:

```
NullReferenceException!
fixing...

val is 19
```

The program creates a class called X that defines a member called x and the Add() method, which adds the invoking object's x to the x in the object passed as a parameter. In Main(), two X objects are created. The first, p, is initialized. The second, q, is not. Instead, it is explicitly assigned null. Then p.Add() is called with q as an argument. Because q does not refer to any object, a NullReferenceException is generated when the attempt is made to obtain the value of q.x.

## Deriving Exception Classes

Although C#'s built-in exceptions handle most common errors, C#'s exception-handling mechanism is not limited to these errors. In fact, part of the power of C#'s approach to exceptions is its ability to handle exception types that you create. You can use custom exceptions to handle errors in your own code. Creating an exception is easy. Just define a class derived from Exception. Your derived classes don't need to actually implement anything—it is their existence in the type system that allows you to use them as exceptions.

The exception classes that you create will automatically have the properties and methods defined by Exception available to them. Of course, you can override one or more of these members in exception classes that you create.

When creating your own exception class, you will generally want your class to support all of the constructors defined by Exception. For simple custom exception classes, this is easy to do because you can simply pass along the constructor's arguments to the corresponding Exception constructor via base. Of course, technically, you need to provide only those constructors actually used by your program.

Here is an example that makes use of a custom exception type. As you may recall, RangeArray supports single-dimensional int arrays in which the starting and ending index is specified by the user. For example, an array that ranges from -5 to 27 is perfectly legal for a RangeArray. If an index was out of range, a special error variable defined by RangeArray was set. This meant that the error variable had to be checked after each operation by the code that used RangeArray. Of course, such an approach is error-prone and clumsy. A far better design is to have RangeArray throw a custom exception when a range error occurs. This is precisely what the following version of RangeArray does:

```
// Use a custom Exception for RangeArray errors,

using System;

// Create a RangeArray exception,
class RangeArrayException : Exception {
   /* Implement all of the Exception constructors. Notice that the
      constructors simply execute the base class constructor. Because
      RangeArrayException adds nothing to Exception, there is no need for any
      further actions. */
   public RangeArrayException() : base{) { }
   public RangeArrayException(string message) : base(message) I }
   public RangeArrayException(string message, Exception innerException) :
      base(message, innerException) { }
   protected RangeArrayException{
      System,Runtime.Serialization.SerializationInfo info,
      System.Runtime.Serialization.StreamingContext context) :
         base (info, context) { }

   // Override ToString for RangeArrayException.
   public override string ToStringO {
      return Message;
   }
}

// An improved version of RangeArray,
class RangeArray {
   // Private data.
   int[] a; // reference to underlying array
   int lowerBound; // smallest index
   int upperBound; // largest index

   //An auto-implemented, read-only Length property
   public int Length { get; private set; }

   // Construct array given its size,
```

```
public RangeArray (int low, int high) {
    high++;
    if (high <- low) {
       throw new RangeArrayException("Low index not less than high.
    }
    a = new int[high - low];
    Length = high - low;

    lowerBound = low;
    upperBound = —high;

 // This is the indexer for RangeArray.
 public int this[int index] (
    // This is the get accessor,
    get (
       if (ok(index)) {
          return a[index - lowerBound];
    } else {
       throw new RangeArrayException("Range Error."};
    }
 }

 // This is the set accessor,
 set i
    if(ok(index)) {
       a[index - lowerBound] = value;
    }
    else throw new RangeArrayException("Range Error.");
    }
 }

 // Return true if index is within bounds,
 private bool ok (int index) {
    if(index >= lowerBound & index <= upperBound) return true;
    return false;
    }
 }

 // Demonstrate the index-range array.
 class, RangeArrayDemo {
    static void Main() {
       try {
          RangeArray ra = new RangeArray(-5, 5);
          RangeArray ra2 = new RangeArray(1, 10);

          // Demonstrate ra.
          Console.WriteLine("Length of ra: " + ra.Length)

          for(int i = -5; i <= 5; i++)
             ra[i] = i;

       Console .Write ("Contents of ra : " ) ;
       for(int i = -5; i <= 5; i++)
          Console .Write {ra [i] + " "} ;

       Console .WriteLine ( "\n" ) ;

    // Demonstrate ra2 .
```

```
            Console.WriteLine ("Length of ra2 : " + ra2. Length);

            for(int i = 1; i <= 10; i++)
               ra2[i] = i;

            Console. Write ("Contents of ra2 : ");
               forfint i = 1; i <= 10; i++)
               Console. Write (ra2 [i] + " ") ;
            }
         }
               Console. WriteLine ("\n"> ;
      } catch (RangeArrayException exc)
         Console .WriteLine (exc) ;
      }

      // Now, demonstrate some errors.
         Console .WriteLine ("Now generate some range errors . " ) ;

      // Use an invalid constructor.
         try (
            RangeArray ra3 = new RangeArray (100, -10); // Error
         } catch (RangeArrayException exc) {
            Console. WriteLine (exc) ;
         }

      // Use an invalid index.
      try {
         RangeArray ra3 = new RangeArray(-2, 2};

         for(int i = -2; i <= 2; i++)
            ra3[i] = i;

         Console.Write("Contents of ra3 : ");
         forfint i = -2; i <= 10; i++) // generate range error
            Console.Write(ra3 [i] + " ") ;

         } catch (RangeArrayException exc) {
            Console.WriteLine(exc);
         }
      }
   }
```

**The output from the program is shown here:**

```
Length of ra: 11
Contents of ra: -5 -4 -3 -2 -1 0 1 2 3 4 5
Length of ra2: 10
Contents of ra2: 1 2 3 4 5 6 7 8 9 10

Now generate some range errors.
Low index not less than high.
Contents of ra3: -2 -1 0 1 2 Range Error
```

When a range error occurs, **RangeArray** throws an object of type **Range Array Exception.** Notice there are three places in **RangeArray** that this might occur: in the get indexer accessor, in the set indexer accessor, and by the **RangeArray** constructor. To catch these exceptions implies that **RangeArray** objects must be constructed and accessed from within a try block, as the program illustrates. By using an exception to report errors, **RangeArray** now acts like one of C#'s built-in types and can be fully integrated into a program's exception-handling mechanism.

Notice that none of the **RangeArrayException** constructors provide any statements in their body. Instead, they simply pass their arguments along to **Exception** via base. As explained, in cases in which your exception class does not add any functionality, you can simply let the **Exception** constructors handle the process. There is no requirement that your derived class add anything to what is inherited from **Exception.**

Before moving on, you might want to experiment with this program a bit. For example, try commenting-out the override of **ToStringC)** and observe the results. Also, try creating an exception using the default constructor, and observe what C# generates as its default message.

## Catching Derived Class Exceptions

You need to be careful how you order **catch** clauses when trying to catch exception types that involve base and derived classes, because a **catch for** a base class will also match any of its derived classes. For example, because the base class of all exceptions is **Exception,** catching **Exception** catches all possible exceptions. Of course, using **catch** without an exception type provides a cleaner way to catch all exceptions, as described earlier. However, the issue of catching derived class exceptions is very important in other contexts, especially when you create exceptions of your own.

If you want to catch exceptions of both a base class type and a derived class type, put the derived class first in the **catch** sequence. This is necessary because a base class **catch** will also catch all derived classes. Fortunately, this rule is self-enforcing because putting the base class first causes a compile-time error.

The following program creates two exception classes called **ExceptA and ExceptB. ExceptA** is derived from **Exception. ExceptB** is derived from ExceptA. The program then throws an exception of each type. For brevity, the custom exceptions supply only one constructor (which takes a string that describes the exception). But remember, in commercial code, your custom exception classes will normally provide all four of the constructors defined by **Exception.**

```
//Derived exceptions must appear before base class execptions

using System;

// Create an exception.
class ExceptA: Exception {
    public ExceptA(string message) : base(message) { }
    public driveride string ToString() {
    }
}

// Create an exception derived from ExceptA.
class ExceptB : ExceptA {
    public ExceptB(string message) : base(message) { }

    public override string ToString () (
        return Message;
    }
}

class OrderMatters {
    static void Main!) {
        for(int x = 0; x < 3; x++) {
            try {
```

```
            if(x==0) throw new ExceptA("Caught an ExceptA exception");
            else if (x==l) throw new ExceptB ( "Caught an ExceptB exception")
            else throw'riew Exception!) ; } catch (ExceptB exc);
        {
        catch (ExceptB exc) {
            Console.WriteLine(exc);
        }
        catch (ExceptA exc) {
            Console.WriteLine(exc);
        }
        catch (Exception exc){
            Console.WriteLine (exc);
        }
    }
}
```

The output from the program is shown here:

```
Caught an ExceptA exception
Caught an ExceptB exception
System.Exception: Exception of type 'System,Exception was thrown.
    at OrderMatters.Main()
```

Notice the type and order of the catch clauses. This is the only order in which they can occur. Since **ExceptB** is derived from **ExceptA, the catch** for **ExceptB** must be before the one for ExceptA. Similarly, the **catch** for **Exception** (which is the base class for all exceptions) must appear last. To prove this point for yourself, try rearranging the catch clauses. Doing so will result in a compile-time error.

One good use of a base class **catch** clause is to catch an entire category of exceptions. For example, imagine you are creating a set of exceptions for some device. If you derive all of the exceptions from a common base class, then applications that don't need to know precisely what problem occurred could simply catch the base class exception, avoiding the unnecessary duplication of code.

## Using checked and unchecked

A special feature in C# relates to the generation of overflow exceptions in arithmetic computations. As you know, it is possible for some types of arithmetic computations to produce a result that exceeds the range of the data type involved in the computation. When this occurs, the result is said to *overflow.* For example, consider the following sequence:

```
byte a, b result;
a = 127;
b = 127;

result = (byte) is * b);
```

Here, the product of a and b exceeds the range of a byte value. Thus, the result overflows the type of the result.

C# allows you to specify whether your code will raise an exception when overflow occurs by using the keywords checked and unchecked. To specify that an expression be checked for overflow, use checked. To specify that overflow be ignored, use unchecked. In this case, the result is truncated to fit into the target type of the expression.

The checked keyword has these two general forms. One checks a specific expression and is called the *operator form* of checked. The other checks a block of statements and is called the *statement form*.

```
checked (expr)

checked {
    // statements to be checked
}
```

Here, *expr* is the expression being checked. If a checked expression overflows, then an OverflowException is thrown.

The unchecked keyword also has two general forms. The first is the operator form, which ignores overflow for a specific expression. The second ignores overflow for a block of statements.

```
unchecked (expr)

unchecked {
    // statements for which overflow is ignored
}
```

Here, *expr* is the expression that is not being checked for overflow. If an unchecked expression overflows, then truncation will occur.

Here is a program that demonstrates both checked and unchecked:

```
//Using checked and unchecked;

using System;

class CheckedDemo {
    static void Main() {
        byte a, b;

byte result
a = 127;
b = 127;

try {
    result = unchecked {(byte) (a * b) ) ;
    Console .Writ.eLine ( "Unchecked result: " + result);

    result = checkedf (byte) (a * b) ] ;      // this causes exception
    Console.WriLeLine ("Checked result : " + result) ; // won't execute
}
catch (OverflowException exc) {
        Console.WriteLine(exc);
    }
  }
}
```

The output from the program is shown here:

```
Unchecked result : 1
System. Overf lowException : Ari thmeti c operati on resulted in an overflow.
    at CheckedDemo . Main ( }
```

As is evident, the unchecked expression resulted in a truncation. The checked expression caused an exception.

The preceding program demonstrated the use of **checked** and unchecked for a single expression. The following program shows how to check and uncheck a block of statements.

```
// Usinq checked and unchecked with statement blocks.

using System;

class CheckedBlocks {
    static void Main() {
        byte 1, b;
        byte result;

        a = 127;
        b = 127;

        try (
            unchecked {
                a = 127;
                b = 127;
                result = unchecked! (byte) (a * b) ) ;
                Console.WriteLine("Unchecked result: " + result);

                a = 125;
                b = 5;
                result = unchecked((byte)(a * b));
                Console.WriteLine("Unchecked result: " + result);
            }

            checked {
                a = 2;
                b = 7;
                result = checked! (byte) (a * b)); // This is Ok
                Console.WriteLine("Checked result: " + result);

                a = 127;
                b = 127;
                result = checked((byte)(a * b)); // this causes exception
                Console.WriteLine{"Checked result:" + result) ; // won't execute
            }
        }
            catch (OverflowException exec) {
                Console.WriteLine(exec);
        }
}
```

The output from the program is shown here:

```
Unchecked result: 1
Unchecked result: 113
Checked result: 14
```

```
System.OverflowException: Arithmetic operation lesulted in an overflow,
    at CheckedBlocks.Main()
```



As you can see, the unchecked block results in the overflow being truncated. When overflow occurred in the checked block, an exception was raised.

One reason that you may need to use **checked or unchecked** is that the default checked/unchecked status of overflow is determined by the setting of a compiler option and the execution environment, itself. Thus, for some types of programs, it is best to specify the overflow check status explicitly.

CHAPTER 8

# Questions

***In this chapter you will read about:***

- Various questions based on the topics read in the chapters of the book.

## Chapter 1 — Introduction to C#.NET 4.0

1. What is C# programming?
2. How would you describe Variables, Data Types, Operators?
3. How is For Loop used?
4. How are Arrays used in C#?
5. How are Events used in C#?
6. What is a Messagebox?

## Chapter 2 — Introducing Classes and Objects in C#.NET 4.0

1. Describe Class Fundamentals.
2. Describe the followings:

   Methods
   Reference Variables
   Parameters
   Return of Value
   Constructors
   Destructors
   Garbage Collection and Destructors

## Chapter 3 — Arrays and Strings in C#.NET 4.0

1. What are Arrays?
2. Describe the following:

   One-Dimensional Arrays
   Multidimensional Arrays
   Jagged Arrays
   Implicitly Typed Arrays
   Strings
   Constructing Strings
   Arrays of Strings

## Chapter 4 — Operators Overloading in C#.NET 4.0

1. What do you understand by Operator Overloading?
2. How would you handle Operations on C# Built-in Types?
3. How would you overload the Relational Operators?
4. Describe the process of Overloading True and False Operatorss.
5. What are Conversion Operators?

## Chapter 5 — Strings and Controls in C#.NET 4.0

1. What is a Concatenation Operator?
2. Describe the method of calculating string length.
3. Describe Button Control.
4. Describe the process of creating the following:

| | |
|---|---|
| CheckedListBoxControl | ComboBoxControl |
| Sorting ComboBox | Access key |
| Cancel button | Count |

## Chapter 6 — Inheritance in C#.NET 4.0

1. What do you understand by Inheritance?
2. How would you create a multilevel hierarchy?
3. When are constructors called?
4. Describe the virtual methods and overriding.
5. How would you use the abstract classes?
6. What is an object class?

## Chapter 7 — Exception Handling

1. What do you understand by Exception Handling?
2. Describe the various Exception-Handling Fundamentals.
3. How would you use Nesting try Blocks?
4. Describe Exception Classes.

# NOTES

# NOTES

# NOTES